The Brandywine

D1598888

The
Brandywine
An Intimate Portrait

W. Barksdale Maynard

PENN

UNIVERSITY OF PENNSYLVANIA PRESS

Philadelphia

Also by W. Barksdale Maynard

Architecture in the United States, 1800–1850

Walden Pond: A History

Buildings of Delaware in the Buildings of the United States Series

Woodrow Wilson: Princeton to the Presidency

Consumed: Rethinking Business in the Era of Mindfulness,
with Andrew Benett and Ann O'Reilly

Princeton: America's Campus

The Talent Mandate: Why Smart Companies Put People First,
with Andrew Benett and Ann O'Reilly

Publication of this volume was assisted by a grant from the Fair Play Foundation and
by a gift from Eric R. Papenfuse and Catherine A. Lawrence.

Published by
University of Pennsylvania Press
Philadelphia, Pennsylvania 19104-4112
www.upenn.edu/pennpress

Printed in the United States of America on acid-free paper
10 9 8 7 6 5 4 3 2 1

Library of Congress Cataloging-in-Publication Data

Maynard, W. Barksdale (William Barksdale)
Brandywine : an intimate portrait / W. Barksdale Maynard.—1st ed.
    p.   cm.
Includes bibliographical references and index.
ISBN 978-0-8122-4677-3 (hardcover : alk. paper)
1. Brandywine Creek (Pa. and Del.)—History. 2. Brandywine Creek Valley
(Pa. and Del.)—History. I. Title.
F157.B77M39 2015
974.8'4—dc23   2014028300

To Susan, Alexander, Spencer, and Elisabeth

Contents

⁂

Preface
American Arcadia
1

Chapter 1
Fish Creek in New Sweden
17

Chapter 2
Pride of Penn's Woods
27

Chapter 3
A River Red with Blood
47

Chapter 4
"Rushing Water and Buzzing Wheels"
69

Chapter 5
Thunderous Age of Black Powder
91

Chapter 6
Industry and War
109

Chapter 7
River of Nature
127

Chapter 8
Literary Pastoral
157

Chapter 9
"Painters of True American Art"
177

Appendix
Bridges of the Brandywine
211

Notes
219

Bibliography
229

Index
241

Acknowledgments
249

Illustration Credits
251

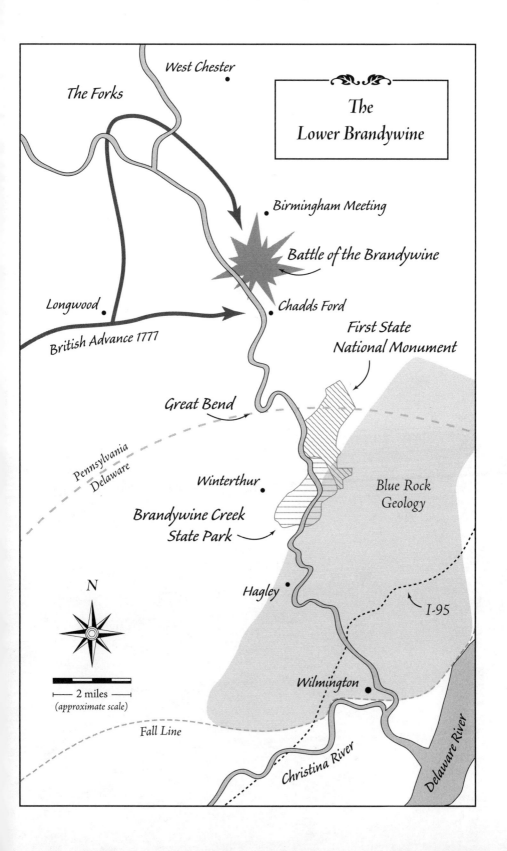

West Chester

The Forks

The
Lower Brandywine

Birmingham Meeting

Battle of the Brandywine

Longwood

Chadds Ford

British Advance 1777

First State
National Monument

Great Bend

Pennsylvania
Delaware

Winterthur

Blue Rock
Geology

Brandywine Creek
State Park

Hagley

I-95

N

Wilmington

2 miles
(approximate scale)

Fall Line

Christina River

Delaware River

Preface

❧ ❧

American Arcadia

It comes down from the Welsh Mountains and twists its way through some of the prettiest countryside in the middle states before gushing along a rocky gorge at Wilmington and meeting tidewater. The quintessential Piedmont stream, running lively over the rocks, the Brandywine finally loses itself into the flat and featureless Christina River, which joins the Delaware Bay.

Centuries ago, the Brandywine wove together two of the thirteen colonies. Finding its source in the wooded hills of the second-largest colony, Pennsylvania, it ended in the second-smallest, Delaware—later the first state. Every traveler who went north to south through colonial America crossed the Brandywine, usually in Wilmington, often stopping to admire its phenomenally productive mills, which made this valley a crucible of the Industrial Revolution. Finally, its importance to the early nation was immortalized by its being the scene of the largest land battle of the American Revolution, the Battle of the Brandywine, fought by George Washington's armies around Chadds Ford, Pennsylvania, one steamy late-summer afternoon, September 11, 1777.

From that day forward, the fame of the Brandywine has never subsided. Early tourists came to see the battlefield and, with the onset of the romantic movement around 1800, to delight in the valley's verdant beauty. Writers visited, and artists, until finally there flourished the so-called Brandywine school of painters, centered on Howard Pyle and

N. C. Wyeth. Perhaps the most famous American painter in the world, Andrew Wyeth, spent nearly a lifetime portraying the Brandywine scene.

Today the Brandywine Valley is famous for its cultural institutions and its outstanding gardens and museums, all of which derive from a long heritage of thoughtful attention to history, pride of place, and quality of life. So important is the Brandywine to the nation, 1,100 unspoiled acres along the creek—called Woodlawn—were recently earmarked for inclusion, advocates fervently hoped, in a brand-new national park, the first Delaware has ever had.

"If proponents prevail," *National Geographic* reported, the country would at last suitably honor the Brandywine "and the outsize course that it has cut through American history." Then in March 2013, President Obama established First State National Monument, the four-hundredth unit of the National Park Service. Its flagship component is the Woodlawn tract on the Brandywine's sinuous shores.[1]

The Brandywine Paradox

A single stream, 150 feet wide, flows beneath the I-95 bridge at Wilmington, where 200,000 drivers cross daily; but in a cultural sense there are actually two Brandywines. One is the everyday river that was dammed to provide power to nineteenth-century industry and is now piped into our homes and businesses for drinking water: a prosaic, workaday watercourse we might call *the Brandywine of milling and manufactures*. And then there is the other river, suffused with historical lore and patriotic meanings, a repository for dreams and high ideals—offering romantic inspiration to poets and artists for generations—*the Brandywine of myth and memory*.

As distinct as they may appear, these two Brandywines are, in fact, inseparable. They weave and coil about each other, running down through the centuries, and the historian must account for both paradigms in every era, a perennial paradox.

For example, when Washington Memorial Bridge was dedicated as Wilmington's civic gateway in 1922, throngs of citizens gathered by the

Brandywine to celebrate the city's role as an expanding center of commerce and industry, as belching smoke stacks along the lower creek boldly attested. And yet the river of myth and memory was lauded too, with speeches referring to the epic Battle of the Brandywine and all the poetic associations that surround one of America's most storied streams. At the end, a parade of 1,200 girls strewed flowers on the water. So did Delawareans take a holiday from their jobs in mills and factories and the offices of chemical corporations to pay moving tribute to their beloved river, a ceremony that seemed almost worthy of the ancient world, when Greeks sought to appease the old, shaggy gods and subtle nymphs that lived along the banks of every stream in Arcadia.

The practical river, the poetical river: we will meet them both in this book, and it is never quite clear where one begins and the other ends. After all, it was the riches that the Brandywine fostered that first allowed citizens leisure to enjoy it and to establish scenic parks along its edge; that made it possible for mill owners to buy framed pictures of their factories showing them embowered in all the forested greenery of the landscape painter's art; and eventually for du Ponts to set aside vast acreage as unspoiled, idyllic tracts, forming what we today call Chateau Country. Without these underpinnings of wealth, the Brandywine might have languished in obscurity, unnoticed and unheralded, like more rural rivers do—who sings, for example, of Tug Fork River in Virginia or Conococheague Creek in Maryland, though they are each longer than the Brandywine? Or it might have been allowed to degenerate into a polluted ditch, as many waterways in Megalopolis have done—including Naamans and Chester Creeks just eastward, with ragged, cinder block margins crowded by shopping malls and subdivisions. Wealth encouraged the broad-minded, expansive urge to celebrate the Brandywine and provided a means to safeguard the river through wise preservation. So the prosaic has ultimately fed and protected the poetic here, until the two mindsets can hardly be disentangled (see Plate 1).

For all the significance of the Brandywine, there has been no lengthy book about its history and culture since Henry Seidel Canby, the best-known Delawarean man of letters, wrote *The Brandywine* in the Rivers of America series (1941), with illustrations by a young Andrew Wyeth. Pieces of the story have been told, but no modern publication has woven together a myriad of colorful episodes, so that they can be seen as inter-related human phenomena happening in a single, surprisingly intimate domain. This book aims to fill that need—to tell the fascinating story of one of America's most appealing small rivers.

That Lyrical Name

Everyone asks, what is the origin of the name "Brandywine"? It dates back to the earliest years of European settlement and refers to a popular drink of the day, Dutch distilled (or "burned") wine, *brandewijn*, nick-named "brandy." Generations have puzzled over how a river came to be named for a beverage. Some have claimed a ship full of brandy sank at the mouth of the creek, and venerable wreckage was sometimes pointed out as evidence. Others say the name originated not with brandy, but with an early settler: a certain Finn, Andrew Brandwyn or Braindwine, lived on the creek around 1660, about the time this stream (originally called Fish Kill or Fish Falls) was variously renamed Brandewyn, Brain-wend, or Brandywine Creek.

But possibly Andrew derived his name from the waterway, not the other way around. To offer two further conjectures: an orchard of med-lar trees is reported to have produced good brandy along the lower creek in the 1670s. Or perhaps the answer lies in the distinctive color that brandy implies: it seems plausible that settlers were struck with how the creek's water, following a thunderstorm upstream, was tinted yellowish-brown with runoff as it poured into the clearer Christina.[2]

Whatever its origin, "Brandywine" is a pleasing name, one that was profitably used to market the finely milled Brandywine flour of the eigh-teenth century, Brandywine gunpowder from DuPont factories in the nineteenth, and the Brandywine School of artists in the twentieth—typically, a mix of purposes both pragmatic and lyrical. The name "Brandywine Corn Meal" was considered so valuable in the West Indies trade, local millers filed a lawsuit in 1857 to protect it. Today the marketing is aimed at tourists who come to see the attractions advertised by the Brandywine Conference and Visitor's Bureau and the bucolic art at the Brandywine River Museum of Art.

By the way, is it a creek or a river? The Brandywine is of in-between size, and both usages have their adherents. "You may call it a stream, a creek, or a river with equal propriety," historian Wilmer MacElree assured an audience in 1911. "The government insists on calling it a 'river,'" a Wilmington newspaper complained in 1944, preferring "creek" as more traditional. In fact, all the very early accounts label it a creek—as stream scientists still tend to—but a 1768 act called for "regulating the fishing in the river Brandywine," and in recent years that term has gained the upper hand.[3]

But surely the ribbon-like Brandywine in its leafy valley barely qualifies as a "river" when compared with great neighboring waterways: its 325 square miles of drainage are dwarfed by the Delaware River with 12,809 square miles and, to the west, the mighty Susquehanna River with 27,580. Probably no other American river of such petite scale is so famous. Although little, it is unusually varied: going upstream, one passes the abandoned, red-brick factories of Wilmington, the wooded ravine at Hagley, swamps teeming with bullfrogs at Chadds Ford, breathtakingly beautiful horse country near Embreeville, a roaring steel mill at Coatesville, and eventually Amish farms where cattle cool themselves in the creek in a scene that looks nineteenth-century.

And the Brandywine's moods are varied: a novelist described it in 1845 as

> at one time, winding slowly, in its silvery silence, through richly-pastured farms; or running broad and rippling over its beautiful bed of pearly shells and golden pebbles . . . until its waters contract and roll heavily and darkly beneath the grove of giant oaks, elms and sycamores; but soon, like the sullen flow of a dark heart, it breaks angrily over the first obstruction.

Thus you may see the Brandywine, at one point, boiling savagely over a broken bed of rocks, until its thick sheets of foam
slide, like an avalanche of snow, into a deep pool.[4]

Daydreams of Englishness

Traveling south in search of his wounded son during the Civil War, Oliver
Wendell Holmes, Sr., passed through Chester County and marveled,

> Much as I had heard of the fertile regions of Pennsylvania, the
> vast scale and the uniform luxuriance of this region astonished
> me. The grazing pastures were so green, the fields were under
> such perfect culture, the cattle looked so sleek, the houses were
> so comfortable, the barns so ample, the fences so well kept, that
> I did not wonder, when I was told that this region was called
> the England of Pennsylvania.[5]

And no particular spot in that whole region seems more English
than the Brandywine. The picturesque stream twists by a flooded
swamp quaintly called "Dungeon Bottom," past historic settlements
named for British towns (West Chester and Birmingham), then edges
alongside Brandywine Hundred in a state named for Lord De La Warr
(land divisions called "hundreds" occur only in Delaware and England).
"You have got a hell of a fine country here," the British officer of 1777
told a Quaker youth admiringly as he surveyed what would soon be a
battlefield.

Further Britishness: Because Quakers intermarried, they built great
family dynasties that cherished their genealogical connection to the
British Isles—to which most had remained Tory loyalists in wartime,
standing aloof from the new American mainstream. By 1853 there were
1,400 descendants of early settlers Abraham and Deborah Darlington,
for example, and the "tribe" held a reunion. Busy at the gathering was
West Chester botanist and amateur historian William Darlington,
back from a genealogical tour of Britain. Not only Quakers boasted of

Ancestral hearth. History-minded descendants preserved the lowly dwelling that Eleuthère Irénée du Pont first inhabited on the creek. In 1952—150 years after the clan arrived—Mrs. E. I. du Pont III paid a nostalgic visit.

their overseas family tree; as Canby noted, many local families sought "to find usually dubious ancestors of impeccable nobility in England."[6]

Seemingly quasi-British, too, is the valley's dainty rural charm: carefully preserved old stone cottages with cluttered colonial hearths, gentrified sports of fox hunting and point-to-point horse racing, and bountiful gardens both public and private. The venerable hunt called "Mr. Stewart's Cheshire Foxhounds" was established on the river's West Branch more than a century ago, named for a county in England and taking the unusual step of eschewing American dogs in favor of more authentic ones imported from Warwickshire, England. Brandywine estates could even claim to rival those of Britain, that Garden Isle: an English gardening expert raved of the du Ponts in 1931, "No one family in America has done more for horticulture." On a bluff over the Brandywine, a cotton-mill magnate assembled one of the finest collections of English Victorian paintings anywhere, the Pre-Raphaelite showpieces now at the Delaware Art Museum. And today local squire George "Frolic" Weymouth is a friend of Queen Elizabeth II, no less, who shares his love of horses.

Along the Brandywine you can visit homes first occupied in the time of Queen Anne, worship in a church erected by English masons before 1700 (though called "Old Swedes" for the ethnicity of its congregation, remnant Scandinavians amid a floodtide of English). The distinctively British tone was noted as long ago as 1866, by Bayard Taylor in *The Story of Kennett*, the best known novel set in the Brandywine region: "The country life of our part of Pennsylvania retains more elements of its English origin than that of New England or Virginia." And here, an enthusiast wrote in 1909,

> the air has a sweet, tonic quality and the oxen plowing the brown hillsides look tranquil and comfortable. To follow the stream through all its wanderings is to pass close to ancient farm walls and bright old-time gardens, under little arching bridges and beside grassy swamps and cressy islands. Far off sounds the shriek of the steam-thresher, and the cries of farmers at their harrowing comes across the fields. . . . Our Chester County stream recalls the rivers of England.[7]

As early as 1805, a romantic writer sequestered at "An Admired Spot on the Banks of the Brandywine" drew a connection to British waterways:

> *Shall Thames and Avon boast the poet's lays,*
> *And shalt thou pass without the meed of praise?*
> *What are their charms the world so much adore,*
> *That do not smile delightful on thy shore.*

The anonymous poet goes on to say,

> *Could I linger on thy tranquil shore . . .*
> *How would my thoughts on rapid pinions soar,*
> *From present to the past, from hence to* England's *shore.*[8]

Given this long tradition of suggestive linkages, it is somehow not surprising that J. R. R. Tolkien named one of the rivers in his imaginary Middle Earth—flowing past the hobbits' peaceable fields and mills in the Shire, that paragon of mystical Englishness—the "Brandywine."

As a matter of demographic fact, Chester County was unusually English for generations, hardly experiencing the diverse immigration so familiar elsewhere in the Northeast. The whole region preserved much of its early ethnic character: Philadelphia long had the highest percentage of native-born stock of any large American city, and, a historian wrote in the 1880s, "It is a singular fact that the white races in Pennsylvania [English, Scots-Irish, and German] are remarkably unmixed, and retain their original character beyond that of any state in the Union."[9]

Lying at the heart of this persistently English-inflected zone, the Brandywine has lured Anglophiles, none more ardent than Howard Pyle, whose vine-clad Wilmington studio in Queen Anne style was described by one visitor as looking "fresh and English." Here he illustrated the tales of King Arthur, immersing himself in English history and lore. Pyle once wrote, "I doubt whether I shall ever cross the ocean to see those things which seem so beautiful and dream-like in my imagination, and which if I saw might break the bubble of fancy and leave nothing behind but bitter soap-suds." Instead of traveling abroad, he and his circle made a little England of their own, here in the heart of colonial America.[10]

As he wrote in one of his first magazine articles, "Old-Time Life in a Quaker Town," Wilmington was a place of "many old-fashioned customs"—until lately there had even been bellmen and criers in the streets—and here the "traditions, manners, customs, and peculiarities of old English life have been handed down from generation to generation, as carefully preserved as an old quilted petticoat in lavender."[11]

Poets who have sung the Brandywine's praises have often been reminded of the Thames. The Brandywine is, by elephantine American
standards, a singularly compact and decorous little river, modestly con-
fining itself to three counties in Pennsylvania and Delaware and hardly
exceeding sixty miles in length: a tidy British scale. Actually the Thames
is much bigger, draining an area sixteen times greater. But both rivers serve
their respective regions as repositories of historical memory, as touch-
stones of local character. As British writer Peter Ackroyd has written,

> The Thames is a metaphor for the country through which it
> runs. It is modest and moderate, calm and resourceful; it is
> powerful without being fierce. It is not flamboyantly impres-
> sive. . . . It eschews extremes. . . . The idealized images of En-
> glish life, with their thatched cottages and village greens, their
> duckponds and hedged fields, derive from the landscape of the
> Thames. The river is the source of these day-dreams of En-
> glishness.[12]

Much the same could be said of how the mythic Brandywine func-
tions in the American Mid-Atlantic—as a kind of traditionalist ideal.
Here (if we avert our eye from industry and sprawl) is an enclave of quiet
agrarian values amid urbanism; here is a beacon of refinement and culture for those who resent the hectic clang of modern life; here is Old
America for the nostalgic antiquarian (see Plate 2). Philadelphia writer
George Lippard, friend of Edgar Allan Poe, captured this feeling as long
ago as the 1840s when, seeking inspiration for a historical novel about
the Revolution, he looked around him at Birmingham Meetinghouse
along the Brandywine in Chester County and saw "a sight as lovely, as
ever burst on mortal eye. There are plains, glowing with the rich hues of
cultivation, plains intersected by fences and dotted with cottages; here
a massive hill; there an ancient farm-house, and far beyond, peaceful
mansions reposing in the shadow of twilight woods." Here, as we shall
often see, the Brandywine seemed an almost old-world antithesis to the
vast, smoky, industrializing city of Philadelphia.[13]

In his nostalgic *Brandywine Days* (1910), poet John Russell Hayes declared that "the old days and the old ways have their natural home in these tranquil valleys; quietude and conservatism are seated here by ancient right." Hayes adored the Brandywine for its antimodern ethos of "reverie & landscape & old folks & old houses & old farms." In the early twentieth century, novelist Joseph Hergesheimer was inspired by the region to take "traditional America for a subject," relishing how "the older lives and days had laid their beneficent tyranny on the present" here. The tenor of such thought—almost a "Brandywine mindset"—can be traced right down to Andrew Wyeth, who wrote of his native hearth in 1965, "I do an awful lot of thinking and dreaming about things in the past and the future—the timelessness of the rocks and the hills—all the people who have existed there."[14]

Generation after generation, the mythical Brandywine has offered solace to thoughtful Americans oppressed by modern life, its relentless pace and chaotic lack of fixity. Here in the realm of spinning wheels and splashing milldams they can find venerable certainties. The Thames has always served a similar function, Ackroyd marveling at its endless capacity for inducing "a mood of nostalgia." "It is in fact remarkable how many writers of the river do comment unfavorably on 'modern life,'" he writes. "The riparian traveler of 1745 is just as likely to condemn 'improvements' as the walker of 2007."[15]

Beauty Changed into Currency

The Brandywine has long functioned as a back-to-nature retreat just westward of Philadelphia, twenty-two miles away (America's very largest metropolis between about 1750 and 1800, then its second largest to nearly 1890), just as does Walden Pond fifteen miles west of Boston or the Thames Valley west of London. These fabled places are all remarkable for the concentrated attention they received from artists and writers as nineteenth-century romanticism reshaped our understanding of the natural world and made escape from crowded cities seem desirable.

Offering a getaway from urbanism, the Brandywine's meandering shores have drawn the wealthy for generations. Pioneering forester Joseph Rothrock urged farmers not to cut down the trees that shaded creekside acres because, someday, their property would become much more valuable for residential development than for corn: "Bear in mind, you through whose land the Brandywine flows, that before long the beauty of your meadows can be changed into currency; that every tree and shaded road along the banks will be an element in the bargain between you and a home hunter." Rothrock seemed to predict today's house-building boom—way back in 1889![16]

Writing after World War I, Hergesheimer bemoaned the increasing intrusion of modernity—especially automobiles and the suburban culture they allowed—into his beloved valley. "The countryside of my imagination . . . long ago ceased to exist," he complained. Classic colonial farmhouses now stood ruinous or had been transformed into upscale "country residences"; old taverns had become tearooms for motorists. With the coming of "great concrete highways," such as U.S. 1 through Chadds Ford, he saw that "the countryside was contracting, it was growing smaller and smaller and some day it would disappear." Never mind that he had moved out here from Philadelphia himself and rebuilt one of those old farmhouses, or that one of the noisy cars was his own.[17]

In the pell-mell Eisenhower years the Brandywine produced William Whyte, America's most eloquent polemicist against suburban sprawl, who lamented what he called the most beautiful valley in the country being chopped up by greedy developers. Alas, many of his worries have substantially come true: today's upscale suburbs with British-sounding names ("Royalwood Estates," "Beversrede") have swallowed rolling farmsteads and great turreted and columned country seats that Philadelphians built long ago as summer places, starting just before the Civil War. Everyone dreams of living here: twenty-first-century Chester County, bisected by the Brandywine and home to horse farms and golf courses, is by far the wealthiest county in Pennsylvania and among the forty richest in the nation.

Prosperity has gilded the name Brandywine ever since Quaker farmers grew wealthy tilling some of the most fertile cropland in colonial America here ("Without doubt the area was one of the most affluent agricultural societies anywhere," a geographer has written), then even richer by milling flour to feed the great cities. They were joined by a French family named du Pont who turned the kinetic energy of rushing river water into the black gold of gunpowder and eventually amassed phenomenal riches as heads of the world's biggest chemical company. Just one of them, Alfred I. du Pont, made more than $3 million in 1915 from stock dividends alone.[18]

Du Pont profits built sumptuous "chateaus" with ornate gardens along the creek in Delaware and allowed the preservation of scenic Brandywine acres that otherwise might have been carved up into industrial sites or housing developments. The opening of these Chateau Country gardens to tourists has lately contributed to giving the region between here and Philadelphia the largest concentration of public gardens anywhere in the nation. The gardening habit goes back many generations in this Anglophile place; botanist Darlington laid out a fine arboretum in a West Chester park and approvingly quoted Washington Irving: "The taste of the English in the cultivation of land, and in what is called Landscape Gardening, is unrivalled. They have studied nature intently."[19]

Affluent as it may be—and advertised as a charming getaway—the Brandywine Valley is far from immune to modern ills. As upscale sprawl creeps over its bucolic hillsides, viewsheds are destroyed, water quality degrades. A *Life* magazine photograph of the Brandywine Battlefield in 1940 showed tumbling barley fields off to the horizon—almost impossible to imagine today, when fancy housing tracts occupy many of those same acres and less than 40 percent of the Brandywine watershed, once a model for the nation in intelligent farming practices, remains agricultural. The three counties through which the creek chiefly flows in Delaware and Pennsylvania are now thronged by 1.6 million people, a number constantly swelling; the watershed alone is home to 235,500.

We voraciously remove thirty million gallons from the little river for various uses—every day.

Since 1967 the Brandywine Conservancy, founded by George "Frolic" Weymouth when the valley at Chadds Ford was threatened by industrial development, has fought to save the scenic beauty of this great American place. The organization today holds 441 conservation easements covering 12 percent of the watershed, keeping these properties unspoiled (by various means, 29 percent of the watershed has successfully been protected). But with every passing decade, development pressures seem to expand: of Pennsylvania's sixty-seven counties, no other was growing so rapidly as Chester County by the year 2000. Until the economy slowed in the Great Recession, five thousand acres were being bulldozed annually there, an expanse equivalent to six of New York's Central Park. The federal government recently called Brandywine Battlefield one of the nation's most threatened landmarks, urgently deserving preservation.

One thinks of Goldsmith's famous eighteenth-century poem, "The Deserted Village," lamenting how the rich were buying up farms in the English countryside and converting them into private estates:

> E'en now the devastation is begun,
> And half the business of destruction done;
> Even now, methinks, as pondering here I stand,
> I see the rural virtues leave the land.[20]

So, too, does Chester County seem a little less rural every year. The Brandywine paradox (capitalists insistently knocking at the doors of Arcadia) is constantly at work here, says David Shields, associate director of the land stewardship program at the Brandywine Conservancy: "The protected land draws great wealth and more people who want to live there—it's a double-edged sword for us."

All the more need for First State National Monument, then. As its debut brochure explains, the park is meant to safeguard "original Quaker settlement patterns . . . woods and pastures . . . scenic rock outcrops and wetlands" along the Brandywine's shores. Federal intervention to save the creek seems warranted, for without question, its role in the life of the country has long been significant. As we saw, much as the Thames Valley has been called a little model for England generally ("an open-air museum of English culture, history and tradition—a microcosm from which a general impression of the whole country can be gained," one historian writes), so too does the Brandywine seem to encapsulate, for many visitors, what they cherish most about the nation's colonial heritage, its original agrarian flavor.[21]

In fact, the Brandywine's early development gave a strong impetus to national trends: One geographer has written that Chester and neighboring counties in Pennsylvania set the pattern in colonial times for the organization of large sections of the greater United States, forming "the prototype of North American development. Its style of life presaged the mainstream of nineteenth-century America; its conservative defense of liberal individualism, its population of mixed national and religious origins, its dispersed farms, county seats, and farm-service villages, and its mixed crop and livestock agriculture served as models for much of the rural Middle West."[22]

And in fact, there are also Brandywine Creeks in western Pennsylvania, Ohio, and Indiana, their names a testament to the dispersal of local settlers to places far removed as pioneers industriously built a republic. These Brandywine notables spread widely. The first booster of Kentucky was John Filson, who spent a childhood on the Brandywine and published his promotional book on the new trans-Appalachian state in, of all places, Wilmington. William Gilpin was born in 1822 at Lafayette's Headquarters, his family home, then spent his childhood at his father's milling village beside the Brandywine in Delaware; later he explored the West and was appointed by President Lincoln as governor of Colorado—never missing a chance to boast that he had been "born on the Brandywine battlefield." Abraham Lincoln himself, a native of Kentucky, was the great-grandson of ironmonger Mordecai Lincoln, who, in 1720, ran a forge "Near ye Branches of the French Creek & the Branches of Brandywine."[23]

As perhaps the most storied little river in America, the Brandywine continues to inspire and delight. The establishment of First State National Monument was a fitting culmination of centuries of public interest in a singularly attractive region. But in the twenty-first century, we face great challenges in preserving this fragile valley at the heart of Megalopolis, which has always existed in uneasy balance between two antithetical impulses—it is a myth-generating paradise, paragon of unspoiled bucolic nature, yet a wealth-generating engine subject to exploitation and overdevelopment. If we are going to save the Brandywine for our children, we need to begin by understanding its fascinating history and why it has always mattered.

Chapter 1

❧ ❧

Fish Creek in New Sweden

Long ago, a little river flowed through desolate, wind-whipped tundra. Mammoths drank from the torrent, Brandywine water freezing to their matted brown fur. Such were the strange sights met with 150 centuries ago in the Ice Age, as the stream rushed through snow-covered wastes toward a shipless sea.[1]

Jump ahead fifty centuries: the mammoth are extinct. Only now, the first humans begin to prowl the land, spears in hand. It is still cold; long reaches of time have yet to elapse before the climate moderates and forests of oak and hickory clothe these hillsides, bleakly draped in low mats of scraggly gorse. In places, freeze-thaw cycles are gradually strewing steep slopes with huge, round boulders of Brandywine blue rock, creating the jumbled landscapes we know today.

Eventually Lenape Indians hunted in these forests, in little bands that came and went with the seasons. They numbered a few hundred at most, making this fertile valley in aboriginal times as sparsely populated as rural Alaska is today. They strung fishing weirs along the Brandywine to catch alewife and shad that clogged the waterways every spring. A cave along the east bank afforded a refuge: Beaver Valley Rock Shelter, where archaeological excavation has yielded arrowheads, stone chips, and clay potsherds from transient hunting parties in the Woodland period, before 1000 A.D.[2]

To keep the forests open and easy to hunt through, the Lenape set fires in winter, filling the air with smoke and sweet fragrance, a smell that wafted for miles and could be detected even out at sea, by men who suddenly arrived in ships from unknown lands far away. For these strangers, the smell of burning forests, torched by the native people, was their first hint of land, of the mysterious shores of the New World.[3]

De Vries at the Rocks

On January 14, 1633, a little ship passed the mouth of the creek—still a nameless stream—and pulled up to an outcrop called the Rocks on Minquas Kill, today's Christina River. (Dutch explorers named creeks throughout the territory of New Netherlands *kill*; "Minquas" referred to a warlike tribe who lived far west of the Christina.) On board ship was David de Vries, a tough Dutch artillerist who had fought many wars at sea, braving Turks and Barbary pirates.

De Vries had come to America to oversee a fledgling colony at the mouth of the Delaware River called Swanendael (near today's Lewes), named for the fat swans that stood out among its abundant birdlife. The whole region newly belonged to the Dutch Republic, and Swanendael was to be the Dutch West India Company's whaling outpost: whale oil was worth a fortune in Europe. Even upriver at Minquas Kill there were whales, de Vries was pleased to note—he saw one spout six or seven times there.

De Vries had come to the Rocks to gather ballast for his ship. Here the crystalline Piedmont touches the oozy Coastal Plain; here stones were available as they almost never are farther down the sandy-shored Delaware Bay. Five years later, de Vries's rivals, the Swedes, would make the lonely Rocks the site of their nation's first permanent settlement in the New World—European states jockeying for position amid the wilds of a little-explored, dauntingly immense continent. But all this lay in the future. As his men hauled stones aboard ship in 1633, de Vries little imagined the Swedes would ever come to threaten Dutch hegemony in the Delaware Valley. He was more worried about the British, starting to

Past the buttonwood. Europeans have known the creek for nearly three centuries. Some sycamores that shaded the early explorers still grow today. Andrew Wyeth, *First Traders on the Brandywine* (1940).

extend their influence north from Virginia, where they had settled at Jamestown twenty-six years before.

And mostly his mind was on the troublesome Indians. Sent to oversee Swanendael just months after its establishment, de Vries had found it burned, its inhabitants massacred, their bones and skulls bleaching in the field where the hapless settlers had been slaughtered while hoeing tobacco and grain. Following this grim discovery, de Vries spent weeks sailing up and down the Delaware River seeking corn and beans from whichever Indians seemed cooperative, narrowly avoiding getting killed himself and finding the Lenapes convulsed with fear of the Minquas, who had sent war parties against them from the west. In these bellicose times they had no food to give him, not even for his best trinkets and knives. The Minquas had flattened their crops, burned their houses. Eventually de Vries would have to voyage all the way to Virginia to buy basic supplies from the upstart British, so he could make the long journey home to Holland and civilization.

At the lonely Rocks that day in 1633, de Vries looked around him in wonderment. The scenery was "beautifully level, full of groves of oak, hickory, ash, and chestnut trees, and also [grape] vines which grow upon the trees." It was a land of unimaginable abundance, he thought, but wasted on bands of quarrelsome Indians. And it was fearfully cold—how could this part of America be so frigid and yet lie at the latitude of Spain, he wondered bitterly.[4]

The Rocks had a fine advantage: here ships could pull in and escape the ice floes that drifted down the mighty Delaware all winter, threatening to crush their wooden hulls. Minquas Kill had the makings of a port—though now it dozed in winter sunlight, uninhabited, huge forest trees rubbing their branches together in creakings no one heard unless an Indian happened to drift by in his dugout canoe. And here, in stately silence, the waters of the Brandywine—perfectly pure—joined the Minquas amid reeds of the tidal marsh where ducks and muskrat teemed.

De Vries was one of the very first white men to visit the Brandywine. It was the Dutch Golden Age—back home, Rubens and Rembrandt were painting—and he had been sent as part of ambitious Dutch efforts to exploit the lucrative fur trade. The Dutch West India Company's hired navigator, Henry Hudson, had first laid European eyes on the Delaware River twenty-four years earlier, and a handful of brave explorers followed. A year after de Vries's visit, a British adventurer named Thomas Yong, recently arrived at Jamestown, sailed up and down the Delaware in a shallop, seeking the Northwest Passage and boldly nailing the coat of arms of King Charles I to a tree in haughty defiance of Dutch claims.

Yong likely saw the Brandywine during this summer 1634 expedition, during which he traded beads, pipes, scissors, and cloth with Indians who pulled alongside in their canoes and offered eels, or beaver and otter skins. The forests were astonishingly dense and dark, except where the natives had hacked out a clearing and planted corn.

Yong gazed upon what seemed to be the mythical land of plenty: the waters of the Delaware River teemed with sturgeon, and there were birds in quantities "so great as can hardly be believed," an "infinite number" of pigeons, blackbirds, turkeys, swans, geese, duck, teal, widgeon, brant, herons, and cranes. A hawk chased a flock of partridges across the wide river, and Yong and his companion shot forty-eight of them as they flew over the boat—that was a haul not greatly out of the ordinary.[5]

The Dominion of Fort Christina

Soon the Swedes would come. The first Swedish settlement of the Delaware Valley in March 1638 marked another huge milestone in the European conquest of the continent, and it all unfolded on the narrow neck where an Indian path linked Minquas Kill and the Brandywine. Here, disdainful of Dutch claims, the Swedes built Fort Christina at the Rocks. Ships *Kalmar Nyckel* and *Vogel Grip* carried brave pioneers as well as their opportunistic leader Peter Minuit, formerly in Dutch service at New Amsterdam and famous for having bought the whole island of Manhattan for sixty guilders. They turned into Minquas Kill, sailed up and down it past Brandywine mouth, firing cannon; but there was no "vestige of Christian people" to be seen in this forlorn place. And so they claimed the land for Queen Christina of Sweden.

Minuit named his fort after her and, in another spectacular transaction, bought from the Indians the whole western shore of the Delaware River from the Atlantic at Cape Henlopen to the falls at today's Trenton, New Jersey—and far inland too—setting up wooden stakes that stood, famous landmarks, for generations. The Indians traded these immense tracts for "awls, needles, scissors, knives, axes, guns, powder and balls, together with blankets," probably thinking the deal was a canny one, since they planned to continue to live and hunt there, unmindful of these puny, legalistic explorers. The Swedes proudly set out to map their vast new territory (which of course embraced the Philadelphia metropolitan region of today), including the Brandywine and all the other "tributaries" and "creeks." A copy was sent to the Crown.

Thus a flamboyant challenge was hurled at the Dutch, who loudly protested this Scandinavian incursion. Minuit, they said, had no authority "to build forts upon our rivers and coasts, nor to settle people on the land, nor to traffic in peltries."

Subsequent governor Johan Printz bolstered the Swedish settlement at the Rocks and defied the imperious Dutch leader, Peter Stuyvesant, who erected the rival Fort Casimir a short way down the Delaware River at today's New Castle, Delaware. Weighing over four hundred pounds, Governor Printz—"Big Guts" or "Big Tub" to the Lenape—inspired awe. When de Vries returned for another American visit, Printz drank his health with a glass of Rhenish wine, toasting the intrepid pioneer navigator. Where de Vries had seen only the Rocks, lonely amid forests and marshes, now there was a sturdy, permanent fort with iron cannon guarding the Christina River and "some houses inside" its walls.[6]

Upon arrival, Printz had immediately shipped 1,300 beaver skins home as evidence of the great abundance of God's bounty in New Sweden. Soon the Swedes were trading far inland with the Minquas for "beavers, raccoons, sables, gray foxes, wildcats, lynxes, bears, and deer." The Lenape vexed Printz with their constant attacks, keeping the Swedes confined to their fortifications. He longed to bring over plenty of troops and guns until he "broke the necks of all of them." Then "we could take possession of the places (which are the most fruitful) that the savages now possess."[7]

In the 1640s, Fort Christina bustled with activity: residents included a commissary, pastor, barber, trumpeter, constable, blacksmith, carpenters, and three soldiers. Outside, stretching to the lazy, tidal-plain Brandywine a short distance away, were fields of tobacco, maize, rye, and barley amid tree stumps, and a roaming herd of cattle and swine. Forests were falling to the steel axes of Finnish settlers, a strapping breed of immigrants brought for just this purpose. Within the walls of Fort Christina debuted the first "log cabin" in America, a typically Finnish housing type, soon to spread everywhere—another Brandywine contribution to the culture of the entire nation.[8]

Printz dreamed of a great "tobacco plantation"—controversial, since some Swedes rued importation of the filthy weed. Just east at the fledgling Swedish settlement of Manathaan (today's Cherry Island landfill),

Two rivers meet. This 1940s view shows the Brandywine, center, as it flows down toward the wider Christina, left. Downtown Wilmington at upper left. Swedish colonial settlement happened at the narrow isthmus, site of Fort Christina at the Rocks.

a cooper set up a cask-making business and constructed small boats, the very beginnings of European industry in the Delaware Valley.[9]

The Swedes recognized the potential for water power on the area's swift streams. Printz built the first "watermill" in the Mid-Atlantic on Cobb's Creek near today's Philadelphia, for grinding grain, replacing an earlier windmill that "would never work, and was good for nothing." He ordered a survey of potential sites ("waterfalls") for a sawmill that could cut oak to be "bartered in the Flemish Islands for wine," and although this came to nothing, Printz was prescient in seeing the opportunities for industry on local creeks, where water rushed powerfully over the boulders.[10]

The last Swedish governor, as it turned out, was Johan Rising, who survived a hellish 1654 voyage across the Atlantic in which a hundred prospective settlers died. Like every new arrival along the Delaware River, he marveled at the many intersecting waterways teeming with geese and ducks. What was later "Brandywine" was being called "Fish Creek" now, appropriately, for "in the creeks there are eel, salmon, thickhead and striped bass." Like Printz, Rising dreamed of mills, and he was surely referring to the Brandywine when he described "the great fall [where] many waterworks could be placed." He planned "to construct there a good dam . . . and then a flour-mill, a saw-mill, and a chamois-dressing mill. . . . If we could here establish powder-mills it would bring us great profit."

Confidently, Rising had engineer Peter Lindeström divide the field between Fort Christina and the Brandywine into building lots, where six or eight houses were soon erected—not so many as the twenty-two the obnoxious Dutch had built at New Castle, but the promising start of a port city. Rising and Lindeström improved the crumbling fort, re-building it "with good ramparts of turf" and palisades against "the attacks of savages." Lindeström drew a map that survives; it shows the fort, the town grid, and the lower Brandywine twisting through its mosquitoey marshes.

But it was not savages who brought doom to Fort Christina: it was those Dutch, whom Rising had fatally antagonized by claiming Fort Casimir for Sweden. In August 1655, Peter Stuyvesant's soldiers, in retaliation, suddenly surrounded Fort Christina, sending boats up the Brandywine to Third Hook, a bluff on the north bank of the creek. From there, they crossed to Timber Island, which Rising owned personally and had partly cleared of its fine trees; it lay in a bend in the Brandywine across from the fort, where the invaders now seized a house and hoisted a flag. Then they dashed up to the Great Falls (today's Brandywine Park) and nearby heights overlooking the Swedish settlement. Stuyvesant had swiftly "invested Fort Christina on all sides."

So began the first European military operation on the Brandywine. Stuyvesant sent a letter demanding that the Swedes surrender, then had his troops fire warning shots from batteries at Timber Island and along the Christina River. His Dutch troops slaughtered cattle, goats, swine, and poultry, and "broke open houses." The Swedish fort was poorly equipped, and a dejected Rising soon met Stuyvesant outside its "sconce" and gave the place up, bringing New Sweden to a humiliating close.

But Dutch rule itself would not last long. The English were pressing in from all sides now, and in 1664 they took control of the entire Delaware Valley.[11]

By the time Dutch traveler Jasper Danckaerts passed through in the fall of 1679, Fort Christina had vanished, swallowed by the mists of history. He came from the north, crossing Schiltpads Kill, Swedish for "turtle" (literally "creek of the toad with a shield on its back"). This was today's Shellpot Creek in Delaware, which has now been diverted and no longer enters the Brandywine.[12]

Along the Shellpot, "a fall of water over the rocks" had allowed construction of a productive grist mill. The Swedish miller showed the curious traveler a dead muskrat hanging up to dry, a creature "numerous in the creeks." Danckaerts then crossed the Brandywine in a canoe, visiting the former site of Fort Christina as well as the place across Christina River where "Stuyvesant threw up his battery to attack the fort." Already these places were of historical interest, and Danckaerts seems to have been our first "heritage tourist," that lucrative industry in modern times. Near the site of the battery, he noted, abundant medlar fruit was harvested by a Dutchman to make "good brandy": a possible clue, as we saw, to the origins of the newly minted name of the river.[13]

By the 1670s these once all-but-trackless woods were being divvied up by Dutch and English immigrants (and remaining Swedes and Finns) into landholdings. Swedish surgeon Tymen Stidham had served as ship's doctor on many voyages, first with the *Kalmar Nyckel*; on one disastrous trip his wife and three small children perished as prisoners of the Spanish. Eventually he settled near Fort Christina and bought huge tracts along the Brandywine, including most of the south bank of the creek from Big Bend (north of the Delaware state line) down to "ye Rattlesnake Kill" in today's Brandywine Park. (Rattlesnakes were once fearsomely common—but are now extinct locally.) A 1671 deed signed by authorities in Manhattan gave Stidham "600 acres of land lying on the north side of ye fish creeke at Brandewyns Creeke just below the falls."

Those falls were extremely valuable: Stidham's sons are said to have opened the first mill on the Brandywine there, near an old Indian ford at the foot of today's Adams Street. In 1678, Cornelius Empson applied for the privilege of establishing a ferry across Stidham's shallow "mill pond." North to south overland travel was gradually increasing, to which the Brandywine proved a vexatious obstacle. When pioneering Quaker evangelist George Fox journeyed south toward Maryland in 1672, he recorded his trepidation when they came to Wilmington and "passed over a desperate river, which had in it many rocks and broad stones, very hazardous to us and our horses."[14]

Along the creek, polyglot citizens of four nations—plus Lenape—were now living alongside each other in these years just prior to the great cultural turning point—the arrival of William Penn.

Chapter 2

☙ ❧

Pride of Penn's Woods

The crucial episode in the settlement of the Delaware Valley came in 1682 with the landing of William Penn at New Castle, where he claimed today's entire state of Delaware as the "three lower counties" of Pennsylvania. Then he sailed upstream to found Philadelphia. Already his promotional map showed the new colony (Latin for "Penn's Woods") embracing the "Brande vine," considered one of the most important waterways of the bountiful region. His new holdings, Penn said, "hath the advantage of many creeks or rivers . . . some navigable for great ships, some for small craft: those of most eminency are Christina Brandywine Skilpott & Schulkill; any one of which have room to lay up the Royal Navy of England, there being from four to eight fathom water."[1]

With great efficiency, Penn's territory was chopped up into parcels and sold off to eager settlers, as shown on the official Thomas Holme map of 1687. "County of Chester" is seen subdivided as far west as the Brandywine—where it abruptly gives way to forest primeval—with plantations confined to the area between Great Bend and the Forks (where the east and west branches of the creek divide), centering on "Brumadgam" or Birmingham, named ambitiously for the prosperous town in the English Midlands. East of the lower Brandywine lies, on the map, "the Proprietary Mannor of Rockland"—a name later famous from paper-milling at the village of Rockland. Many of the original, west-running parcel lines still appear as modern property divisions in Chester County, more than 330 years later.

More British maps would follow, including one of the famous "circular line" dividing today's Delaware from Pennsylvania. First drawn in December 1701 with the "horsedyke" at New Castle as its radius, running due north to an oak tree with twelve notches on the west bank of the Brandywine near Great Bend, the round shape of the boundary is unique in all the American states. In 1750 another twelve-mile radius was drawn, meant to clarify the original. Tradition holds that the New Castle courthouse cupola was appointed the center of this circle, but, in fact, the boundary was difficult to draw and not nearly precise enough to line up on one building—so irregular, in fact, it actually had multiple centers from which it was measured. First State National Monument embraces the green on which the courthouse stands in New Castle as well as the historic No. 14 Bound Stone, part of the circular border, in the park's Woodlawn section on the Brandywine.[2]

The flood of Quaker settlers—Pennsylvania's population broke twenty thousand by 1700—seemed to spell doom for the Lenape Indians (see Plate 3). Their chieftains sold spacious inland tracts to Penn in 1683 but reserved one mile on each side of the Brandywine for hunting and fishing. Under the leadership of Checochinican (Person of Few Words), they huddled for security at Queonemysing, or Indian Town, in Great Bend. This settlement did not last long, however; soon the Lenape had fled west or perished, the last, locally, being the itinerant basket maker "Indian Hannah," who died near Embreeville on the West Branch in 1802 and whose grave, with the coming of romanticism, became something of a shrine for poetical types. Today the site of Indian Town dozes beneath rolling fields, one of the most important archaeological sites in all the Mid-Atlantic, though barely explored.

Further upstream, old Lenape graves were frequently excavated by curious settlers, and farmers collected artifacts of the vanquished native peoples. When West Chester celebrated its centennial in 1899, locals put their findings on public display: an iron tomahawk, heaps of stone tools and colorful trade beads, an Indian skull and jawbone, and more than five thousand arrowheads, or "darts."[3]

Gone, too—mostly within just a few years of the Quakers' arrival—was much of the superabundant wildlife every seventeenth-century settler had commented on. Penn himself had glowingly described "elk, as big as a small ox, deer bigger than ours, beaver . . . turkey (forty and fifty pound weight) . . . phesants, heath-birds, pidgeons and partridges in abundance . . . . brands, ducks, teal, also the snipe and curloe, and that in great numbers . . . wild cat, panther, otter, wolf." Now all were greatly reduced or driven to extinction. In the 1740s, Swedish naturalist Peter Kalm could report that "things are greatly altered"; gone were the days you could kill eighty ducks in a morning. A farmer in his field along the Brandywine at Wilmington shot the last beaver in 1770, it was said (though these pesky tree-fellers are now back). As late as 1838, "wagon loads of the *passenger pigeons* were brought into Philadelphia and were seen in heaps in the market," but they too subsequently vanished from the scene. "Many of those [animals] which originally inhabited our woods have gone, with the red men of the forest, never to return," botanist William Darlington declared in an 1826 speech, "and others are daily becoming more rare."[4]

Despite all the ecological changes, numerous ancient trees survive today from the first years of English settlement, the glory of our much-altered landscape—a concentration of giants virtually unrivaled anywhere else along the Eastern Seaboard. A tulip tree older than our nation, twenty feet around, stood at the DuPont Experimental Station above Rising Sun Bridge—a tall sentinel patched with concrete that unfortunately died in 2013. For a century artists showed this giant in their paintings of Walker's Mill. On the Winterthur estate stands a tulip tree seventeen feet eight inches in circumference and soaring to 162 feet, the tallest tree in the state of Delaware. "It would be a tree of note even in the Smokies," a visiting expert marvels. On the main lawn of the house grew a white oak that, according to my ring count after it was sawed down, sprouted in the late seventeenth century. Such extraordinary trees have outlived every other living thing from that remote era—certainly every animal and person has long since been swept away—and yet these venerable veterans still burst into green life each spring, as if they were three years old and not three hundred.

Recently there has been a flurry of tree-measuring by the Native Tree Society. Their results are astonishing. At 138 feet tall, a Winterthur beech is the tallest of that species the group has measured anywhere in the country. Sixty-seven trees at Longwood qualify as Pennsylvania State Champions. A tulip tree there hits 164.2 feet—incredibly, the tallest hardwood standing in the northeastern United States. A visit to just one section of Brandywine Creek State Park revealed more giants: seventy-three tulip trees over 130 feet tall (one at 160 feet), sixteen of these more than fourteen feet in girth—no wonder Thomas Jefferson called this species "the Juno of our groves." Society members across the nation responded excitedly to the announcements: "That's more big poplars than Steve and I have measured in the entire state of Ohio." "There just aren't many places with so much quantity and quality. I'm astounded."[5]

The survival of these specimens owes much to the du Pont family's traditional love of trees, dating back to the romantic era when immigrant Eleuthère Irénée du Pont signed his traveling papers "botaniste." Winterthur historian Maggie Lidz tells me,

> It's crucial that there has been a continuous history of tree care, right back to the 1830s, when the Winterthur property was described as "as wild as the mountains of Virginia." The family kept the house surrounded by trees, which was a choice not followed much elsewhere—they valued the trees that highly. Later on, Colonel Henry A. du Pont wouldn't let anybody cut the trees, and he had Charles Sargent down from the Arnold Arboretum to document them. Today, we couldn't have Azalea Woods or March Bank without the tree cover. Trees are what

give the garden such a strong sense of identity, not just locally but nationally and internationally.

Brave Brick Houses

With the British settlers came real, permanent architecture. Thousands of years of Indian occupation have left virtually no trace today, except for the occasional arrowhead in a muddy cornfield. And few if any authentically Swedish or Finnish log cabins remain. By contrast, the Brandywine Valley has dozens of sturdy structures surviving from the earliest years of Quaker settlement—homes of industrious farmers who built them to last.

The ideal, said one observer of seventeenth-century Pennsylvania, was houses "built of brick, some of timber, plaister'd and ceil'd, as in England"; "brave brick houses," Penn himself called them. The surprisingly many homes that survive from these early years help make Chester County second in the Commonwealth of Pennsylvania in National Register of Historic Places properties, with more than three hundred total. Only the city of Philadelphia boasts more.

Well-built houses of extremely early date testify to the great wealth that now began to accrue—this being, by lucky chance, some of the most fertile farmland on the entire Eastern Seaboard. Penn was delighted to find "a fast fat earth, like to our best vales in England, especially by inland brooks and rivers, God in his wisdom having ordered it so . . . the back-lands being generally three to one richer than those that lie by navigable waters." No wonder settlers hurried inland, away from the Swede-infested Delaware River, and crowded the Brandywine's banks in the district they called Birmingham.[6]

And the houses they built have become famous for their picturesque charm. Even in the 1860s they were considered well worth visiting, as novelist Bayard Taylor wrote of one of them in *The Story of Kennett*: "A hundred years had already elapsed since the masons had run up those walls of rusty hornblende rock, and it was even said that the leaden window-sashes, with their diamond-shaped panes of greenish glass, had been brought over from England, in the days of William Penn." As a lad of fifteen, the antiquarian Taylor had drawn a picture of a colonial farmstead on a diamond pane "taken from the window of a house erected in the year 1716."[7]

West of Chadds Ford, the primitive-looking brick Barns-Brinton House (1714), today a museum, served early settlers as a tavern on "Ye Great Road to Nottingham" in the colony of Maryland. Andrew Wyeth showed it in a painting, *Tenant Farmer*. Nearby is that time-capsule of a place, Kennett Meeting, a sober, whitewashed hall of Quaker worship (c. 1713) that briefly formed a defensive position for Americans in the Battle of the Brandywine. Soldiers lie buried in its graveyard, a little German flag today marking Hessian remains.

On the river near West Chester at Taylor's (or Black Horse) Run, at the upper end of North Creek Road, stands the Abiah Taylor House, with a 1724 datestone and 1753 barn (oldest extant in Pennsylvania) across the way. Even in the nineteenth century it was "pointed out to strangers as the original dwelling" hereabouts. This brick landmark, built by a farmer and miller who arrived from Didcot, England, shortly after 1700, was recently restored by architect John Milner with leaded casement windows of the kind early homes inevitably had.[8]

The much-photographed John Chads House (c. 1725), now owned by the local historical society, stands on a steep slope at Chadds Ford, looking down on its original springhouse. Chads (originally the family name was Chadsey) inherited five hundred acres here from his father and operated a ferry over the creek, serving travelers. His crossing fees varied from one shilling six pence for coach or wagon to four pence for a horse and rider or an ox, cow, or heifer down to three halfpence for a hog. Chads's redoubtable widow, Betty, remained in the house throughout the battle, hiding "her silver spoons dailey in her pocket." The fieldstone dwelling with pent eave, sheltered by a white pine already sizeable in a drawing of the 1840s, is another fine example of early construction by the pioneering English. Milner praises its harmonious relationship with the land, being "hunkered into the hill and protected from the north winds. The way settlers sited their buildings to take advantage of water sources and protect them from weather creates the Brandywine aesthetic in terms of architecture and function. These structures have such incredible personality."[9]

One of the oldest and best of this nationally important collection of colonial dwellings is the Brinton 1704 House. As we have seen, Penn's Quakers quickly pressed right up to the Brandywine in Birmingham, recognizing the fertility of the creek bottoms and seeking to avoid established settlers on the Delaware. Cutting down the magnificent forests was followed by the planting of winter and summer wheat, buckwheat, rye, barley, oats, and Indian corn. Turkeys, wild geese, and ducks were for the moment plentiful, and venison could be purchased from the Indians. "We had Bearflesh this fall for little or nothing," a new British arrival reported. "It is good food, tasting much like Beef."[10]

Among the early Quaker immigrants to this place of nature's largesse was seventeen-year-old William Brinton, who came with his parents in 1684 from Staffordshire. They settled near the Brandywine close to today's Dilworthtown—then in the trackless wilderness—and spent the first winter in a nearby "cave." The Brintons quickly built a house and began preparing the land for agriculture. So successful were they, William Brinton was able, within twenty years, to erect an exceptionally large dwelling of stone, today's Brinton 1704 House. Its interior frame made lavish use of thick oak and walnut, so abundant was timber in those days.

Well into the nineteenth century, the history-minded Brinton family showed visitors the site of their very first family cabin—an indentation in the ground with an old pear tree nearby, and a swarm of blue-bottle flowers. Brought from England by the Brintons, this plant subsequently became an agricultural pest in the region.

Thousands of people today can trace their genealogy to these intrepid Brinton colonists, and the Brinton Association of America maintains the house as a museum. William Brinton's four-greats-grandson led the Union armies in the Civil War (General William Brinton McClellan); his sister Elizabeth was the ancestor, eight generations down, of President Richard Nixon, himself a Quaker. Immigrant James Nixon settled in Brandywine Hundred by 1731, and his son from whom the president was descended fought as a private in the Battle of the Brandywine.

Restoration of the Brinton 1704 House in 1954 re-created the original twenty-seven leaded casement windows, which give it such a medieval feel. Early artifacts on display include poignant objects brought over on the ship by the Staffordshire family: a mortar and pestle, a glazed-redware ink stand, a pocketbook, and a 1629 London Bible with flame-stitched covers. All these somehow survived the ransacking of the house by British troops in the Battle of the Brandywine, the last hours of which raged in nearby fields, where, at sundown, General Washington observed in dismay the collapse of his army.[11]

Another great American family founded on the Brandywine was that of Gilpin. Joseph Gilpin, an English weaver from Dorchester, near Oxford, sailed with his wife and small children in 1695, landing at New Castle. They set out on foot for their plantation in Birmingham, already assigned to them, but could only go ten miles before night set in. They asked for shelter at a settler's home but were refused. Fortunately there were Indians camped nearby, so they picturesquely "lodged there for the first night on shore, in America." Hardships were just beginning: "They had at first to dig a cave in the earth and went into it, in which they lived four or five years and where two children were born."

Eventually Joseph Gilpin built a frame house with walls of wattle and daub and, in 1754, the masonry home that became General Howe's headquarters during the battle (on today's Harvey Road, Chadds Ford; a second Gilpin house was headquarters for Lafayette). The Gilpins had fifteen children in all, and there were forty-five grandchildren when he died, start of a huge cohort of Gilpins that would fan out across a growing nation. In time, one descendant was a U.S. senator from Idaho; another lived in Duluth and treasured an iron spiral candleholder set into an oak stand—inscribed date, 1686—which Gilpin had brought with him to America. The descendants of Joseph and Hannah Gilpin had an extraordinary impact on the region around the Brandywine: they included the founders of the tree collections at today's Longwood

Gardens and Tyler Arboretum, the industrialists who helped get serious milling underway on the Brandywine at Wilmington, and the men who first envisioned the Chesapeake and Delaware Canal across Delmarva.[12]

Glazed Headers, Pent Eaves

All these early Chester County houses are nationally important for their deep history and their craftsmanlike excellence. Architect Milner lives in the Abiah Taylor House he restored and has described the power these old dwellings have exerted in creating a modern tradition of neocolonial design—the past directly shaping the present in this Brandywine region of such heightened historical susceptibility:

> The early vernacular architecture of southeastern Pennsylvania has had a profound influence on my own work for the past three decades. The treasures of this region afford almost limitless inspiration for the restoration of historic buildings as well as for the design of new buildings in the context of an exceptional landscape. The more I work on these remarkable structures, the more I feel a connection with the craftsmen who created them, and the more I am inspired to carry on the tradition.[13]

Milner greatly admires the architect Brognard Okie, a staunch antimodernist of the early twentieth century who restored the Betsy Ross House in Philadelphia and re-created William Penn's mansion on the Delaware River, in addition to developing a charming style of country house based on early colonial examples. "He responded to the spirit of colonial woodwork," Milner notes, "but applied his own personal style." Okie remodeled the Dower House outside West Chester for novelist Joseph Hergesheimer, an exercise that says much about the dyed-in-the-wool traditionalist culture of the valley. For Hergesheimer, the Dower House (1712) had "the air of the past, of an early Quaker pastoral, had remained like the tranquil scents of a simple garden." In Okie he found a man of "fanatical honesty" who, even more than the novelist, "lived

On the patio. In the 1920s, novelist Joseph Hergesheimer "re-created" the Dower House, turning the 1712 farmhouse into an enclave of timeless values where he could flee the frantic twentieth century.

almost wholly in an immaterial world, not of words but regretted old Pennsylvania houses" long since demolished.

Together Hergesheimer and Okie tackled the restoration. Okie insisted on using solid oak beams for the door frames, joined with oak pins: "That was the old way to do it. That, then, would be our way." (Thus they "repudiated the use of screws in the Dower House" as excessively modern.) They began a search for venerable lanterns, cupboards, latches, box locks, and "the smallest brass knobs imaginable," along with hinges of H, L, and clover shape. Old wood came from barns, stone was cut from abandoned quarries, huge boxwoods were trucked in from homesteads in the region. Local antique expert Francis Brinton helped; Hergesheimer said the meeting between Brinton and Okie "was very affecting—two men lost in their singleness of allegiance to the past in Pennsylvania."

Not that the Dower House restoration was wholly authentic; windows were enlarged and a sleeping porch added. But the final results deeply impressed the nostalgic Hergesheimer, who brooded on the ancientness of the place: when in 1712 "the pins were thrust home above the latches, the doors, the house, was fastened upon a forest hardly broken by the settlement" of Penn. "Slipping into the night it was absorbed in a silence that, emphasized by the wind in the trees, the nocturnal animals, reached across the continent from ocean to ocean. . . . It's impossible now to conceive of such a silence, such a deep resonant hush. How soon it vanished!"[14]

Surely the Dower House—still standing proud today at 100 Goshen Road, West Chester—and its various peers make Chester County, all in all, just about the best-preserved colonial landscape in the nation. There are so many of these houses—because the settlers built in brick and stone, more likely to endure. Driving the twisting back roads, usually with some frantically impatient suburbanite on your tail, you glimpse these dwellings out of the corner of your eye, their lumpy walls of robust stone, raised by hand so long ago. The most exciting are often the ones not yet restored, with moldering window sash and crumbling slate-tile roofs and improvisational Victorian additions, such as bay windows surrounded by fish-scale shingles, or scroll-saw porches, and with tattered curtains of parti-colored fabric behind half-broken window panes, and the bricks at the top of the chimney knocked loose and about to fall. Where the whitewash has flaked away, perhaps a row of glazed header brick peeps forth, the ruddy clay and Coke-bottle-green glaze as snappy as in the very best work in old Philadelphia. Or maybe you can find joist holes filled with rotten wood where a pent eave once jutted, that distinctively Pennsylvania feature. It seems priceless to discover these unrestored houses, because possibly the next time you drive by, they will be undergoing yuppified restoration—or even reduced to a pile of rubble by a snorting yellow backhoe.

Such houses, now so aged, were once ultramodern symbols of the dynamic transformation of the American countryside as forests gave way to fields and crops. The Brandywine was emerging as, one might say, the model farming district for the nation. From his Como Farm beyond Marshallton on the West Branch, John Beale Bordley, a founder of the Philadelphia Society for Promoting Agriculture, experimented with crop rotation, giving advice to farmers everywhere in his popular books published after the Revolution. Already Colonial newspapers had been full of advertisements boasting of the riches of the Brandywine bottomlands. For example, one John Gillylen sold a farm near Downingtown in 1765

> containing 468 acres, with . . . 113 acres cultivated; the whole plantation is plentifully stored with springs and streams of water, one of the forks of Brandywine runs near a mile through the land; an orchard of 9 acres with near 500 of the best fruit trees. . . . The land is all new, the crop that is now in the ground is but the third. . . . Likewise to sell, a negroe boy, aged 13, and a negroe girl, aged 15, both have had the small pox, and sold for no fault. I design to pay all my debts, and forewarn any person or persons from cutting hoop poles, or any timber . . . off my land.[15]

When President Barack Obama created First State National Monument, part of the intention was to preserve what remains of these kinds of early Brandywine agricultural landscapes. The official proclamation notes that the 1,100-acre Woodlawn section of the monument contains at least eight structures from the eighteenth century. "Because Woodlawn has been relatively undisturbed, it still exhibits colonial and Quaker settlement patterns that have vanished elsewhere."[16]

At Old Swedes Church

Much as Roman Londinium reverted entirely back to forest before eventually being resettled as medieval London, so the old Swedish town beside the lower Brandywine at Fort Christina vanished during the years of rapid English inroads, finally being resurrected after sixty-seven years as the city of Wilmington. During the intervening period, little remained as a reminder of New Sweden except for the surnames of local farmers and a single place of worship, Old Swedes Church, built for remnant Swedes in English days. Historical interest in Fort Christina remained, however; when traveler Peter Kalm came through in the 1740s, he was given a relic, a Swedish silver coin of 1633, dug up when a new fort was built on the site of the old to protect the British against French and Spanish privateers.[17]

Fort Christina's occupants had buried their dead not in the wide, waterlogged marshes but on a slight rise northward, where Old Swedes Church now stands (in Virginia, Jamestown settlers did much the same). Three Lutheran missionaries arrived from Sweden in 1697 to serve the remaining Swedish colonists; they included the energetic Reverend Eric Björk, who pressed for a new place of worship. By now the Quakers were pouring ceaselessly into the Delaware Valley, and in fact there is little or nothing "Swedish" about the architecture of Old Swedes: an English mason named Yard brought his crew down from Philadelphia, joined by English carpenters John Smart and John Britt. The cornerstone was laid in May 1698, and bluestone walls were up by fall. Lime for mortar was brought from Maryland in a boat. Björk left an account that describes fir pews on either side of a wide aisle, separating the sexes, and a circular precinct at the east end with seats for ministers.

The smith Mattias de Foss wrought dozens of iron letters for inscriptions on the outside walls, including "LUX-L.I. TENEBR. ORIENS-EX ALTO" ("Light from on high shines in the darkness"). With its massive stone walls and a red brick bell tower, Old Swedes has attracted artists since the 1840s, including Howard Pyle, Robert Shaw, and the young Andrew Wyeth. A late nineteenth-century renovation upset Pyle, who loved the fabled building and always pointed it out to companions from the train. He loathed "the garish yellow shingles and the crass new woodwork. . . . Old buildings and fragments of the past are to me very and vitally alive."[18]

For generations, the vicinity of Old Swedes Church was a sleepy rural environs, as Pyle reported in his magazine article, "Old-Time Life in a

Three hundred years of worship. Few American structures anywhere remain in regular use from the seventeenth century. Howard Pyle illustrated Old Swedes Church for Woodrow Wilson's book, *A History of the American People* (1902).

Quaker Town." One parishioner recalled how swallows built mud nests under the rafters and darted over the heads of the congregation; cows trundled over whenever they heard the sound of the church bell, knowing the churchyard gate would be left open and they could graze amid the tombstones. "Once our cow left her companions," the congregant recalled, "and followed grandfather to his pew door." In a painting now in the Brandywine River Museum of Art, *The Last Leaf*, Pyle showed an elderly man visiting his wife's tomb here, with the church in the back-ground.[19]

Today, modern industry and a somewhat blighted neighborhood surround Old Swedes, an evocative place nonetheless: it has been called the "oldest church in North America still standing as originally built and holding regular worship services." Here the visitor's mind turns back to the long-ago seventeenth century and the very earliest phases of European colonization. When First State National Monument was es-tablished, planning immediately began to add Old Swedes to its hold-ings, the park being meant to "interpret the story of early Swedish, Finnish, Dutch, and English settlement in the region."[20]

Back when the 1938 tercentenary of the Swedish landing ap-proached, commemorations were planned, and it was noted that two million Americans were of Swedish descent. The Swedish crown prince solicited donations from all citizens of his country for the erection of a monument at the Rocks. The park was a joint effort, with Swedish art-ist Carl Milles providing a sculpture and a Philadelphia landscape design firm preparing the site—a dump in the midst of an industrial district along the oily Christina River. American Car and Foundry stood directly across the street, backing up to the Brandywine, and again, not a trace remained of the fort the Swedes had built nor of the marshes that surrounded it protectively upstream and down. During the dedication, an entourage of Swedish dignitaries disembarked from a ship in a lashing rainstorm, accompanied by President Franklin D. Roosevelt.

To leap ahead seventy-five years: in 2013, the 375th anniversary of the coming of the Swedes, the king and queen of Sweden visited the site amid great panoply—along with the president of Finland's parliament—and archaeologists speculated about the precise site of Fort Christina. On hand was a 1990s replica (berthed nearby) of the three-masted, Dutch-built pinnace *Kalmar Nyckel* that had brought the first Swedes, a re-doubtable ship that crossed the Atlantic eight times, whereas no other vessel of that era made more than two trips.

A New Town Rises

In 1731, today's Wilmington was born just west of Old Swedes. The enterprising settler Thomas Willing laid out a grid in emulation of Philadelphia and predicted a great grain-port metropolis would soon rise. Four years later, Quaker William Shipley and friends bought lots in the fledgling place, which rapidly developed as a center for the shipment of grain.[21]

Artist Pyle liked to tell a story of how Shipley, an immigrant from Britain who lived near Philadelphia, first happened to come to Wilmington—a glorious founding myth in which the Brandywine plays a starring role. He said Shipley's devoutly religious wife, Elizabeth, had a dream: "She was traveling on horseback, along a high road, and after a time she came to a wild and turbulent stream, which she forded with difficulty; beyond this stream she mounted a long and steep hill-side; when she arrived at this summit a great view of surpassing beauty spread out before her." This, she perceived, was a kind of Promised Land where her family was surely destined to settle.

A few years later, Pyle said, Elizabeth Shipley undertook an actual trip through the Mid-Atlantic in which she crossed "a roaring stream that cut through tree-covered highlands, and came raging and rushing down over great rocks and boulders"—the Brandywine. "The cawing of crows in the woods, and a solitary eagle that went sailing through the air, was all the life that broke the solitude of the place. As she hesitated on the bank before entering the rough looking ford, marked at each end by a sapling pole to which a red rag was fastened, the whole scene seemed strangely familiar to her."

From the hilltop she saw the bright Christina River, and her vision was suddenly reality. It was here that she and her husband settled in 1735; here the city of Wilmington flourished; and here, William and Elizabeth Shipley's son, Thomas, founded a dynasty of millers on the Brandywine.[22]

Milling was revived on the creek (after the brief Swedish attempt) by Samuel Kirk at the foot of today's Adams Street in Wilmington in the

1720s, beside the former Stidham mill. Here the creek is shallow, the Indians having used the spot as a ford; later, as we saw, the important Old King's Road running north to south through the colonies crossed without a bridge. Kirk's pioneering enterprise became legendary as the Old Barley Mill, a rather primitive "undershot" facility that stood immediately below its dam on the south bank. Sketchy remnants of that dam can be faintly perceived even today, and a millstone lies nearby as a mossy relic.

One of nineteenth-century artist Robert Shaw's best-known etchings shows Old Barley Mill—a print that hung in the better homes in Wilmington for generations as a nostalgic token of the early years of Quaker settlement. In 1742, milling expanded when Oliver Canby built a dam downstream from Old Barley Mill and shipped processed grain to Philadelphia and even the West Indies—start of serious merchant milling. Within twenty years a complex of mills had begun to spring up around Market Street Bridge.[23]

Once again the English settlers wrought ecological havoc. Construction of dams profoundly changed the nature of the creek by cutting off the runs of fish in springtime, species that had, for millennia, come up the waterways to spawn. Shad had once been fantastically abundant—on the Schuylkill, Penn said, you could catch six hundred with a single swipe of the net—but now their numbers crashed.[24]

The Lenape had long depended on the fish, lining the creeks with weirs to catch them, and were horrified by the effects of the Kirk dam, about which they complained to the British governor. A 1727 legislative act called for all dams to be removed from the Brandywine to allow the fish to run, and as late as 1760 four dams were breached by officials; but thereafter dams multiplied (eventually to more than 125 on the whole creek) and several species of fish became extinct. Today there are plans underway to remove or breach several dams on the Brandywine—long disused for any industrial purpose—so that shad, in particular, can run again. As a gesture in this direction, Brandywine Conservancy removed two such dams on the East Branch in 2012, freeing eighteen stream-miles from obstruction after more than a century.[25]

Two Stargazers

As English pioneers pressed ever westward, the question of the boundary between Pennsylvania and Maryland became troublesome. To settle it, the Mason-Dixon Line was drawn, a drama in which the Brandywine played a part. Culturally, that line ratified what everyone already knew: the Brandywine Valley, on the fortieth parallel, was the southernmost outpost of a thoroughgoing Northern culture, in contrast to Maryland, just a dozen miles away, which belonged to the South.

Elkanah Watson of Massachusetts traveled northbound in 1778 and admired the high level of cultivation, the neatness of agriculture in the Brandywine region: "The contrast, so obvious and so strong, in the appearance of these farms and of the southern plantations, will strike every observer, and can be imputed to but one cause"—the blight of slavery. At the same time, it was said that anyone going south knew they had left Chester County behind when, upon knocking at a door, "the landlord behaves with politeness to you." Quaker coolness and Southern gentility formed a striking dichotomy.[26]

The uncertain boundary between Maryland and Pennsylvania had sometimes been contested with violence. To finally settle the matter, surveyors Charles Mason and Jeremiah Dixon arrived from England in 1763 and, with sensitive apparatus carefully packed atop a feather mattress, bounced in their wagons thirty-one miles due west of Philadelphia to a marker that had been laid on a prior survey in 1736. That stone lay near the farmhouse of John Harlan, which still exists, amazingly unchanged and quaintly unrestored, in rural seclusion on the West Branch of the Brandywine at Embreeville. Here the surveyors erected a wooden observatory and made astronomical measurements in bitter January cold before setting up the Stargazers Stone, which also survives. It was the start of what one historian calls "the most ambitious geodetic survey ever conducted," one that would set all future standards for the world.[27]

From Stargazers Stone they ran a line fifteen miles south into Delaware—immediately crossing the coiling West Branch three times—

to place the "Post Mark'd West," the spot which determined the precise latitude of the Mason-Dixon Line. The industrious Mason and Dixon repeatedly returned to Harlan's farm during their multiyear survey and spent the colder months there. Once they recorded a frigid temperature of minus twenty-two degrees, though the latitude lay south of balmy Naples. Dr. Benjamin Rush later called their measurement (January 2, 1767) the most intense cold ever noted in the Philadelphia region, re-markable even in that era—hardly conceivable today—when the Dela-ware River froze solid every winter and Philadelphia shipping was entirely suspended until early March.[28]

Mason and Dixon are famous for the line they drew, but the greater scientific achievement was their successful measurement of one degree of latitude, part of a larger contemporary effort to understand the true shape of the Earth. This took nearly five months to do, as they recorded the distance all the way from Harlan's farm to the Nanticoke River in the swamps of southern Delaware. The process began at Christmas 1766, in a tent in Harlan's backyard, where Mason set up a long-case astronomical clock that had been loaned to him by the Royal Society in London; already it had been used for scientific inquiry at faraway Saint Helena and Barbados and (by Dixon) to study the transit of Venus at the Cape of Good Hope. At Harlan's, Mason watched the "immersion" of a moon of Jupiter as it passed behind the planet.

Before returning to England, the surveyors came back one last time to say farewell to John Harlan. Shortly thereafter, Harlan is said to have drowned in the Brandywine, which runs right in front of his door.[29]

The Mason-Dixon Line had ended the chance of bloody conflict between two great colonies. As the 1770s began, the Brandywine Valley seemed about the most prosperous and peaceful locale in the New World—but war clouds would eventually gather, and a huge invading army would soon be on these shores.

Chapter 3

❧ ❧

A River Red with Blood

Not one but two "September 11ths" darken the chronicles of American history. The often-forgotten one happened in 1777, when the trouncing of George Washington's army at the Battle of the Brandywine marked the military nadir of the Revolution.

Philadelphia was then the largest city in America, and to defend it seemed imperative. Armies attacking from the south would have to cross the Brandywine, a formidable barrier with steep-sided hills and strong watery currents. And so it was on the banks of the Brandywine that Washington drew his defensive line in September 1777 as a British invasion force approached—having landed at the head of the Chesapeake Bay and marched north. The bucolic countryside settled by peace-loving Quakers was about to witness what is said to have been the largest and longest land battle of the Revolutionary War, with some thirty thousand soldiers engaged as Generals Washington and Howe faced off in their only head-to-head matchup.[1]

This may have been the most titanic battle ever fought in this hemisphere prior to the Civil War—and yet the mighty contest is little known today. Compare it to Gettysburg, fought three counties to the westward, eighty-six years later: preserved land there comprises six thousand acres, whereas at Brandywine there are only fifty acres officially preserved at Chadds Ford, with most of the rest of the battlefield in private hands and, thanks to recent sprawl, often cluttered with housing developments. Gettysburg has a thousand markers and monuments; Brandywine has just a handful. Of course Gettysburg was a much bigger spectacle, with five times more soldiers on the field. But the biggest difference is that the American army was defeated at the Brandywine, and defeats rarely get commemorated.

The American rout was the result of one of the more ingenious flanking maneuvers in military history—"a capital stratagem," novelist Washington Irving later called it. As Howe's army approached, some eighteen thousand strong, Washington, with about fifteen thousand tattered troops, failed to identify all the Brandywine fords upstream from his position at Chadds Ford (see Plate 4). Moreover, someone fed him the false information that there were no fords at all above a certain point. The British took brilliant advantage of his ignorance. The portly, toothless Howe was that day "at his very best," according to the great British military historian Sir George Otto Trevelyan, not his sometimes sluggish self but "the high-mettled warrior who had stormed the redoubt at Bunker's Hill."[2]

As Howe's massive army neared the Brandywine on the foggy morning of September 11—their ultimate objective Philadelphia—he sent a small group to strike Washington's center at Chadds Ford, purely as a distraction. At the same time, the main body of the British army went left by back roads to cross the Brandywine upstream from Washington's army at Jefferis's Ford, a locale the American commanders were unaware of. The Continentals were closely guarding the Brandywine fords they knew about—seven crossings from Pyle's Ford north to Buffington's Ford—but unfortunately not the ones higher up (see Appendix). Local loyalists made the flanking maneuver possible by guiding the British, at whose head rode General Charles Cornwallis, erect in the saddle, an awesome sight to farmers who, forgetting their haymaking, stared in astonishment as history passed their door: "His rich scarlet clothing loaded with gold lace, epaulettes &c occasioned him to make a brilliant and martial appearance."[3]

At midday, Washington finally realized he had a huge enemy force advancing across the hills toward his vulnerable right. He swung his troops into action, and fighting was fierce around Birmingham Meeting-house. But as the hot day ended, his army was fleeing in disarray. The defeated Americans would spend the winter camped in near-starvation conditions at Valley Forge on the Schuylkill River northwest of Phila-delphia, the very trough of the young nation's fortunes.

Bayonets Bright as Silver

Before the battle, Washington, then age forty-five, made his headquar-ters at farmer and miller Benjamin Ring's house, now reconstructed at the state park. Here he conducted his councils of war, and here he got the chilling word that the British were suddenly on his right. All his storied officers were gathered in the Ring parlor, including Charles C. Pinckney, later U.S. ambassador to France and a presidential candidate, and Casimir Pulaski, making a striking American debut with his mous-tache and snappy hussar uniform.[4]

Nearby still stands Lafayette's Headquarters: the Gideon Gilpin House, a quaint old place built of stone and occupied at that time by an innkeeper. The Marquis de Lafayette was only nineteen and little-known, having just arrived from France that summer to assist the patri-ots' cause, but the events of the day would bring him boundless fame and help knit American and French hearts permanently together. In the havoc after the battle, the Gilpin House was plundered, its owner later putting in a claim to the federal government for lost cows, oxen, sheep, and swine, plus fifty pounds of bacon, a history book, and a gun.

The smaller of the two British forces, sent to attack the American center, was commanded by Lieutenant-General Wilhelm von Knyphau-sen, a Prussian officer with a livid saber scar from eye to chin. The first shots of the battle rang out as his troops reached Kennett Meeting on today's U.S. 1. Washington supposed the British would cross the Bran-dywine directly in front of him, facing cannon fire from Colonel Thomas Procter's Artillery on a knoll behind today's Sanderson Museum in Chadds Ford. But Knyphausen pushed only briefly across the ford, then fell back as Americans retook the west bank under command of Captains

Porterfield and Waggoner and then General Maxwell. Again, only the British knew that their assault was merely a feint.[5]

Procter's Artillery consisted of four brass cannon pulled up behind a hastily built breastwork of earth and logs in front of an orchard. It looked across blooming fields of buckwheat toward the creek—"Meadow Ground" on the General Weedon map, drawn that day and the only American cartography that shows the battlefield. This battery fired all day at Knyphausen in one of the really spirited artillery duels of the war. The cannonading could be heard like distant thunder as far away as Philadelphia—by Congress then meeting at Independence Hall and by Thomas Paine, who wrote to Benjamin Franklin in Paris, "I was preparing Dispatches for you when the report of cannon at Brandywine interrupted my proceeding."[6]

At noon, Washington rode up and down the American line, stopping off at the Chads House. James Parker, a Loyalist from Virginia, was secretly observing him from a British battery on the far heights, across the Brandywine. He watched as the general left the house accompanied by officers and two white flags, climbing the hill behind it to view the battlefield with a spyglass. Parker had the British fire their cannon, and "my prayers went with the ball that it might finish Washington & the Rebellion together." As the shells whistled down, Washington said calmly to some civilians who were tagging along, "Gentlemen, you perceive that we are attracting the notice of the enemy. I think you had better retire." Thus did Washington narrowly escape being killed, which might have changed the whole future history of the North American continent—and the world.

Meanwhile the British were executing their stealthy flanking maneuver. After wading across the West Branch at Trimble's Ford (today, southeast of the intersection of Camp Linden and Northbrook roads), the main Redcoat force made its way to obscure Jefferis's Ford on the East Branch. Farmers watched in astonishment at the sight, never to be forgotten, of "the army coming out of the woods into the fields belonging to Emmor Jefferis on the west side of the Creek above the fording place." As young local Joseph Townsend later recalled, "In a few min-

utes the fields were literally covered over with them, and they were hastening towards us. Their arms and bayonets being raised, shone as
bright as silver, being a clear sky and the day exceeding warm."

For four hours Cornwallis's huge army splashed across at Jefferis's
Ford—"horse and foot, artillery, baggage, provision wagons, arms and
ammunition, together with a host of plunderers and rabble." Rousted
from his farmhouse, the terrified farmer Emmor Jefferis was forced to
guide General Howe through the confusing lanes of the countryside
east of the river. As the battle fully erupted, the Quaker ducked bullets
that whizzed nearby. "Don't be afraid Mr. Jefferis, they won't hurt you,"
Howe said with amusement. Meanwhile British troops ransacked
Jefferis's house. They rolled kegs of liquor out of the cellar, knocked off
their heads, and got drunk on his lawn.[7]

After wading across at the ford, the Crown forces marched through a
"terrible defile" into the hamlet of Sconneltown—the Americans could
have ambushed them in the ravine, had they only known they were
coming. They passed Strode's Mill on Plum Run, where soldiers' rude
graffiti on beams and rafters would be pointed out for generations.
Finally they paused at high Osborne's Hill after many miles of rapid
march. (A marker on today's Birmingham Road at Country Club Road
indicates the spot.) The view across the fertile fields and forests of September was lovely, and a British officer told young Townsend, "You have
got a hell of a fine country here."

Townsend's reminiscences form one of the most striking eyewitness
accounts of any battle during the war as he revisited, years later, with
intense clarity what had plainly been the most extraordinary day of his
life: the youthful wonder at seeing the magnificent soldiers who seemingly materialized out of nowhere; the spectacular uniforms; the sea of
scarlet across the green landscape; the innumerable spurs and swords
and shiny boots. At Osborne's Hill the ground was strewn with heaps
of blankets and baggage as the troops readied for their grim advance.
Cornwallis, wrote the historian Trevelyan, now "deployed his whole
force as coolly and methodically as if he were in Hyde Park," and in
stately, awesome formation they began to march forward, a scene one of

their officers called "the most Grand & Noble Sight imaginable." It was about 4:30 in the afternoon. So thrilled was Townsend by the beautiful spectacle, it came as an astonishing shock when a thousand guns suddenly began blazing and scarlet-clad warriors pitched forward into the dust.[8]

A Most Infernal Fire

Across Street Road and up the slope toward Birmingham Meeting came the Redcoats, both British and Hessians, and the Americans could see how deftly they had been flanked. That stone structure for Quaker worship had been erected in 1763, replacing an earlier building. Hopelessly outnumbered Virginians fired at the British from behind the graveyard wall. As they fell back, a battery on the hill to the south fired furious volleys of grapeshot down the road in front of the meeting-house, shredding the roadside hedges, and British soldiers scrambled for shelter behind the wall. Others struggled up the slopes toward the meetinghouse. A lieutenant recalled, "There was a most infernal fire of cannon & musketry—smoak—incessant shouting—incline to the right! incline to the left!—halt!—charge!"[9]

At a fork in the road south of the meetinghouse, an old cannon installed in 1877 commemorates the American battery that blasted away at the British from the hilltop behind it. Washington himself belatedly rushed there to direct the fighting, trying to turn around what one historian calls his worst battlefield performance of the war. Just getting from the Ring House to the battle scene proved difficult; an American officer forced an aged Quaker named Brown, on threat of running him through on the spot, to jump onto a charger and guide the top commander over hill and dale. Washington's horse galloped at Brown's flank, leaping fences, the Father of His Country constantly shouting, "Push along, old man!"[10]

It took almost two hours for the British to take the heights, American general John Sullivan reported. "The hill was disputed almost muzzle to muzzle in such a manner that General Conway who has seen much service says he never saw so close and severe a fire. . . . We were obliged to abandon the hill we had so long contended for, but not till we had almost covered the ground between that & Bremingham meeting house with the dead bodies of the enemy." The left fork in the road, to Dilworthtown, wound through woods and crossed Sandy Hollow. Fighting was intense on both sides of the road here. Cannon and musket fire tore through the forest in some of the most vicious fighting of the entire Revolution. "A cannon-ball went through Captain Stout," a New Jersey soldier said, "and through a sergeant that stood behind him."[11]

South of the road, young Lafayette galloped up and tried to stem the rout, the fighting happening in what he later remembered as being "in front of the thinly wooded forest." Dismounting, he shouted to the men to fix bayonets, and he shoved them in the back if they tried to turn and flee. But the American line collapsed, and a bullet tore through the Frenchman's left calf. Lafayette's aide-de-camp hoisted him onto the saddle, and he escaped—with the patriotic wound that would make him instantly famous and beloved among all freedom-loving Americans. Among those who tended his injury, it is said, was young James Monroe, future American president, one of a whole roster of famous men who were on the battlefield that day, including Nathanael Greene, Alexander Hamilton, Henry Knox—and John Dickinson, supposedly the only signer of the Declaration of Independence to experience combat during the war. Here too was Lemuel Cook of Connecticut, who would live to see the Civil War—last survivor of all Revolutionary War veterans.[12]

Almost Cut to Pieces

As the battle thundered at Birmingham, the British finally attacked the American center to finish off the distracted Continentals. Knyphausen, wrote Trevelyan handsomely in the 1890s,

> sent his infantry across Chads's Ford in a dense succession of
> regiments, distinguished one from another by numerals which

are all of them so many titles of honour in the estimation of an old-fashioned Englishman. The Fourth Foot, the Fifth Foot, the Seventy-first Glasgow Highlanders, and the Twenty-Third Fusiliers splashed through the water, scrambled up the bank, ran over the ditch and parapet, and captured a hostile breastwork with many of the defenders, and all the cannon. They drove the Republicans before them, in a running fight. . . . The Americans were exactly in the same plight as the Austrians at Sadowa, and the French at Waterloo.[13]

It was about 5:30 in the afternoon when that assault on the ford began. Some troops waded across at the main ford, under fire from Procter's battery who "raked the ferry . . . with grape." The grapeshot "did much execution," one of the Queen's Rangers said; "The water took us up to our breasts, and was much stained with blood." The Redcoats were dangerously exposed as they marched in a column down the road east of the ford, hemmed in by "the Morass on their Flanks," and were "galled by Musketry from the Woods on their right and by round and grape Shot." Others waded "up to our middle" at Chads's Lower Ford, about where today's railroad bridge stands, and took hits from a four-gun American battery on Rocky Hill, near where the N. C. Wyeth Studio is now.[14]

As the soaked army of invaders advanced through fields and orchards eastward of the Lower Ford, American soldiers "rallied afresh and fought Bayonet to Bayonet," a British sergeant recalled. The powerful Redcoat force made short work of the Rebels. One group trapped "in a Buck Wheat field was totally scivered with the Bayonets before they could clear the fence round it" and escape. Among the Third Virginia Regiment eyeing the rout from the hills above Chads's Ford was Captain John Marshall, future supreme court justice. The moment, however discouraging, was significant for patriotic symbolism: the Seventh Pennsylvania Militia who fought Knyphausen flew a red banner with a red-and-white stars-and-stripes canton, perhaps the first iconic-type "American flag" ever seen in battle.[15]

Attack on the river. Chads's Lower Ford came under fire from an American battery on Rocky Hill as British soldiers splashed across, in an imaginative 1940 depiction by Andrew Wyeth, who grew up on the distant slope.

Now the British overran all the Continental positions along the Brandywine, and artillerist Procter's black horse was shot out from under him as he fled. In the mayhem, Colonel Samuel Smith of Maryland—later a U.S. Senator—was separated from his unit and feared capture in the night. He pounded on a Quaker's door and demanded to be taken to Chester, toward which Washington's army was hastening. "If you do not conduct me clear of the enemy," Smith bellowed, "the moment I discover your treachery I will blow your brains out."[16]

Also escaping was Colonel John Cropper, one of many Virginians on the field that day—including "Light-Horse" Harry Lee, the father of Robert E. Lee, himself the architect of some Civil War flanking maneuvers of an audacity that recall Brandywine. Stories of the battle long echoed in the South: Cropper's grandson, Henry A. Wise, later a Confederate general, recalled fondly of his boyhood,

The children would never tire of hearing [Cropper] relate the story of the bloody fight at Brandywine, when the Seventh Virginia, the command of which had devolved upon him, was almost cut to pieces, and he himself was wounded by bayonet thrust; and how when the ensign had been killed and the colors captured, he drew a ramrod from a musket, tied his red bandanna to the end, and hoisted it as a flag.[17]

Cropper's remnant troops spent the hours of darkness hiding in a newly felled wood before joining the headlong exodus toward the east. All during that hellish night, scores of wounded lay moaning on the battlefield: at least six hundred Americans were injured, and four hundred British. The dead numbered some three hundred on the patriot side, and an uncertain number of the king's troops. Young farmer Townsend helped carry casualties to Birmingham Meeting, where doors were torn off and used for operating tables. Bodies and amputated limbs were dumped in a ditch in the graveyard. (Years later, in 1814, Townsend would offer medical aid to those who fell in the Battle of North Point at Baltimore, by which time he had become a leading Quaker of that city, noted for his devoutness and "tinge of quaint eccentricity.") Other wounded were brought to the hamlet of Dilworthtown, where the British encamped for several days.[18]

Among the doctors who hastened to Dilworthtown under a flag of truce from Philadelphia was Benjamin Rush, who had helped bind up the wounded on the day of the battle and had almost been captured by the advancing British before escaping. Surgeon-general for the army and a signer of the Declaration of Independence, Rush was struck by the politeness of the Redcoat officers and the commendable orderliness and discipline of their troops, compared with the Continentals. Ahead lay a brutal winter at Valley Forge, sixteen miles north, which would prove the ultimate test of these battered Americans' resolve.[19]

As dusk fell on the night of the battle, George Washington was seen on the road to Wilmington, a mile below Dilworthtown, pointing his fleeing troops toward Chester in a scene that his namesake biographer

Washington Irving would describe as "headlong terror and confusion. . . . The dust, the uproar, and the growing darkness, threw everything into chaos." Hours later, a fateful letter was delivered to Congress:

> CHESTER, September 11, 1777. Twelve o'Clock at Night.
> SIR, I am sorry to inform you that in this day's engagement we
> have been obliged to leave the enemy masters of the field. Un-
> fortunately the intelligence received of the enemy advancing up
> the Brandywine, and crossing at a Ford about six miles above
> us, was uncertain and contradictory, notwithstanding all my
> pains to get the best. This prevented my making a disposition
> adequate to the force with which the enemy attacked us on our
> right. . . . The Marquis La Fayette was wounded in the leg. . . .
> I have the honor to be, Sir, your obedient humble servant, G.
> WASHINGTON.[20]

With his brilliant military stroke, General Howe had nearly destroyed Washington's Army—and might have finally done so, had he pursued the foe vigorously. Instead, he distracted himself by occupying Philadelphia fifteen days after the battle —and then winter came, the Americans slowly regrouping to fight again.

The Quakers of Birmingham were left to repair the damage to their farms and homes. For generations they would grumble about the pillaging done by the invaders, the pilfering of valuable clocks and heirlooms. British campfires in the wheat fields had been stoked with costly mahogany furniture, even as nearby fence-rails were left untouched. Heavy rainstorms washed soldiers' mangled bodies out of their shallow graves, Townsend recalled, and "beasts and wild fowls" picked at them until he and others undertook reburial, a ghastly chore. One descendant of local settlers remembered, "Grandmother asserted that great numbers were killed in the [Brandywine] . . . and that the farmers for several days afterward were fishing dead bodies from the water."[21]

Downstream, Wilmington did not escape this epic military campaign entirely, even if the Crown forces never attempted their Brandywine crossing there, as Washington had expected some days before. After the battle, Howe sent nine hundred troops of the Seventy-First Regiment of Foot to seize the town and secure accommodation for the wounded; as Howard Pyle would evocatively write, they "stacked their muskets along the stony streets in the moonlight." Soldiers broke into the home of Delaware's top political leader, President John McKinly, in the middle of the night and took him prisoner. Offshore were the men-of-war *Roebuck* and *Liverpool*, shelling the panicked town of 1,250. A militia captain named Stidham, descendant of the family of Swedish settlers on the Brandywine, saw the *Roebuck* coming into the creek in pursuit of his soldiers: "The balls rained down upon the roof" of the old homestead. Then Hessians came ashore, chasing Stidham through the house; he narrowly escaped by hiding in a hollow oak tree out back where he had once played hide-and-seek as a boy.[22]

Long Live Lafayette!

The battle proved the single most spectacular event ever to happen along the Brandywine—and remains so today. The historical associations that had already begun to cluster around the creek now found intense focus in this dramatic episode. At an early date, tourists came and reveled in historical memory here. The first were very illustrious: Lafayette himself, accompanied by a fellow officer, the Marquis de Chastellux. With a group of French friends from Philadelphia, they rode down to tour the battlefield in December 1780, even before the war was over.

They brought along a copy of the battlefield map by engraver William Faden, official geographer to King George III. Published at Charing Cross, London, in 1778, *Battle of Brandywine in which the Rebels Were Defeated* relied on military surveys made in the hours following the fight (including one by Lieutenant S. W. Werner, Hessian artillerist) but was nonetheless so inaccurate it ultimately sowed much confusion about the events of the battle, which historians are still trying to disentangle. The distinguished tourists also employed the services of an American major who had fought that day and now lived in a house on the battlefield. In the woods where the Virginians had fought and Lafayette was wounded, "most of the trees bear the mark of bullets or cannon shot," the excursionists noted. But already, just three years after the battle, they expressed perplexity and disagreement about what had happened where.[23]

More than four decades later, the elderly Lafayette undertook a triumphal tour of America amid hysterical enthusiasm for the last living superstar of the Revolution. He revisited the Brandywine on July 26, 1825, in the company of prominent locals, including Captain Jacob Humphrey, whose forehead was laced with a scar from a musket ball that grazed him in the Battle of Trenton. Lafayette rode up from Delaware in a barouche drawn by four gray horses, having spent the night with Eleuthère du Pont at Eleutherian Mills on the Brandywine; among the party was U.S. congressman and future secretary of the treasury Louis McLane, who owned a mill site on the river. On passing over the bridge at Chadds Ford, Lafayette remarked, "It could not be here we crossed. It must have been further up," astonishing everyone with his accurate recall: the new bridge was in fact a little below the old ford. But specific memories of the battle had faded locally; when Lafayette asked where the "bridge of rails was across the Brandywine"—erected hastily during the campaign—nobody seemed to know.[24]

Then he visited the dying Gideon Gilpin, with whom he had headquartered, before riding to Dilworthtown and Birmingham, followed by a huge crowd shouting "Long live Lafayette!" "Show me where is the meetinghouse," he requested, and upon seeing it again he began to speak at length in French about the battle to du Pont and his other companions, pointing out where he had been wounded near Sandy Hollow, now Jacob Bennett's cornfield. He lunched in the cannon-scarred Samuel Jones mansion north of the meetinghouse and was shown a collection of military relics dug up by farmer Abraham Darlington on the surrounding battlefield.

Then Lafayette went past Strode's Mill to West Chester, escorted by volunteer soldiers. There were ten thousand patriots in the streets, it was said, and Lafayette smiled and exclaimed, "Happy people! Happy people!" He was treated to a dinner in the grand jury room of the court-house. He rose to speak of his memories, recalling how it was "my first action under the American Standard, and our great and good Commander-in-Chief, in company with your gallant Chester County-man, my friend Gen. Wayne." He called it an honor "to have mingled my blood with that of many other American soldiers, on the heights of the Brandywine." Toasts followed, including one by banker-botanist William Darlington (who commanded the local troops during that festive com-memoration) to "The fields of the Brandywine: irrigated, on the Cadmean system of agriculture, with the blood of Revolutionary patriots—the teeming crop must ever be Independent Freemen." The Greek hero Cadmus had sowed dragon teeth in a field, from which brave soldiers sprang.

The next day, Lafayette left West Chester by going southward over Cope's Bridge on the East Branch, continuing his American tour. In the District of Columbia and Virginia he would meet former and current presidents Jefferson, Madison, Monroe, and John Quincy Adams; soon after, he returned to France on a new U.S. frigate named, in his honor, *Brandywine*, a ship that saw distinguished service up through the Civil War. As Andrew Wyeth liked to tell, when Lafayette was eventually bur-ied, soil from the Brandywine Valley was sprinkled inside his coffin.[25]

Turning up Bones

Lafayette may have been the most famous nineteenth-century tourist of the Brandywine, but there were many more, their names largely unre-corded. All battlefield tourism centered on Birmingham Meeting, where fighting had been especially fierce. That venerable building was enlarged to the east in 1818, a year before an octagonal schoolhouse was built nearby. For decades after the battle, digging for graves in the cem-etery turned up bits of red cloth from British uniforms. Visitors were shown dark spots on the wooden floor, said to be ineradicable blood-stains. An overeager tourist of 1861 tried to cut them out with a pocket-knife as souvenirs.[26]

The evocative meetinghouse is remarkably unchanged even today, and the visitor can find penknife graffiti on the wooden bench-backs dated as early as 1791 and 1813. A glass-fronted bookcase contains, alongside ordinary modern paperbacks, evangelist George Fox's *Journal* in two volumes, Philadelphia 1808, red leather labels cracking off from brown tooled spines; Fox brought Quakerism to the region when he visited New Castle in 1672, surviving his crossing of the "desperate" Brandywine before returning to tell Penn about America firsthand. Big trees in the graveyard may include a few of the dozen planted in 1879 by a patriotic Philadelphian as "living landmarks for the benefit of future generations."[27]

In 1828, a West Chester resident urged Philadelphians to visit the battlefield. At Chadds Ford they could see

> the little redoubt, still perceptible [and] pick up an occasional bullet or grape-shot, and see the passage-way which two cannonballs made for themselves through the gable-end of an ancient mansion on the hill. . . . Or you may visit the Birmingham grave-yard, and as you see the sexton turning up, some two feet below the surface, the bones of a British soldier, with fragments of his red coat still retaining its color, his stock-buckle, pocket-glass, flints, and buttons stamped with the No. of his regiment, contrast the peaceful scenes which now surround you.[28]

Many Philadelphians accepted West Chester's invitation to visit, especially since the Quaker City was swelling into a major metropolis (population 220,000 in 1840), dense and dirty. Philadelphia editor Charles Jacobs Peterson took a pilgrimage to the battlefield in 1844, writing it up in full romantic vein for *Graham's Magazine*, where he and staff writer Edgar Allan Poe had lately experienced a rocky relationship. Gazing around him at the Chadds Ford bridge, he said, "I found it all it had been pictured, one of the loveliest scenes in nature." In the nearby village he was shown venerable remains: "Every tradition, however exaggerated, every relic, however doubtful, had absorbing interest for me."

Antiquarian exercise. Around 1900, Amos Brinton, age ninety, pointed out the site of colonial Chads's Ferry. Historians of the 1777 battle had been uncertain where the crossing lay.

But the best locale of all was Birmingham Meeting, where Peterson stood in the dilapidated graveyard where sheep wandered and the rains had opened yawning cavities in the earth. He looked over the sunset valley as a distant plowman called to his oxen. As if on cue, an aged grave digger appeared and told of having dug up the bones of English officers, identified by their regimental buttons; he pointed out that the church's mortared walls were perforated by musket balls; he pulled out his knife and sketched the plan of the battle on a shingle of the coping of the graveyard wall. That wall, he explained, had seen the frantic last stand of the Americans, whose bodies now lay underfoot or beneath the "huge" earthen mound by the gate.

The old-timer told sensational stories until "grave-yard, hill, woodland and valley were putting on the cloudy mantle of night. . . . The rolling brow of Osborne Hill was half lost in the gathering gloom." Deeply moved, Peterson predicted that future generations would forever make pilgrimage to this place—America's equivalent to the "baronial ruins" and "ivied abbeys" of Europe.[29]

A Tour of Battle Hill

The Brandywine was proving a must-see for anyone seeking a comprehensive understanding of the American Revolution, including famous historian George Bancroft, who spent a day there. In 1846, the Historical Society of Pennsylvania undertook a thorough study of the place, publishing a *Plan of the Battleground* by researchers John S. Bowen and J. Smith Futhey and requesting detailed information from elderly locals, pestering them especially for the correct colonial names of those confusing Brandywine fords.

In 1848, New York editor and wood engraver Benson Lossing embarked on an eight-thousand-mile tour of battlefields, sketchbook in hand, as preparation for his blockbuster, *Pictorial Field-Book of the Revolution*. In the late fall he rode into West Chester in a wagon drawn by his faithful horse, Charley, and Joseph Townsend (nephew of the man who so memorably witnessed the battle) showed him around the battlefield. They rode down to Jefferis's Ford, then followed the line of British march to Birmingham Meeting, where they took shelter under the porch from wind and sleet and studied Bowen and Futhey's map. Once, Lossing mused, this had been a "wild ocean of carnage." The traveler learned that thousands of pounds of cannonballs had been plowed up along the Brandywine. He tied Charley beside the stream at dusk and sketched the site of Chads's Upper Ford, where so much cannonading had happened. The ford, he was told, was 160 feet north of the covered bridge, where a little gully could still be detected.

Brandywine tourism grew and grew throughout the nineteenth century, building to the crowd of one thousand that showed up for centennial ceremonies in Chadds Ford in 1877. A railroad guidebook published at the start of that decade gives a good account of what tourists saw:

To the north east is Osborne Hill, whence the portly and pomp-
ous Howe surveyed the growing lines of our men, on another
eminence just east of the Meeting, remarking, as he looked,
that "damned rebels form well." The position thus taken was
the scene of the defeat which lost the day. There Sullivan and
Deborre's divisions were thrown into confusion, and Lafayette
vainly striving to rally the broken line, was wounded. Inside the
grave yard wall, which is attached to the quaint old edifice,
Stirling threw a detachment of the men, who checked, for a
brief period, the torrent of pursuit. All around the meeting
house the battle raged, and to the south eastward, gallant and
staunch Greene, with his steady reserves, covered the retreat.
Half a mile away is the ravine, where he made his final stand,
and held the enemy at bay, while the beaten patriots gathered
and formed again in his rear, to hurry off the road to Chester.[30]

An even bigger crowd assembled on September 11, 1895, to dedicate
a little memorial column near the site of Lafayette's wounding—not on
the exact spot, because nobody could agree where that had been. The
Chester County Historical Society had recently been formed, with one
of its top priorities to identify the precise location on "Battle Hill." Members interviewed old men who had seen Lafayette point it out during his
tour seventy years earlier; but most everybody now seemed baffled. No
matter—as many as eight thousand people came that day by carriage,
horseback, and electric railway to witness the stirring ceremonies.[31]

Residents of the old valley were incorrigibly history-minded. When
West Chester celebrated its centennial in 1899, local families donated a
mountain of artifacts for exhibition at the courthouse; seemingly everybody had colonial porringers, spoons, tea sets, stoneware jugs, or spinning wheels. Many owned relics from the battle: a Hessian's hat; a
mahogany spice chest that had been used as a medicine box to tend the
wounded; a sword dug up at Birmingham Meeting; an eighteen-pound
cannonball found at the Abiah Taylor farm; even the razor that Washington had used to shave before the fight. Some chinaware came with

the explanation, "Grandmother Jefferis had just finished baking and this platter was filled with turnovers for the children when the Hessians appeared and ate up all the food in the house." There was an armchair in which Lafayette rested during his return visit, a mahogany high-post bed in which he spent the night. As locals admired this hoard of historical memorabilia far into the evening, a big searchlight atop the courthouse tower was aimed dramatically at Valley Forge, the Paoli Battleground—and the Brandywine.[32]

Washington's Headquarters proved a perennial favorite for tourists. The modest stone house was already a focus of historical interest when Chastellux and Lafayette revisited the battlefield in 1780. When historian Lossing came, owner Joseph P. Harvey gave him a piece of Revolutionary grapeshot he had recently plowed up. In 1910 a marker was installed by the Chester County Historical Society, which five years later marked points of interest across the entire battlefield. The coming of the concrete highway (today's U.S. 1) around that time swelled the tourist ranks; over nine thousand visited Washington's Headquarters in 1921 alone, from across the country. During these busy years, local antiquarian Christian Sanderson rented the place and joyously showed off his collection of relics. He had reluctantly moved away when, in 1931, news came that the venerable house had burned. What stands today is a reconstruction.

For generations, locals tilling fields or widening roads unearthed every kind of rusted artifact from bayonets to pistols. Sawmills sliced into trees studded with cannonballs, including a four-pound American ball found in 1819. A farmer plowing along the creek above Chadds Ford dug up an unexploded shell in spring 1856, still full of powder, "a perfect missile of death." Philadelphia artist Russell Smith painted *Brandywine Battlefield* in 1870, showing two fence-digging farmers who have unearthed a cannon. Even today, relics are discovered, including an apparent bombshell fuse holder found with a metal detector in a suburban front yard in 2006. And so the mighty battle lives on, more than 230 years later.[33]

On Holy Ground

In spite of urgings from the American Legion and other groups, efforts to preserve the Brandywine battlefield long proved fruitless. Some blamed certain Quaker farmers who showed little interest in memorializing a bloody conflict. Even the installation of the small column in 1895 was controversial, a speaker at the dedication stressing, "Nor is this shaft meant to glorify the spirit of war." Congress resisted enshrining the site of George Washington's worst defeat, so a proposal to create a national park celebrating the first Stars and Stripes flown in battle came to nothing. Elsewhere in Chester County, Paoli Battlefield was preserved as open space for military drilling even before the Civil War, and Valley Forge became a state park in 1893—but nothing was done at Brandywine.[34]

Six thousand acres between Chadds Ford and West Chester saw marching and shooting, but as we saw, only fifty form today's state park along U.S. 1, belatedly established in 1949—barely adequate for visitors seeking immersion in the past. Strenuous recent efforts have helped preserve 42 percent of the entire battlefield, much of it by private conservation easement. But the parcels are scattered, making it difficult for a tourist to envision the sweep of armies as is possible at Gettysburg.[35]

The problem is shared with many Revolutionary sites. What a contrast with the Civil War—within three decades of that national trauma, Congress launched a grand push to buy up key battlefields, and lately the private Civil War Trust has rescued twenty-nine thousand additional acres. Efforts on behalf of the Revolution have been comparatively feeble. Analyzing 677 historic sites associated with the Revolutionary War and the War of 1812, the National Park Service recently found that more than four hundred are entirely unmarked, much less preserved as shrines.

In the economic boom of the late twentieth century, the price per acre of buildable farmland at Brandywine skyrocketed from $2,000 to $40,000. "The developers ran roughshod," says David Shields of the Brandywine Conservancy. Local governments proved ineffectual in safeguarding a resource flung across five municipalities in two counties.

Old Quaker families that resisted setting aside acres as a memorial to militarism instead cut multimillion-dollar deals with developers. Outrageously, expensive homes peppered the very heart of the battleground where Cornwallis's troops surged across Street Road. "I watched that battlefield disappear in the 1980s and wondered, 'Why doesn't somebody do something about this?'" recalls historian Tom McGuire. Sandy Hollow, where fighting raged and near which Lafayette was wounded, narrowly escaped destruction and is now abutted by luxury homes. McGuire observes sadly, "It reduces the scope of using your imagination when you have to say, 'The British Grenadiers came through those backyards up there.'"

Far from expanding its boundaries, in recent years the state-owned park at Brandywine struggled to keep the lights on. As with Washington's Crossing elsewhere in Pennsylvania, budget cuts pushed the park to the brink during the Great Recession. "We fought the Redcoats in 1777," jokes friends' group member Linda Kaat, "and now we're fighting red ink." When the government closed Brandywine in 2009, her organization scrambled for private cash to bring it back again. Many worried that the park's historic buildings that housed Washington and Lafayette would deteriorate from lack of funding.

On battlefields large and small, the war for America's freedom spilled the blood of 25,700 dead and wounded patriots. When it comes to preservation of those sanguine landscapes, there are few easy answers. Nobody pays attention, says historian Robert Selig, an expert on the Revolution, until developers are at the door and "people wake up and realize this battlefield will disappear." Then efforts become frantic, passions run high. "Whether you build there or not is an emotional issue," he told me. "People talk about 'holy ground,'" and compromise seems impossible. In few places are these issues so urgent as at Brandywine. And as we saw, so intense have development pressures become, the federal government has named it one of the nation's very highest priorities for preservation.

Chapter 4

❧ ❧

"Rushing Water and Buzzing Wheels"

In July 1798, William Wordsworth and his sister, Dorothy, took a three-day walking tour of England's Wye Valley. A few miles upstream from the famous medieval ruin of Tintern Abbey, they stopped and marveled at the scenery. There on "the banks of the Wye" William Wordsworth began to compose what has become his most cherished poem. "Tintern Abbey" was not written down but rather chanted aloud by the poet as he walked back down the valley, heading home; so it is not only the quintessential poem about a river, it was created in the very process of traversing that river's lovely shores, each rhythm a footfall on the grass.

The Wordsworths were part of an army of tourists of the picturesque for whom the Wye had become an irresistible goal. In every pocket was William Gilpin's book, *Observations on the River Wye . . . Relative Chiefly to Picturesque Beauty*, which made history in the 1780s as the first illustrated tourist guide and helped launch a transatlantic mania for excursions and escapes into natural scenery. Here in America, the Brandywine (sixty miles long) came to serve a similar function as the Wye (134 miles). It was accessible from cities and yet deliciously scenic, with all four of Gilpin's "ornaments" in evidence: irregular ground, hoary woods, tumbled rocks, and venerable buildings. When Gilpin describes a particularly rough stretch of the Wye, we may recall the Brandywine where the placid river suddenly bends, then foams over the boulders at Hagley's Birkenhead Mill: "The violence of the stream, and the roaring of the waters, impressed a new character on the scene: all was agitation, and uproar; and every steep, and every rock stared with wildness, and terror."[1]

But the real Wye, like the Brandywine, was no pristine waterway at the heart of an unspoiled paradise. Its hillsides were laced with tourist paths, "viewpoints" having been cut out of the native forests as early as the 1750s to accommodate throngs of visitors. Moreover, the Wye Valley was a prosperous center of English milling, known for the production of paper, iron, and wire: before 1700, it became, one historian notes, "arguably the crucible of the Industrial Revolution." Academics argue briskly whether Wordsworth had any right to ignore all this modernization in writing an escapist poem to his beloved "sylvan Wye! thou wanderer thro' the woods." But of course he looks away from ugliness: his artistic purpose is to establish the Wye as an antidote to "the fretful stir / Unprofitable, and the fever of the world." One modern historian notes that the Wye presents "two, contrasting stories"—the river exploited and spoiled, versus the river celebrated for its naturalness—which is exactly the paradox we find on the Brandywine from 1780 on as the milling industry undergoes a rapid and epoch-making expansion.[2]

The Genius of Oliver Evans

The American Revolution disrupted commerce nationwide, but it did not entirely stop the growth of industry on the Brandywine. By the time of that great conflict, merchant milling was well underway at Market Street Bridge in Wilmington, where the creek reaches tidewater. By cutting long races through the stubborn rocks on either side of its banks—starting about 1757, two on the north and two on the south—Quaker millers seized its fast-flowing water for use in turning millwheels on a site otherwise not practicable, in the deepwater harbor just below the bridge.

Thus did they ingeniously combine two extraordinary assets of this first-rate waterway, the Brandywine: Piedmont whitewater right next to Coastal Plain navigability. Epic improvements in milling technique were promoted by the genius inventor Oliver Evans in his *Young Millwright and Miller's Guide* (1795), to which Washington and Jefferson subscribed. Evans grew up on a Delaware farm but found rural enterprises dull, so he apprenticed with a wheelwright; even then, he showed lively curiosity and was seemingly able to foretell the distant technological future: "I labored to discover some means of propelling land carriages, without animal power." Later he lived in Brandywine Village "nearly opposite the Academy" and demonstrated his innovative milling machinery at his home.[3]

As can be seen today in a detailed miniature-model at Hagley Museum, Evans invented five mechanical devices that could move grain and flour up, down, and sideways through a mill, freeing the millers' aching backs. These were the screw-like *conveyor*, *drill*, *descender*, *elevator*, and a revolving rake called the *hopper-boy* for the panting lad whose job it claimed. His seemingly miraculous achievements in automation were described in a newspaper account of 1791:

> Every part of the machinery in which those improvements consist, is now in use at Brandywine Mills, and is highly approved of. The wheat elevator has been lately applied, for the first time, to unload a shallop; it elevates three hundred bushels per hour, and enables the miller to convey his wheat to any granary in the mill without the assistance of manual labour. To such perfection are our grist and merchant mills brought, by the assistance of those improvements, that we may say, perhaps without boasting, that they are not equalled in the world. The machinery is so well applied, that from the time the wheat leaves the waggoner's bag, the measurer's half bushel, or the vessel's hold, as the case may be, no manual labour is required, but the wheat is converted into superfine or other flour, fit for packing, entirely by the effect of the machinery.[4]

The result of all this was the profound transformation of American milling and a major step in the nascent Industrial Revolution (see Plate 5). The Brandywine enterprises at Wilmington became the top-producing flour mills in the New World, helping feed not only American cities but Europe and the West Indies, a point of immense satisfaction in a nation that seemed to pride itself, foremost, on its ability to innovate and make fistfuls of money.

The industrial potential of the lower Brandywine was obvious early on. Joseph Tatnall proudly described his site in 1773 as

> an extraordinary MERCHANT MILL, situated in the Borough of Wilmington, on Brandywine Creek, below the Bridge, on a never failing stream. Said mill has two water wheels, two pair of burr stones, and every thing compleat for the manufacturing of superfine flour. Shallops of a considerable burthen may load or unload without any difficulty, it being performed by water. . . . The situation of the abovementioned mill, need not be more particularly described, as it is well known to many, and has the advantage for the sale of flour of two considerable markets, viz. Philadelphia and Wilmington.[5]

Unfortunately, time has completely erased these historic mills at Market Street, except for one rebuilt south millrace, which carries cool, dark Brandywine current to the pumping station that supplies the modern city with drinking water. Its flow is silent but powerful, a visceral evocation of the kinetic force of water as it drops from a higher level (Third Dam) to a lower. The old mills may be gone, but Brandywine Village Historic District preserves several millers' homes, recalling the Quaker dynasty that once ruled here: Oliver Canby, Joseph Tatnall, Thomas Lea, James Price.

So important were the flour mills to the economic health of the colonies—and to the bellies of the Continental Army—that General Washington sent his trusted officer, "Mad Anthony" Wayne, to live in Joseph Tatnall's home for several weeks before the Battle of the Brandywine. "I cannot fight for thee, but I can and will feed thee," Tatnall promised the Americans. But after the defeat on September 11, 1777, Washington feared that Tatnall and his pragmatic Quaker peers would end up supplying the British army instead. Continental troops arrived in Wilmington in November and plucked the grinding stones from the Market Street mills, halting production for ten months.[6]

Later, as U.S. president, Washington routinely reviewed patent claims and read with fascination about Oliver Evans's achievements. During one tour, he revisited Tatnall's Brandywine mill to study the Evans machinery, followed by a crowd of excited boys. Two of Evans's brothers traveled to Mount Vernon in 1791 to help Washington improve his gristmill on Dogue Run. And later he sought more assistance, beginning a letter flatteringly, "MOUNT VERNON, April 15, 1798. Sir: Knowing that no place is more likely to furnish a good Miller than Brandywine. . . ." Lafayette inspected Tatnall's mill during his return trip to America, too—one of many tourists to make a point of seeing these shrewd mechanical operations, which promised great things for the economic growth of the young republic.[7]

Brandywine Village was happily spared much twentieth-century redevelopment and today preserves something of its original flavor. In 1770, a decade or so after the first overshot mills were begun on the south bank of the creek, one James Marshall excavated a millrace on the north. With the Brandywine blue rock thus made available, he built a five-bay Georgian house, which Thomas Lea, prominent miller and banker, bought in 1785. It survives today, emblematic of the prosperity that water-powered industrialization brought. A handsome row of early stone houses extends up the street and includes the Tatnall Houses, No. 1803 (first part, c. 1770) and No. 1805 (c. 1850), these having been rescued some decades ago from being demolished for a high-rise apartment building.[8]

A Fine Range of Mills

The years following the Revolution saw a dizzying explosion of industry on the creek in Delaware. A partial enumeration in 1793 listed fifty merchant mills, grinding and packing 91,500 barrels of flour annually; fifty saw mills cutting one thousand feet per day of plank and boards; eight forges producing seventy-five tons of bar iron annually each; seven fulling mills; four grist mills; four paper mills; two slitting mills; one furnace, making fifteen tons of pig metal and three tons of castings per week; one snuff mill; and one tilt hammer.[9]

Travelers commented ecstatically about those lofty mill buildings at Market Street, which Philadelphia artist Charles Willson Peale stopped to sketch on October 23, 1789, making a record for posterity of this history-making locale. There were now ten mills close together, with twenty pairs of millstones capable of grinding two thousand bushels of grain per day. A system had been devised whereby, when one pair was "dressing up" or cooling, another constantly ran—so that travelers marveled at the sounds of industry going both day and night. Here was a foretaste of the relentless pace of the Industrial Revolution that would soon reconfigure the life of every American.[10]

By 1804, thirteen mills on the lower Brandywine were grinding four hundred thousand bushels of grain every year. "A fine range of mills, perhaps the completest of their kind in the United States, are just below [Market Street] bridge," said *The Travellers Directory*—for this continued to be the nation's most important center for flour milling throughout the Federal period. As Brandywine mills became a considerable tourist attraction, Jedediah Morse hailed them in his *American Gazetteer* as the "greatest seat of manufactures in the United States."[11]

Meanwhile, property on the creek was becoming ever more desirable. Back in 1771, Vincent Gilpin had advertised his holdings, two miles upstream from Wilmington on "the creek called Brandywine," already recognizing their potential:

> The mill house is of stone, 35 feet by 30, boulting and bran-rooms adjoining, two pair of millstones, one whereof French burrs, fanns, screens, boulting cloths, and hoistings all good, and go by water; suitable for manufacturing wheat, in the best manner, to the amount of 20,000 bushels, or upwards, yearly; as there is no want of water, handy to navigation, and a good neighbourhood for wheat country business, and timber, a great stroke of business may be carried on; the forebays and running works were all repaired last summer; the plantation contains

120 acres, 70 whereof cleared, four acres of watered meadow, the rest extraordinary good wheat land, and well manured; with a good orchard, a new stone dwelling house, three rooms below, and four above, a good draw well, a frame barn, and stone stabling under a hay house, with other outhouses, and two small tenements for tradesmen or labourers.[12]

Another farmstead sold in Delaware in 1785, five miles upstream from Wilmington, was glowingly advertised as having

400 acres, 150 of which are cleared, the remainder covered with heavy timber, suitable for ship-plank, staves and fire-wood, which being so convenient to a landing and market renders it valuable. There are on said plantation, a good stone dwelling-house, a log barn, stables and hay-house, a large orchard of the best grafted fruit; the meadows at present a little out of repair, but may be made equal to any in that part of the country. This place being situate on the Brandywine, has a beautiful seat for mills, forge, or other water-works.[13]

All this milling drew public attention and comment akin to that directed at our high-tech tablets and smartphones of today, because it, too, seemed so revolutionary—factories that ran day and night, and all by themselves! A huge literature on the subject delved into the arcana of French burr stones, balance-rynes, cock-head spindles, cog-wheels, wallowers, and trundle sluices—again, generating its own argot like certain technological crazes of our own times. In terms of game-changing innovation, the Brandywine Valley at Wilmington was effectively the Silicon Valley of its day.

Arts and Sciences

Even as wealth quickly accumulated, Wilmington was earning a reputation as an ideal place to live. A doctor in 1792 surveyed the healthfulness of towns up and down the Eastern Seaboard and found Wilmington the best of all, its Piedmont setting offering relief from "marsh miasmata and other noxious exhalations." "The hills of Brandywine," he concluded, "furnish as healthful a district of country as any in America."[14]

For proud Wilmingtonians, the old Swedish dream of building a significant port city was at last coming true. Ships appeared from all over the world, "rounding to" into the Christina, sometimes then slipping into the Brandywine. Merchants watched with spyglasses for sails on the horizon and listened for cannon shots announcing new arrivals. Local chronicler Elizabeth Montgomery once watched a "dark, dirty-looking" vessel creep in, sails lowered. A steamboat chugged down to tow her up the river as boys ran through the streets shouting, "A whale ship!" Piles of glistening shells were offloaded, along with whalebone, and curious townsfolk offered gifts of tools, knives, and beads to a feather-bedecked New Zealander who wandered ashore: "O, shocking!" Montgomery recalled. "He was a cannibal."[15]

With increased wealth came culture, and from the Brandywine mills flowed money that promoted arts and science in Delaware. Edward Tatnall, a botanist who owned Wawaset Nursery on the banks of the creek ("Wawassan" was a Lenape name for the Brandywine), used a telescope on his balustraded rooftop at No. 1805 Market to observe the heavens. William Canby lived amid a lush garden by Market Street Bridge on the south bank, perusing Alexander Pope's *Essay on Man*—that Englishman too was a lover of rivers, resident alongside the Thames—and corresponding with Jefferson about theology.[16]

Following the violent slave revolt in Haiti in the 1790s, a lively community of French émigrés settled in Wilmington, some forty families, and built bathhouses on the millrace banks west of the creek above Market Street Bridge. Their servant girls sat on benches in the fast-flowing race to wash clothes, drying them on the grass to "snowy whiteness." The French-speaking expatriate colony in Wilmington would soon include an industrious family from France named du Pont.[17]

Among the intellectuals drawn to Wilmington in these years were British-born architect Benjamin Henry Latrobe (later designer of the U.S. Capitol) and sharp-tongued English satirist William Cobbett— "Peter Porcupine"—who taught school on Quaker Hill overlooking the Christina, wrote about the prosperous Brandywine mills in *Porcupine's Gazette*, and later brought the bones of patriot Thomas Paine back to America for burial. On his first visit here, Cobbett spent several days examining the corn mills, cotton factories, woolen-mills with dye houses, and powder mills, and admiring the larger setting:

> This river is very rapid, running upon a stony and rocky bed. In the valley, I saw vines as thick as my arm.... The country round, is high, pleasant and healthy, and the fruit abundant. The roads are good. The inhabitants are not subject to the fever and ague.[18]

Another fresh arrival was Irish patriot and former prisoner Archibald Hamilton Rowan, who settled on the Brandywine's banks just below Old Barley Mill in Wilmington, which he fitted up for calico printing and dyeing. Children delighted in visiting this eccentric gentleman, entering with awe his book-filled "cottage of rough boards ... with several small rooms, each having a fine name. On the inside he pasted paper to make it look neat." Rowan's only companions were his dogs, Sally and Charles, named for his wife and son left behind in Ireland; he addressed them as if they were people. Rowan took long walks along the creek and through the woods of today's Brandywine Park, swinging his sword-cane with compass atop. In his pocket was a pedometer, a gift from his wife when he was imprisoned overseas and needed adequate exercise around the jail yard. The sound of his flute charmed boaters on Barley Mill Dam. In winter Rowan played a Scottish game called "golfing" on the ice, using a round stone fitted with a handle. After his crude house burned, he relocated right across the creek.[19]

Spanning the Brandywine at Wilmington. Market Street Bridge stood at the heart of America's best-known milling district. This vital crossing (seen here in its 1839 version) was rebuilt time and again after destructive floods. Photo ca. 1880.

The mills at Market Street were famous partly because they were so visible, the bridge here forming a vital link in the main north–south road along the Eastern Seaboard—making it a predecessor to Interstate 95, which today crosses the Brandywine a short stroll to the west. The social reformer Francois de La Rochefoucauld, a refugee from the French Revolution, stood on Market Street Bridge and admired the "delightful" scene: the fifty houses of Brandywine Village standing near the creek that roared over huge rocks as cattle placidly grazed along the banks; eleven mills busily rattling within sight of where he stood.[20]

Today's Market Street Bridge is the sixth span to cross the creek at this historic place. The first went up about 1766, as milling got under way: "Whereas there is proposed to be built, in the King Road leading from Chester to New Castle, a substantial Bridge over Brandywine Creek," designers were invited to submit proposals. The bridge stood high above the water on three thick masonry pillars, but frame ones were substituted after floods repeatedly dislodged the stones. Finally the bridge was smashed by an ice jam and was replaced by a pioneering, very early iron-chain suspension span in 1810, by prolific bridge builder James Finley. Its 145-foot "chord" was one of the longest in America, though not so great as the Merrimack bridge in Massachusetts or the Schuylkill bridge in Philadelphia. It, too, washed away when chunks of ice and logs hammered it during the 1822 freshet. "I was present when this bridge fell," miller William Lea recalled, "and the crashing of the chains, shrieks of fire was awful." Three men drowned.[21]

The lost structure was immediately replaced by a covered bridge designed by engineer Lewis Wernwag, which appears in a painting by Bass Otis, one of an increasing cohort of topographical artists to visit the area. Washed away in 1839, that bridge was also replaced. The river crossing was a vital one, not only for travelers but for farmers' wagons and thundering droves of cattle.

Rochefoucauld marveled to report that there were nearly eighty mills on the Brandywine in Delaware alone. He was given a thorough tour of Tatnall's "flour manufactory," where, as we have seen, automation was so highly developed: amid clouds of white dust, a mere six employees ground 100,000 bushels annually. Sloops brought slave-grown grain from Virginia and Maryland right up to the walls of the mill, which touched the tidewater basin below the bridge. Looking back, historian Henry Seidel Canby marveled at how the Brandywine formed the junction between Northern industry and, starting with the Coastal Plain at its mouth, Southern agriculture—nowhere else in America, he said, was there so sudden a change in geography.[22]

Tatnall's workers (including twenty-four who ran the ships and built barrels) were English or Irish and prone to drunkenness; Frenchmen would have been better, being more industrious, Rochefoucauld was told. Tatnall refused to hire blacks, who "do not work with the whites; but are slow, and bad workmen." There was seemingly no limit to the potential for milling on the Brandywine, Rochefoucauld saw. Nearby was a mill for bolting Georgia silk, and just opened was a water-powered manufactory for printing linens brought from India, which a dozen girls finished up at home before the cloth was then sold in Philadelphia.

Watermarks

Upstream stood Gilpin's Mill, at the foot of today's steep Three Mill Road on the west bank. The Chadds Ford family of Gilpin first made their presence known in Delaware before the Revolution when Thomas Gilpin undertook the development of valuable mill sites on the Brandywine, traveling to England to investigate the possibilities of trade with the mother country. An enlightened man, he was an original member of the American Philosophical Society, but his Quaker refusal to assist the American cause led to his arrest in his Philadelphia office days before the Battle of the Brandywine. Exiled to Virginia, Gilpin died six months later.[23]

It was left to his young sons, Joshua and Thomas, eventually to carry on the Brandywine mills. As a teenager, Joshua avidly read Latin classics and wrote erudite poems and essays; Thomas excelled in math, science, and literary pursuits. In 1795, Joshua, age thirty, traveled to Europe to further acquaint himself with manufacturing and trade. Along the way, he assembled a valuable cabinet of mineralogy and socialized with the Swarthmore-born artist Benjamin West, a Gilpin relation. Thomas, nineteen, took charge of the mills.

At the Three Mill Road location in 1787—site of a former snuff mill—Joshua Gilpin and Miers Fisher founded the first paper mill on the creek, sending samples from this "Brandywine Mill" to Benjamin Franklin, printer in Philadelphia. In part owing to the purity of the creek water, paper with "Brandywine" watermarks soon became well-known for its quality—still appearing bright white today in rare copies of the *Mirror of the Times* newspaper, for example, published in Wilmington in 1799. Gilpin and Fisher specialized in banknotes, making paper for bills used from Rhode Island to North Carolina.[24]

Then, in August 1817, Brandywine Paper Mills made history, becoming the first place in the country to manufacture paper by machine, using the pirated Cylinder Mould Machine design of Englishman John Dickinson, assembled amid great secrecy. Milling was a high-stakes business marked by intrigues and spying: Joshua Gilpin twice visited Apsley Mill on the River Gade, at Hemel Hempstead northwest of London, to observe what went on there, taking copious notes from memory afterward.

Apsley Mill was where Dickinson developed his famous, top secret machine for making paper. It featured a hollow brass cylinder rotating in a vat of pulp, instead of the traditional wooden frame immersed in the soggy liquid. To steal this revolutionary technology, Gilpin hired away a man named Laurence Greatrake by offering him a huge salary. When Dickinson learned that Greatrake had left England and taken with him one of the priceless brass cylinders, he was livid.

Witnessing the miracle of the Industrial Revolution firsthand, a visitor marveled to see Gilpin's revamped Brandywine Mill run by only two men and a boy, not the dozen men and six boys usually required to manufacture paper. They dumped in rags, then didn't touch them again until out came, like magic, "perfect paper, at the opposite side . . . where it winds on with great velocity what may be termed one endless sheet . . . smooth as satin." The speed was incredible, sixty feet a minute, not to mention the endless nature of the ream, which glowed white like "fine damask cloth." Philadelphia publishers clamored to get the oversize machine-made Brandywine paper, including those who issued the *American Daily Advertiser* newspaper and Lavoisne's *Atlas* (see Plate 6). Despite all precautions, Gilpin's plans were soon stolen by others, however, and the mechanical papermaking technique spread widely—among other things, facilitating an explosion of American media and publishing in the years leading up to the Civil War.[25]

Papermakers identified their products with watermarks, visible when the sheet is held up to the light. Fine wires forming letters or pictures were placed in the mold before the paper pulp was poured in; where the wires had been, the paper is slightly thinner, resulting in a translucent watermark. The top expert on American watermarks was DuPont Company retiree Thomas Gravell of Wilmington, who began his research in 1970. Watermarks are notoriously difficult to photograph, but Gravell found an easy, fast way using DuPont Dylux 503 photosensitive paper and fluorescent lights. J GILPIN & CO BRANDYWINE say the watermarks of Gilpin-made papers; rival William Young's say DELAWARE.[26]

Truly Romantic Spot

The industrializing Brandywine is immortalized in artist Thomas Doughty's painting, *Gilpin's Mill on the Brandywine* (ca. 1825–1830), later published by James Smillie as a popular engraving with the erroneous but crowd-pleasing title, *The Battlefield of Brandywine*. A young Philadelphia leather merchant who taught himself to paint, Doughty was one of the first landscape painters in the country to embrace the romantic style. His early career consisted of making views of gentlemen's estates, and presumably he intended this one to be bought by the millwrights Gilpin. Other artists depicted the scenic locale too; as far away as England, the ceramic illustrator Enoch Wood showed *Gilpin's Mill on the Brandywine Creek* on decorated china.

But here the Brandywine paradox starts to become visible: the place is famous for industry, yet simultaneously celebrated for its naturalness. Artists of the picturesque habitually found a way to merge both stories into a single image of beauty-and-utility, progress in harmony with nature. In a late example, the 1872 book *Picturesque America* pondered the juxtaposition of the two themes along the river: at the densely wooded powder yards of Hagley, for example, "the beauties of Nature and the toils and dangers of industry strangely mingle. . . . Throughout the length of this Eden run the iron lines of a horse railroad." At Riddle's Cotton Mills at today's Mill Road, "One lingers in the dense shadows of the forest-covered bank with delight, and discovers, in the mingled sounds of rushing water and buzzing wheels, a strange charm. Repose and activity, the hush of shadowy woods, and the hum of labor, seem to blend in delicious harmony."[27]

The effusive age of Wordsworth and Coleridge brought an outpouring of literary appreciation for the Brandywine, even as tourists thronged. A merchant who rented a cotton mill from the du Ponts in 1831 raved that "it would add ten years to his life to reside here in such a spot." A friend chimed in: "It's very romantic!" British traveler Joseph Gurney enjoyed "roaming about the romantic banks of the Brandywine river" in 1838. Joshua Gilpin took breaks from milling to write pastoral poems in the manner of Virgil, and his daughter Mary, strolling on the creek banks with a friend, confessed her hope of "writing a work like the journal of a naturalist about this country." A reporter rapturously described the DuPont powder works, which, despite the technology and profit-making there, was the most scenic locale of all:

> The place itself is beautiful beyond description: the high hills on either side, covered with lofty trees rich with verdure, bright with brilliant sunshine on their towering tops, and rich in their dense shadows below; the lucid stream gently gliding over its stony bed, its glassy surface reflecting its woody sides and the bright cerulean sky.[28]

Already by the late eighteenth century, the creek was drawing many of these lovers of the picturesque, that aesthetic philosophy that effortlessly bled into romanticism. Looking upstream from Market Street Bridge right after the Revolution, German botanist Johann Schoepf noted that "the narrow gorge through which the stream flows makes a view particularly pleasing and rough." Rochefoucauld visited Gilpin's Mill, adding further to our knowledge of its operations—rags brought from up to three hundred miles away were pounded by vertical wheels, then made into paper ranging from fine vellum to coarse brown; workmen were Irish and prone to inebriation. But much of his enthusiasm was reserved for the setting: even with the factories, here was a "truly romantic spot" embracing "a view rather gloomy, wild and uncultivated, yet pleasing."[29]

He noted how the creek raced through a gorge almost covered in woods, coursing over jumbled rocks that gave the whole landscape the effect of the famously beautiful forest of Fontainebleau in France. Gilpin lived in a mansion on the hilltop (Kentmere at today's Riddle Avenue) with a fine view of the creek and forested valley.

After his tour of the mill, Rochefoucauld crossed the swift river to reach the home of one Reverend Dr. Wharton in Brandywine Hundred. He traveled through woods of oak, chestnut, and hickory and saw numerous conifers, including abundant Virginia cedars and pines (strangely absent today). Cedar provided poles for wooden fencing and planks for clapboarding. Wharton was an entirely self-sufficient farmer, Rochefoucauld found. The flax of his tablecloth had been grown on his estate, as had the wood of the table itself. Wharton owned seven slaves who, the clergyman explained rather heartlessly, needed much less food than whites: he fed them cornbread, with meat only at lunchtime.[30]

Picnics and Promenades

Elizabeth Montgomery, that chronicler of early Wilmington, fondly recalled the fun she had on the Brandywine in her youth. "This is a romantic stream, long celebrated in story," she said, and she enjoyed numerous outings that must have been typical for many Wilmingtonians. As a child in the 1780s, for example, she was taken up to the old snuff mill on the north bank (later Augustine Mills), where a workman gave her a cherished souvenir: a paper wrapper from a tobacco roll, with an engraving of men smoking pipes around a table and saying in turn, "Good tobacco. Yes, excellent. Who made it? Isaac Jones."[31]

The "narrow rugged path" to the snuff mill was a popular walk, Montgomery added, with scenery that grew ever bolder and wilder even as the industrial establishment grew nearer. Here as a young woman, she and her friends undertook a memorable "evening excursion to this romantic place." Starting up the north bank, they passed under a "mammoth willow." Dog's Head Rock was a favorite spot to carve initials; here two of the party, a young couple, fell off the outcrop and into the race with a splash "as if the flood-gates had given away." Montgomery's friend cried, "How shall I go through town, or enter my house in such a dripping dress?" A local poet had expounded upon this same "lofty rock / On which was written many a name," and, somewhat surprisingly, it still survives in our time, unnoticed along a half-derelict park roadway, with initials and carved and painted dates of the 1820s still faintly visible.[32]

On other occasions Montgomery joined her associates in promenading up and down the Brandywine raceways, with the gristmill near Third Dam and Rattlesnake Run (which drains today's Trolley Square) a popular picnic destination. June was the ideal season for strolling the walks under forest trees as water spilled over the dams and dashed and foamed through the floodgates in a scene recalling the English riparian paintings of J. M. W. Turner or John Constable. "Whole schools of young people" went "skipping along the banks, climbing the rocks, and fancifully decorating their heads with wild flowers." The stream could be crossed by an alarmingly high footbridge of "slender boards, that rock with your weight, and the only support is a wire not as thick as your finger."

Much picnicking centered on Old Barley Mill at the foot of Adams Street. Like many mills on the stream, it underwent constant changes over the years, being used successively for grinding barley, calico printing, spinning, carding, and spindle-making. Its milldam served as the city's swimming hole, where "flags and lilies of rare beauty" pushed up from the muddy banks and unfolded in the sunshine. From his little cabin downstream, full of pasted pictures children had brought him, hermit-like Isaac Kendall offered swimming lessons to boys.

In winter, Old Barley Mill Dam saw skating, townsfolk lining the snowy banks to admire feats of dexterity: men cutting ciphers or pulling little girls on their coattails; boys riding a dangerous "whirligig" of sleds fastened to a pole and spinning so fast, a dense mist boiled up. Around 1820 some schoolgirls came to slide on the thawing ice, but one fell through and drowned. "Crowds were running towards Brandywine" and soon brought the stiffened corpse home to the widowed parent.

"This was an agonizing scene," Montgomery recalled, "to see the be-reaved mother lay her hand on the breast of her darling child, in hopes some warmth still remained."

Many accounts survive of the growing importance of the Brandywine to Wilmingtonians. A woman who spent her girlhood in town in the 1840s recalled long walks beside that "far-famed stream": old, moss-grown flour mills; The Walk, with brick mansions of the mill proprietors, green blinds on the windows and ornamental grounds laid out in fantastic curves, half-moons, and triangles; the clang of the cooper's hammer; Bish-opstead (the old Canby place) full of the scent of clambering rose bushes. Farther up, "high hills, skirted by woods, rose on the left, and, on the right, terminated in a deep gorge, through which little brooks tinkled. . . . There was the same old log, serving for a rustic bridge, where we had an-gled for minnows many a day." Her eye was for, exclusively, the Brandy-wine of myth. One would hardly know that this was the same river that had revolutionized American industry and continued to export flour, cloth, gunpowder, and paper in vast quantities to the world.[33]

Skating at Rockland Dam. The large white paper mill (Jessup and Moore) still stands today as condominiums, but much else is gone, including the 1839 covered bridge and the colonial mills at right.

Paper Mills at Rockland

The Janus-faced blend of Brandywine milling amid scenic beauty was not confined to the lower creek. Upstream at Rockland, Delaware—where today's Rockland Road crosses a concrete bridge—milling got under way early, in spite of the wild remoteness of the spot. Gregg and Kirk's grist mill went up on the west bank in 1724, before there was any bridge, only "Kirk's Ford." By 1733 there was a fulling mill; and Kirk's grist mill, demolished only in recent decades, bore a 1749 datestone. The paper mill of William Young followed. Jessup and Moore expanded the latter during the Civil War—eventually it was said to be the nation's largest papermaker—and experimented with using straw instead of rags to meet burgeoning demand. The Settling Pond allowed sediment to filter out from creek water, so the supply was clear. So much water went through the factory, it poured back into the river in thundering waterfalls. In 1863, Wilmingtonians complained about the sodium chloride that was dumped into the creek at Rockland, which made their tap water taste bad—one of the first public admissions that the Brandywine, that beloved Arcadia, was becoming seriously polluted by industry.[34]

Up Mount Lebanon Road—almost the only steep grade in all of Delaware, which has the lowest mean elevation (just sixty feet) of any state—a venerable oak marks the stone ruins of Rockland Presbyterian Church, near where Rocky Run cuts through a virgin woodlot. Huge tulip trees guard Mount Lebanon Methodist, established in 1812. Young artist N. C. Wyeth and his bride Carolyn liked to visit this "beautiful secluded spot," studying quaint inscriptions on gravestones and strolling through avenues of ancient boxwood. Two days before Christmas in 1906, they buried their newborn daughter here, in a tiny grave that seems to have left no trace today.[35]

Suburban wealth has waved its wand across Rockland. Gone are the ramshackle workmen's houses and shops that once lured Sunday painters (population two hundred in 1880); today, upscale condominiums rise in their place. Of the numerous mills that lined the stream on both banks, only Rockland Mills survives, now an exclusive gated community. Its stone walls trembled to the making of paper from the 1850s to 1933 under Jessup and Moore; later it was Doeskin Products, until finally closing in the early 1970s. It was served by an intricately constructed stone dam, in our time inexorably washing away and scheduled for partial demolition in order that anadromous fish may "run," as they have not since the eighteenth century.

The early history of Rockland is dominated by the personality of William Young. A Scottish bookseller, he immigrated to Philadelphia in 1784 and ran a shop and printing press on Chestnut Street not far from Independence Hall. Seeking to avoid expensive importation of paper (the first copies of the Declaration of Independence, for example, had been printed on paper from Holland), he opened Delaware Paper Mill at Rockland in 1794–1795. His major client was the U.S. government, then sited in Philadelphia, which needed paper for stamps, bonds, certificates, and legal forms. Because linen rags were costly, Young experimented with making paper from mulberry tree roots and the bark of the tropical guaiacum tree.

In 1813 Young expanded his operations, creating the adjacent Delaware Woolen Company mill for making blue cassimere (suit-cloth) and working up coarse wools into a satin-like fabric. The next year, his paper mill burned down. In 1822 he established a cotton factory, which contained some of the earliest powered cotton-spinning machinery in the country. Three years later came Rockland Manufacturing Company, making woolen cloth, which his sons ran until it burned in 1846. Young's stately Federal-style home still stands uphill on Black Gates Road, a reminder of the wealth that early industrialization brought. It is surrounded by modern developments and a country club, and a new suburban house supplanted its squarish, fort-like, stone-walled barn in 2013.[36]

A recent series of oral interviews with old-timers who could recall Rockland early in the twentieth century provides an invaluable record of the "crik" before industry sputtered out and suburbanization washed over the landscape. The riverbanks were planted with willow trees in soldier-like rows, their twigs used to produce charcoal for powder-making. Little sawmills dotted Wilson's Run. The Brandywine Canoe Club operated just above Rockland Dam. Men and boys fished for bass or hunted squirrel, rabbit, and muskrat in the chestnut woods all the way up to Smith's Bridge, bringing home supper for the family. (Smith's Bridge was the scene of a small tragedy back in 1865 when William Twaddle, age fourteen, "was out for the purpose of shooting ducks, and was standing on an elevation, with the butt of his gun resting on the bridge" when he "accidently struck the trigger with his foot, causing it to go off . . . killing him instantly.")[37]

The mill workers lived in close proximity to the gentry: Round Top on the Winterthur property, where Brandywine Creek State Park headquarters now stands, was a favorite place for the upscale sport of beagling. Local boys were hired to run up and down the hills, dragging burlap bags in which foxes had been kept, so du Ponts could exercise their hunting dogs. (Those boys also carved their names in Round Top's beech trees with pocketknives; recently I saw a big dying tree there with the graffito "Henry Gray Del. 1889.") As the children climbed the hill to their schoolhouse near Black Gates Road, they dodged the du Ponts who tested fancy new automobiles on the steep incline.[38]

Today, all the milling is gone, and there is almost no way to visualize more than one hundred mills grinding and creaking, up and down the valley. Broken walls overgrown with briars don't give much suggestion— even ninety years ago, novelist Hergesheimer saw only "grist mills tangled with blackberry bushes, the mill wheels collapsed in the empty races." But at Hagley Museum, a single wheel has been reconstructed within the once-ruinous walls of the Birkenhead, an 1824 powder mill. Amateur archaeologist Roland Wells Robbins came down from New England in 1955 to dig in the mud of the sodden mill race, looking for traces of the early apparatus. He was famous for earlier digs at the Saugus industrial site in Massachusetts and for having discovered the location of Thoreau's cabin by Walden Pond.[39]

Standing inside the Birkenhead today, one gets a sense, however partial, of what river-powered industry must have felt like—the splash of the water, the low groan of the steadily turning wheel. But a visitor one recent February found the wheel immobile for winter, with only a cavernous stillness inside the blue-rock walls. The millwheel made a huge loop, with soft, gray light leaking in wanly through the crack between wheel and walls. All the moving parts, the polygonal shaft, the long arms, the planked inner face of the wheel, the toothed gears, were powdered with crystalline snow that had sifted in with the wind in the night. Winter or summer, water-powered industry along the Brandy-wine was always interesting to see, always picturesque.

Chapter 5

❧ ❧

Thunderous Age of Black Powder

For many, the name "Brandywine" is synonymous with the du Pont family, who arrived in 1802 in flight from the bloody French Revolution and its aftermath. For the historian, the du Ponts present the whole Brandywine paradox in microcosm: at the cutting edge of modernization and high technology, yet arch-traditionalist in their attitude toward cultural heritage and the landscape. The du Ponts were newcomers, and yet they settled down deeply into the valley with a profound sense of belonging. They were French—bequeathing us such local place-names as Granogue, Guyencourt, Cossart—yet they exhibited even more than many natives the typically English traits so often remarked in the region. For example, to this day their passion for family history equals that of any earl or duke puffing his pipe in a London club: they actually employ a genealogy office that keeps careful track of more than three thousand descendants (each given a coded pedigree number), 1,200 of whom recently showed up to celebrate the two-hundredth anniversary of the family's arrival in America. If the Brandywine has a nostalgic, antiquarian tone, the du Ponts have done much to foster it.

From an early date, du Ponts exhibited the kind of natural aristocracy that many conservative writers longed to see in a fast-changing America. The famous horticulturist Andrew Jackson Downing sounded a hopeful note in his 1841 classic, *Landscape Gardening*: "As a people descended from the English stock, we inherit much of the ardent love of rural life," and what was now needed, he felt, amid a churning populace filled with "enterprise and energy" and the "uncouth and discordant" was a "society more fixed in its character." He saw promising glimpses of such a future in certain families who inhabited long-settled regions of the Eastern Seaboard—for example the Latimers who built the Wilmington estate called Latimeria (decorative fragments of which are now at Winterthur), with its "high keeping, richly stocked gardens and conservatories, and much natural beauty, heightened by judicious planting, arrangement, and culture." Downing declared that in "a strong attachment to natal soil, we must look for a counterpoise to the great tendency towards constant change, and the restless spirit of emigration, which form part of our national character." The Brandywine would seem to fit his purposes exactly, matching as it does his description of the ideal "romantic valley" with "steep rocky banks" and "tangled thickets of deep foliage." As the crowning touch, Downing had written, "let the stream turn the ancient and well-worn wheel of the old mill."[1]

The Brandywine as *counterpoise*—Downing's term is perfect to describe how the creek has long served, in its mythological dimensions, the quixotic American need for something old, fixed, settled. The Janus-faced river impressed many visitors with its paradoxical capacity to calm and soothe the soul. "Despite its services in the gigantic flouring-mills, or even its dark deeds in the manufacture of gunpowder," the Victorian book *Picturesque America* notes, "it is throughout a great part of its course a peaceful woodland rivulet."[2]

Powder-Making at Eleutherian Mills

Melancholy young Eleuthère Irénée du Pont—his name in Latin means "liberty and peace"—learned how to manufacture gunpowder under brilliant chemist Antoine Lavoisier at the National Powder Works in France. After immigrating to America in 1800, he scouted unsuccessfully for mill sites near Washington, DC, before detouring to Delaware, where he knew several French refugees from Santo Domingo: "I shall stop off in Wilmington for a day to see the Brandywine," he wrote his father back home, Pierre Samuel du Pont, an ardent lover of freedom and friend of Jefferson and Lafayette.[3]

The fast-flowing creek looked uniquely promising: in a four-mile stretch it dropped 120 feet, ready to power many new mills. In a deal that lawyer Alexander Hamilton helped draft, Eleuthère bought ninety-five acres in April 1802 from a signer of the U.S. Constitution, Jacob Broom, whose burned mill of 1795 stood forlorn on the west bank below Rockland. Broom had operated a carding, woofing, and spinning facility that produced cotton stuffs, using Arkwright's English plan and employing an all-English workforce. The fire was blamed on a foreign saboteur determined to prevent America from violating Britain's monopoly on manufactures. Broom was a patriot whose map of the Brandywine Valley proved invaluable to General Washington in the defense of Philadelphia, but he lived adjacent to rugged creekside property named after an English garden: Hagley in Worcestershire was a thousand-acre estate famous for its waterfalls and occupying, as Thomas Jefferson described it on a visit, a beautiful "descending hollow."[4]

Eleuthère, age thirty, moved his family to Delaware in July 1802, occupying a small stone house that still stands below Hagley Library. Its location "in the damp air of the creek" was unhealthy, he feared, so he built a much bigger dwelling on a brow just uphill—the handsome Eleutherian Mills, open to the public today. "When I began building my establishment here, it was like settling in the back country," he recalled. "No road, no decent house, no garden . . . in the midst of our woods."[5]

A powder works of the same name was erected down along the river bank where Eleuthère could oversee its bustling activities from the piazza of his home. By summer 1803 he wrote President Jefferson (who had just bought Louisiana, an idea first suggested by Pierre du Pont) bragging of his successful processing of saltpeter, a granular white powder that was the most expensive ingredient of gunpowder, imported from India. Soon he received an order to process saltpeter for the U.S. Army, too. Months later, gunpowder was finally made—just in time to propel cannonballs from Navy ships against Barbary pirates at Tripoli. The War of 1812 would offer a further boost to du Pont's nascent

Eleutherian Mills. E. I. du Pont's hilltop home overlooked the upper powder yards, of which little trace remained in 1952 when E. I. III and his wife visited on the sesquicentennial of his family's arrival on the Brandywine.

enterprise: 750,000 pounds of gunpowder were ordered by the army as they fought the invading British.[6]

With the coming of that war, many feared an attack against the Brandywine flour mills and powder works. Camp Shellpot was established to protect the lower reaches of the creek. Eleuthère organized the Brandywine Rangers, who flew a flag with eagle and stars surrounding a swarming hive, its slogan reading, "Bees in Peace, Hornets in War." His sister-in-law Josephine du Pont listened anxiously to the soldiers' drumming from her home at Lower Louviers, across the creek from Eleutherian Mills. Designed by Eleuthère, supposedly with the assistance of Jefferson, Lower Louviers has a tall portico overlooking the water. Josephine's flowerpots were now swept from the windowsills and mantelpieces, replaced with a martial decoration of cockades, pistols, and sabers. When Philadelphians panicked after the British attacked Washington and Baltimore, they sent professional militias to guard the powder works, who established Camp DuPont and Camp Brandywine.[7]

The 1812 conflict led to a burst of new industry on the creek. An American embargo on the import of British goods stimulated the local textile industry. Meanwhile, in defiance of a British ban on the export of mechanics or machines, talented millers flocked to America pretending to be farmers, with milling equipment wrapped in cloth and labeled "fruit trees."[8]

Two mills with du Pont family connections were built downstream from the powder yards in 1813. In the one known today as Henry Clay Mill, honoring a celebrity visitor of 1833 (now Hagley Museum's visitor center), a cotton-picking machine and dye vats occupied the basement; a carding machine stood on the first floor; spinning mules and looms on the first and third floors. Surviving time sheets show that workers (one-third were women) toiled from dawn to 8:00 p.m., six days a week. Later the place was used for the manufacture of sturdy metal kegs for DuPont gunpowder.[9]

Picturesque brick-and-stone Breck's Mill was built by Wilmington lawyer (and future U.S. secretary of the treasury) Louis McLane and his brother-in-law George Milligan for the spinning of cotton. Two pencil sketches by traveling architect Benjamin Henry Latrobe, dated October 1, 1813, show "Milligan and McLane's New Mills" without its present tower, in a wooded valley that is pleasingly little changed two centuries later. By the 1820s, this mill and another one almost touching it to the south—the vanished Rokeby Mill—together housed 2,300 spindles, ten hand looms, twenty power looms, and employed seventy-nine workers. Decades later it served as a recreation hall for DuPont employees, Henry Seidel Canby recalling in his youth how, "between dances, couples hung out the windows to watch the moonlight on the roaring water over the dam."[10]

William Breck took charge of Breck's Mill in 1832 but sold out to Charles I. du Pont seven years later, who converted the facility to woolen cloth manufacturing. His house with a "C. I. D. 1823" datestone still stands nearby. Uphill, the "14 acres woodland" around the Federal-style house called Rokeby—named for a poem by Sir Walter Scott—that were shown on a map by surveyor Jonas Fairlamb in 1826 still remain forested today in this stretch of the valley known for huge old trees.

Immediately across the dam from Breck's Mill is the whitewashed and bell-towered Walker's Mill, built by Philadelphia merchant Joseph E. Sims for making cotton yarn and muslin during the War of 1812. Sharing space in that facility was Hodgson's Brandywine Foundry, where two English immigrants manufactured spinning machines used in the textile industry. Artist Charles Willson Peale sent his sons Titian and Franklin to learn the miller's trade here prior to working in Peale's own cotton factory in the outskirts of Philadelphia. Their uncle James, also a well-known painter, had fought in the Battle of the Brandywine and painted some views of the creek. Franklin Peale went on to introduce steam presses at the U.S. Mint in Philadelphia, and Titian became an intrepid artist and naturalist who explored the West. In later times, Walker's Mill reflected in the river was a beloved subject for plein air painters, appearing in one of N. C. Wyeth's very first efforts as a student.[11]

The Seat of Industry and Beauty

Eleuthère du Pont's rapid achievements in the making of gunpowder along the Brandywine were the amazement of all. An observer reported in 1815,

> This is a gigantic undertaking and almost incomprehensible
> that one man alone was able to conceive and carry out all the
> work and the mechanical and hydraulic constructions, to make
> the design, to apply it to the terrain, superintend it, and carry it
> to completion in a valley which offered only a mass of rocks
> bristling, an uncultivated desert; being continuously harassed

by extreme fatigue, exposed to frightful dangers, and able to employ only workmen whom it was necessary for him to instruct and whose language he had to learn.[12]

The ever-capable Eleuthère expanded his powder operations by purchasing, in the wartime boom of 1813, the downstream Hagley tract of Rumford Dawes, a Philadelphia merchant who enjoyed the "agreeable murmur" of the stream. Dawes had advertised his first-rate site in 1791:

> The iron-works and mills on Brandywine . . . consisting of a forge, rolling and slitting mills, smith's shop, coal-house, and sufficient stabling for several teams of horses. The slitting and rolling mills are in good order, having several pair of rolls, cutters, and every necessary tool for slitting nail-rods and rolling sheet iron. . . . There is plenty of wood to be had in the neighbourhood for coaling at a reasonable rate. . . . Also a saw mill, and a large convenient three story stone merchant mill, having two water wheels, three pair of burs, boulting works complete, and a stone corn kiln. . . . All the above works stand within a short distance of each other, and as they have the advantage of all the Brandywine, with 17 feet fall, there is water sufficient to drive them all at one time in the dryest season. There is likewise a convenient seat for a paper mill.[13]

Visitors to Hagley Museum can see twin bald cypress trees by the creek, planted in the yard of Dawes's home centuries ago, near his slitting mill (where sheets of iron were cut into rods for blacksmiths). Other venerable trees include the tulip poplars on Holly Island, near Henry Clay Mill. That island is shown wooded on a map of 1812, but a survey of 1743 describes it as "barren having neither trees nor grass on it but grown over mostly with bryars & shrubs." Holly Island is noteworthy for having never been developed and still retaining a primeval quality, even now.[14]

The powder mills at Hagley Yard were expanded after the original Eleutherian Mills facility ("Upper Yard") was devastated by explosions in March 1818. Such blasts were occasional in all powder yards, but this one was especially severe, killing forty workmen and being felt as far away as Lancaster, Pennsylvania. So hideous was the carnage, rescuers fainted at the grisly sights.

Growth at Hagley Yard was epitomized by the Birkenhead Mill, where the innovative Eleuthère first used cast-iron wheels to mix powder ingredients in a "rolling mill," a means more efficient than the old stamping process. In typical powder-mill design, the stone walls were massively thick and buttressed against explosions, but open on the side facing the creek and with a flimsy shed roof designed to disintegrate in a blast—aiming the fiery concussion away from the yards (to "go across the crick" was synonymous with violent death on the job). The water level at the dam nearby is thirty-three feet higher than that at the next dam downstream, this "fall" once powering the entire Hagley Yard with its thirty-three mills, many of which still stand as hoary ruins.

Famous visitors often came to Eleutherian Mills, including, it is said, President James Madison in 1816. Lafayette spent a night during his 1825 American tour, penning a warm note: "After having seen the banks of the Brandywine a scene of bloody fighting nearly half a century ago, I am happy to find it now the seat of industry, beauty, and mutual friendship." He mourned at the grave of Pierre Samuel du Pont in nearby Sand Hole Woods off Buck Road, the family patriarch having caught his final illness not long after accidentally falling off a boat into the Brandywine. Countless du Ponts have been interred in this, one of the most private and exclusive of cemeteries, a tranquil resting place for a family that in time became the single wealthiest in America.[15]

By 1832, one-seventh of all U.S. gunpowder was made by the Du-Pont company, much of it used for hunting, as pioneers with flintlocks subdued a wilderness continent. "Brandywine" was synonymous with the best gunpowder product available, and rivals as far away as Connecticut stole the name. Powder was sold in cans with colorful labels: a hound holds a lifeless pheasant in his jaws or rips into the flanks of a deer; an Indian warrior with feather kilt and headdress stalks through a tobacco patch with a knife; a slaughtered stag lies sprawled, its feet entangled in the words "Smokeless Rifle Powder"; an eagle hovers in the sky amid a crackling burr of lightning bolts, holding in its beak a banner, "Duck Shooting." Such cans survive in considerable numbers, modern collectors find: "No true Yankee would throw away a half can of perfectly good powder, so the can was put on a barn rafter or in an attic and forgotten."[16]

Powder Yard, Garden, and Deer Park

Eleuthère du Pont's attention was almost completely absorbed by industry, but he did have another strong interest: his traveling papers when he came to America listed his profession as "botaniste," a subject he had studied at Paris's esteemed Jardin des Plantes. In case he failed as a powder maker, he had a backup plan: he would win himself a post at the French forestry commission by supplying that nation with valuable trees from the New World. "My position in the midst of forests will make it an easy task," he wrote to some botanists in Paris almost as soon as he arrived on the Brandywine.[17]

This scheme came to little—although he did provide forty boxes filled with acorns and seeds to botanical expert André Michaux, who occasionally visited him—as did another plant researcher, Constantine Rafinesque, who discussed with du Pont the classification of hickory nuts and gathered enough information to write a "Florula Delawarica." Du Pont routinely planted rare trees near his home, including a hybrid pink buckeye, now a giant; perhaps this was the one he brought from Georgia to Delaware as a nut as he returned on horseback from a business trip to New Orleans in 1817. Hagley today boasts eighteen trees that are the largest of their species in the state, and a gnarled osage orange in front of Eleutherian Mills is said to be the second biggest in the nation.[18]

Eleuthère encouraged an interest in botany among his growing family. Daughters Eleuthera and Sophie described both natural history and social happenings along the Brandywine in their sketchbooks and in the whimsical hand-drawn "Tancopanican Chronicle" they kept in the early

1830s (the title refers to one of several Lenape names for the creek). These young ladies spent much time drawing, transmitting to us the appearance of long-lost homes and mills nearby. They received instruction from visiting professionals: French naturalist Charles Lesueur visited in 1822 and sketched the children on the piazza of Eleutherian Mills, big trees beyond, along with a glimpse of the sprightly wooden rocking horse that is still in the home today.

Eleuthera and Sophie's charmingly inexpert sketches open to us a Brandywine world largely vanished. We see, for example, innumerable small farmhouses enlarged piecemeal over time, often of incongruous materials. One is low and three-parted—brick, log, frame, whatever happened to be available. The visual effect is haphazard and full of surprises, a source of delight for the young sketch artists. We see shaggy trees that overgrow the rooftops, chickens prowling dusty yards, and fences of myriad types everywhere. Farm women sit in doorways in the summer sunshine. What a difference the passage of 180 years has made: think how dumbfounded the du Pont daughters would be if they could explore the suburbanized Brandywine near Hagley today and find no functioning mills, no wooden sluicegates, no covered bridges, no wagons, no horses, no farms.

The "Chronicle" makes note of tourists visiting the valley. They had long been coming: "The remarkable grandeur of the Brandywine can be better viewed than described," said an appreciative visitor of 1814. "The confused noise of the mills is no sooner lost (when ascending the stream) than the ear is saluted with the sound of the descending waters dashing over the falls in torrents." In 1830, some visitors named Percival "strolled about to see the beauties of the Brandywine, but not having a guide, they only saw *our village* & walking thro' the powder yard & the [deer] park, debouched thro' the gate into the Kitchen yard!, where by way of welcome Cupid tried to bite Mr P's hand."[19]

A more pleasant encounter came in May 1831, when two artists, Patrick and Parker, visited Wilmington "for the purpose of taking some of the charming scenery on the Brandywine." They "came to see the place and were escorted over the mills by Mr. du Pont in person. . . .

View from the piazza. E. I. du Pont could keep a close eye on the black powder operation from the porch of his home, which enjoyed a picturesque prospect of forest and river. Drawing by Baroness Hyde de Neuville, 1817.

They informed Mr. du Pont that some of their views might in future be 'lithographed.' . . . Their views afforded Papa great entertainment particularly one of the island and cotton factory in which the faithful copier of nature had carefully omitted *all* the rocks."

The clannish du Pont family occupied fine houses on both sides of the Brandywine, some of which still stand, and there was constant visiting "across the creek." A lady visitor in 1832 became alarmed at the low-riding, rope-drawn candlebox boat "in crossing the stream, and evinced her agitation by getting every moment nearer to the end of the boat: as she went backwards she did not see that she was gradually pushing Miss E. du Pont in the creek."[20]

Few realize it today, but the powder yards were always kept heavily wooded, hardly resembling the typical industrial site—because trees provided a buffer in case of explosion. Some of the huge sycamores at Hagley are far older than the crumbling ruins they shadow, having seen the powder-making era come and go. In fact the whole environs long retained a semi-wilderness flavor, even as late as the second decade of the nineteenth century, when a Catholic priest went out to attend to the Irish powder workers:

> Started about 10 a.m. for Hagley Brandywine. Arrived over rocks, through woods, amidst stumps, down precipices, up perpendicular (almost) steeps and bumping loose stones against my wheels at every step, across Squirrel Run. . . . From thence through abominable rocky, loose, stoney roads through Hagley tan-yard, down Brandywine Creek. . . . To Peter Quigley's on a bank as high as the third story of the big cotton factory, gave private baptism to his infant child.[21]

The Dashing of the Torrent

Du Pont had made extraordinary progress in expanding his gunpowder yards, but he and fellow Delaware millers faced a recurrent problem: flooding of the Brandywine. Deforestation was the cause, as the upper reaches of the creek in Pennsylvania were increasingly denuded for farmland, from which heavy rains drained rapidly.

Felling trees had been the proudest accomplishment of the early settlers: William Penn had urged the woods of his sylvan colony be "clear'd" quickly in part to "refine" the air of pestilence and disease that otherwise hovered around dense forests, "the multitude of trees, yet standing, being liable to retain mists and vapours." The coming of romanticism introduced a new appreciation for woodlands as places worth keeping, but not everyone was convinced. As late as the 1820s, a British traveler could voice fear of the American forest primeval: it was filled with "fallen trees in every possible stage of decay," where "congeries of leaves that have been rotting since the Flood, cover the ground and infect the air."[22]

Deforestation produced unintended consequences, however. Dropping water tables in time of drought caused valuable mills to go idle; huge freshets in rainy seasons invaded factories, smashing machinery. These troublesome phenomena began as early as the mid-eighteenth century. Traveling through the Mid-Atlantic region in the 1740s, Peter Kalm noted that certain mills that were highly productive sixty years ago could now only run after rain or snowmelt, water in their streams having dwindled since the forests began to be cut.[23]

Every few years, gigantic floods tore through, each becoming a subject of lore. Old-timers reminisced about the Great Freshet of September 1775, for example, or subsequent ones in 1783, 1795, and 1809. Bayard Taylor included one such flood in his novel, *The Story of Kennett*. It was impossible to predict when the next would come. Worried millers watched the stream, noting its height as it surged through the headgates of the races and whether it went suddenly "turbid" with sediment starting to wash down from a heavy rainfall upstream.

On February 21, 1822, sudden warm weather caused rapid snowmelt, triggering one of those floods that became legendary. No one could remember the creek ever rising so high at Downingtown, where it formed "an object terribly interesting. On its ruffled and perturbed surface, was continually beheld floating evidences of that wide spread destruction which accompanied its impetuous march. The dashing of the torrent against impeding objects and the loud, and solemn roar it produced, was calculated to recall to one's mind, the idea of the *Apocalyptical voice*."

One of the local worthies named Downing waited until the afternoon of that foggy day to remove his cattle from the barn, by which time the water was so high, he had to tie a rope around their horns and pull them out on horseback, swimming. At Dowlin's industrial establishment nearby, a forge, gristmill, and sawmill were swept away, as were Richard Bicking's paper mill and Dr. Lukens's ironworks dam at Coatesville on the West Branch. Downstream, brand-new Wister's dam and new bridge were destroyed and Painter's dam above Chadds Ford was "very much injured."

Then the flood rolled into Delaware. As we saw, Wilmingtonians watched in dismay as ice and logs caromed into Market Street chain bridge, collapsing an abutment. The entire bridge then tumbled into the raging creek. A newspaper reported of the day's events, "One life lost—apprehensions of more—damage beyond conjecture."[24]

Only when the water receded could the destruction be fully assessed up and down the Brandywine. Dams were burst, headgates swept away. Gilpin's paper mill got two feet of water across its floors, resulting in severe damage. At Rockland, where the water rose three feet higher than even in the 1795 freshet, Caleb Kirk and William Young and Company suffered huge losses, and the wooden bridge that carried the public road across the river was destroyed. Mr. Kirk traveled downstream interviewing distraught mill owners, finding that enormous quantities of road soil had been washed into all the mill races.[25]

Rebuilding began immediately. A newspaper reported, "The destruction produced by this freshet, has provided more employment for various classes of laborers, than would a dozen of improvement bills." Philadelphia bridge designer Lewis Wernwag was called in to replace the spans at Rockland and Wilmington. Citizens admired how Wernwag and a dozen assistants hammered together the new Market Street Bridge in just days from prefabricated timbers brought in by boat. It promised to last forever—but would in turn wash away seventeen years later.[26]

That 1839 event damaged Bancroft Mills below today's Delaware Art Museum, a site destined to become famous for textile production. English-born Quaker Joseph Bancroft had been trained in cotton weaving in Lancashire; then he served as superintendent upstream at Rockland before buying a gristmill in 1831, at a time when grain milling was on the decline, owing to midwestern competition. He switched it over to cloth-making, specializing in glazing fabric for awnings, tents, and especially window shades. But it was all erased in 1839, a terrible blow to Bancroft's fledgling business. An eyewitness said that river water came "sweeping through the mill with resistless violence." There was no warning: workers had left for midday dinner, and when they came back, the creek had risen into the lower floor, ruining the sixty looms with $1,500 of warps in them.

"The stream at this place is confined to a narrow channel by high and precipitous banks which prevent all overflowing," an observer said, "crowding the vast volume of water to a fearful height." The surge climbed thirteen feet in three hours, high enough to damage Bancroft's carding engines and drying equipment on the second floor. The boiler (used to heat the mill) and its house were swept away, as was the dam, and the race was choked with debris. The water rose twenty-two feet above ordinary level, fully five feet higher than in 1822.[27]

The freshet ravaged the Brandywine from Dowlin's Forge all the way to Wilmington, where the water rose more than twenty feet. "Floors and roofs of buildings, and numerous articles of furniture" were strewn along the banks, and "the mills at Brandywine village, were very much injured." Residents of the valley came to expect such disasters, which occurred with distressing frequency. "Wrecked bridges and floating timbers are dashing frantically together," an observer reported in 1872, "while the grunts of a protesting pig . . . mingle with the clamor from an eddying hen-coop."[28]

Westward Ho!

After every flood, bridges were quickly repaired, because they were vital for commerce and general travel. Countless settlers migrating west crossed the Brandywine somewhere along its length, including on the road from Philadelphia to Lancaster—America's first inland city—crossing the East Branch at Cope's Bridge (see Plate 7). Earlier, as Taylor's Ford, this place must have seen distinguished members of Congress as that august body fled to Lancaster after the Battle of the Brandywine. A substantial stone bridge of three arches went up in 1807 and is still used by highway traffic today, a notable relic of the Federal era when transportation networks were steadily improving as trade burgeoned. A line of four-horse stages regularly thundered across the bridge, linking seaboard cities with inland settlements; and there was a constant rumble of farmers' heavy wagons. A little milling community grew up at Copetown, amid towering oaks and hickories: there was a grinding mill as well as the

Brandywine Works machine shops and foundry of E. T. Cope & Sons, which made paper-mill machinery, turbine water wheels, and threshers.[29]

Downstream, seventy-foot-high Deborah's Rock protrudes dramatically toward the Brandywine. According to legend, Deborah was a Lenape maiden who jumped to her death; in reality, this was the name of the wife of an early settler. Deborah's Rock was popular for swimming and fishing, and a commercial icehouse was established there in wintertime. The vicinity was described, in 1856, as "the sweetest of all the pleasant nooks on our beautiful and classic stream." In 1815, Creek Road had been extended down the east bank and later became a favorite pleasure drive for citizens of West Chester. It passes Bowers Island, once home to a paper mill—a place wooded for as long as anyone could remember and ideal for raccoon hunting, as well as for bass fishing at Tussy's Pool.[30]

Even as progress "improved" the Brandywine, the lure of western settlement was beginning to draw ambitious young people away from the old banks of the river. One was John Filson, booster of Kentucky and the first popularizer of Daniel Boone. Raised on a farm on the West Branch above Mortonville, Filson liked to tell of an adventure he had as a schoolboy: Hurrying to the mill with a bag of corn, he tried a shortcut across the Brandywine. His horse was forced to swim, Filson clinging to its mane for dear life and watching helplessly as all his corn bobbed away.

Later Filson worked as a surveyor and schoolteacher, but a Revolutionary War wound is said to have prevented him from using his arm to thrash the children sufficiently. In fall 1783 he left, in his early thirties, for Kentucky in the distant West. As a land speculator, he purchased tens of thousands of acres and wrote a book that extolled the virgin territory, *The Discovery, Settlement and Present State of Kentucke*, which has been called one of the most important documents on the western expansion of the United States.[31]

There were no printing presses in the West, so Filson returned to Wilmington in summer 1784 and had Irish-born pressman John Adams produce the book. Its most sensational section was the appendix, "The Adventures of Colonel Daniel Boon," based on interviews with the explorer, born a Quaker in Pennsylvania. Thus did Filson make Boone famous in the romantic era—it is even said that his book was consulted by Lord Byron in England. Filson briefly taught school in Wilmington and drew a map of the town before returning west for good and founding Cincinnati. Shortly afterward, in 1788, his surveying party was attacked in the wilderness by Shawnee Indians, and the colorful Filson was never seen again.[32]

Adams was long the only printer in Delaware, but others eventually followed. The best known was Hezekiah Niles, born on October 10, 1777, at Jefferis's Ford on the Brandywine, less than a month after the battle. His parents, from Wilmington, had taken refuge from the British, little realizing the king's army would come storming right through their sanctuary. In adulthood he moved to Baltimore and established *Niles Weekly Register*, one of the best-known journals of the time. Apparently he got considerable mileage out of his origins on the battlefield, a contemporary satirist joking that Niles's mother would have been run through with a Redcoat's bayonet except that the ruffian received a timely "blow across the gob" with a cheese-toaster. Niles was of one many talented Americans who traced their origins to the banks of the Brandywine but now achieved fame in places far removed as the nation steadily expanded: "WESTWARD HO!" read a West Chester newspaper in 1854 as several local clans set out for a new life in fledgling Battle Creek, Michigan. Eleven hundred miles west of the Brandywine, Kansas City boomed under the industrious eye of Coateses and Chandlers, family names long familiar along the old river.[33]

Chapter 6

❧❧

Industry and War

In the middle of the nineteenth century, the lower Brandywine was transformed by the huge growth of Wilmington and its industries. Increased wealth brought the construction of fine new buildings in Brandywine Village, including the Episcopal church of St. John's, under a soaring tower of blue rock (1858)—the final documented church by John Notman, noted Philadelphia architect.

But the vicinity suffered a calamity in 1854 when the fashionable district along the South Race was devastated by the explosion of three DuPont powder wagons in the public roadway. The stretch was called "Brandywine Walk" for its appealing promenade, a "romantic road" along the river. The covered wagons, drawn by five horses each, were following their customary route through town to unload 450 powder kegs at a wharf. Suddenly at the foot of Orange Street they detonated, one after another, with a sound like innumerable cannon going off—some thought it was the day of judgment.

Plaster ceilings fell and windows blew in, all over the city. Nearby stately homes were shattered: one was left a "tottering mass of ruins," another was "literally burst," and a stable was reduced to a "heap of burning rubbish." The celebrated garden of the Episcopal bishop was "a sickening scene of devastation," its ornamental trees now merely blackened stumps and the ground strewed with horseflesh. Two of the three hapless wagon drivers were identified from body parts, but the third man simply vanished, "blown to atoms."[1]

A horrified city cleaned up the damage. Cracked furniture would be pointed out in local homes for generations. (At his desk years later, Henry Seidel Canby wrote *The Brandywine* to the ticking of a tall-case clock injured that day.) Officials resolved that black powder should travel in future by railroad, not by wagon. Henceforth, explosions would be confined to the powder yards, such as the fearsome one in 1859 that killed seven men at Hagley. One victim was found dangling in a tree, and the headless trunk of another flew far across the creek.[2]

Wilmington's growing affluence came largely from its very early railroad line, which crossed the Brandywine near Old Swedes Church in 1837—the same route followed by Amtrak's Northeast Corridor today, along a right-of-way originally surveyed by prominent architect and engineer William Strickland. The morning the first trains ran, an old man told excited crowds in the streets about a prophecy he once heard from inventor Oliver Evans: "In the future, people will travel from Philadelphia to Baltimore in one day—on carriages without horses." With the epochal coming of the railroad, the most modern technology touched the venerable shores of the Brandywine, chronicler Elizabeth Montgomery now eyeing "flocks and herds in rich pasture . . . fields of waving grain . . . meandering streams; vessels under full sail; steamboats plying; railroad cars whizzing past."[3]

The Philadelphia, Wilmington & Baltimore line triggered explosive growth of industry in town—just in time, since the rise of midwestern farming had badly hurt local milling, Brandywine production seemingly being "done for" by 1836. But by the 1850s there were more than five thousand mill and manufactory workers, some right on the banks of the Brandywine. Prosperity had returned in force: in the two hundred years before the railroad came, Wilmington grew to 7,800 souls; in less than twenty years subsequently it swelled by another ten thousand.

The railroad bridge over the creek was a 440-foot covered wooden truss with painted-tin roof, standing on stone piers in the water. A pivot-draw allowed ships through. President Franklin Pierce and his cabinet, including Secretary of War Jefferson Davis, saw it up close in 1853 when they took the steamer *John Stevens* out of the Brandywine on their way to Philadelphia after a local fete.[4]

That Brandywine bridge proved dangerous: in September 1848, two trains collided south of it, killing a machinist and a brakeman. In July 1853, the bridge tender fell asleep and failed to give the "drawbridge open" signal by waving his lamp; a northbound freight train plummeted into the creek, and its engineer and fireman were drowned. The distraught tender went "almost crazy" with remorse and tried to drown himself, too.[5]

Another bad accident occurred during the Civil War, in September 1863:

> On Thursday night, about 10 o'clock, the draw of the railroad bridge over Brandywine creek being off so as to admit vessels to pass, a train of peach cars coming at that time, and the signal not being discovered, the locomotive, tender and three cars were precipitated into the creek. The sound of the crushing cars was terrible. Two men were mortally wounded. Next morning it presented an awful, heart-rending spectacle; the locomotive, tender and one car hid, the other two a mass of ruins, wood, baskets, and peaches floating. Men, women and children were gathering them.[6]

The railroad spurred much industry. Along the Brandywine near Old Swedes, the iron-casting foundry of Bush & Lobdell got under way in 1830. With the advent of trains it expanded rapidly into the making of railroad wheels, using a patented "double plate wheel" famed for durability. These were cast-iron wheels, cheaper than wrought iron, with special "chilled" running surfaces that could last eighty thousand miles. An historian has called Lobdell Car Wheel Company "one of the first large manufacturers of producers' goods in the United States"; it helped pioneer modern techniques such as research and development and even the hiring of traveling salesmen.

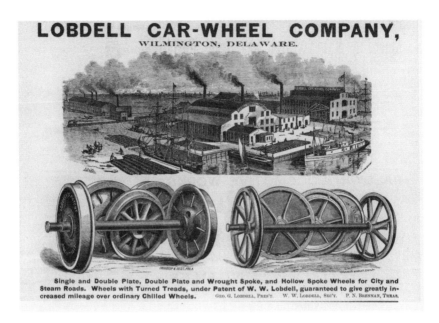

Chilled wheels. Ultra-strong wheels manufactured on the Brandywine in Wilmington were fitted to thousands of American railroad cars and locomotives as the Industrial Revolution boomed.

Output grew from 150 railroad wheels per day in 1844 to 230 in 1860, by which time Lobdell had more than two hundred workers (including many German immigrants) and was selling three hundred thousand wheels annually, 22 percent of all U.S. production. Starting in the 1850s, the *Maria Fleming* and another schooner sailed from its wharf on runs to ports from Baltimore to Boston; coming home, they hauled coal, sand, and scrap and pig iron. Much of Lobdell's business was in the South and dried up after Fort Sumter; but wartime subsequently brought an expansion of business as the U.S. Military Railroad ordered thousands of wheels.[7]

The great national boom in railroading was felt at Chadds Ford, too. The Philadelphia & Baltimore Central Railroad bridge was opened across the Brandywine in November 1859, by today's Brandywine River Museum of Art, which occupies the former Hoffman's Mill of 1864. This line transformed the sleepy village into a popular summertime retreat for Philadelphians. The bridge crossed the Brandywine about where the British army had waded over at Chads's Lower Ford.

A newspaper reported,

> REMAINS OF A SOLDIER FOUND.—We learn that the workmen engaged in forming the embankment of the Baltimore Central railroad, near the Brandywine, exhumed, on Tuesday last, remains supposed to [be] those of a soldier killed in the memorable battle, fought there on the 11th of September, 1777. The bullet which, in all probability, deprived him of life, was found among his bones. There were, also, a large brass belt buckle, and a number of lead buttons. From the latter, we have but little doubt that these were the remains of an English soldier, although they were found in [Delaware] county, or on the east side of the stream—the position occupied by the Americans. Some of the bones were in a state of tolerable preservation, and, together with the bullet, bucket and buttons, were eagerly appropriated as relics by the workmen and spectators.[8]

The Sage of Cedarcroft

By the time that bridge opened, the fast-growing United States faced its greatest crisis since the Revolution: a sundering of the national fabric over the slavery issue. Already the region had felt the shocks of the impending calamity; the line drawn by surveyors Mason and Dixon, headquartered at Harlan's peaceful Brandywine farm, had turned into an infamous symbol of ideological division. Standing on Smith's Bridge, one gazed upstream into Pennsylvania, a state that had been the first ever to pass a gradual abolition act (1780) and in which slavery was now extinct; a half-turn and one looked downstream into a border state where 1,800 African Americans were subject to living in chains. Incredibly, the Delaware legislature would not get around to ratifying the Thirteenth Amendment (outlawing slavery) until 1901, by which time the

"Peculiar Institution" had long since been eradicated everywhere by a great bloodbath, 2 percent of Americans giving their lives—equivalent to the loss of six million people today, or six-and-a-half times the current population of Delaware.

Abolitionism thrived in Chester County. Farmers John and Hannah Cox—she was the niece of the Peirce's Park horticulturalists—gave land for Longwood Meeting around 1853 (today a tourist information center beside Longwood Gardens) and an adjacent cemetery. The white-framed meetinghouse became a hub of Quaker abolitionist agitation, and famous reformers John Greenleaf Whittier, William Lloyd Garrison, Wendell Phillips, Frederick Douglass, and Lucretia Mott are said to have harangued crowds there. The Underground Railroad was feverishly active: Thomas Garrett in Wilmington smuggled in runaway slaves from the South by boat, who landed near the Brandywine's mouth at Old Swedes; then he would forward them on to Chester County with a cryptic note addressed to his coconspirators, "I send you . . . bales of black wool." The Brandywine had long proven a formidable obstacle for northbound runaways, a Philadelphia newspaper advertising in 1782 for "SLAVES, One yellow, the other black, RUN from New Castle, in Delaware, the 20th of February, and were seen at Brandywine bridge; their intent must have been New York."[9]

In meadows along the creek at Chadds Ford on September 11, 1860, a crowd of twenty-five thousand assembled for a People's Party rally—a faction aligned with the Republicans, but mild on slavery—amid banners, twenty blaring bands, and a thundering brass cannon. Thousands of bluecoat soldiers marched and maneuvered, and Ohio congressman John Sherman spoke two hours in a spectacle that local squire Chalkley Harvey helped organize—a sometime occupant of the former Washington's Headquarters, Harvey was a great enthusiast for the Revolutionary battle and could discourse upon the subject endlessly. A newspaper reported,

> The trains from Philadelphia and elsewhere, which arrived almost hourly, were constantly adding large accessions to the

monster assemblage, and the various uniformed clubs of IN-
VINCIBLES, WIDE AWAKES, CONTINENTALS, &c.,
of which five thousand members were present, accompanied by
bands of music, bearing innumerable transparencies, torches,
&c. lent an attractiveness to the scene. . . . The spot selected for
holding the meeting was very appropriately that upon which
the Battle of Brandywine occurred, 83 years ago, than which
one more fitting in all respects, could not have been chosen. . . .
One of the most striking features of the scene were the long
lines of carriages of every conceivable description, which to the
number of thousands, were crowded into every available spot,
whilst rapidly moving teams, jubilant clubs, and merry crowds
lent a life and animation to the scene which may not be described.[10]

For many the highlight was the stirring speech by Bayard Taylor,
renowned writer and world traveler. Taylor lived near Kennett Square
at a mansion called Cedarcroft (1858–1860, surviving today on Gate-
house Drive north of town), where Emerson and other luminaries regularly visited him. As the war neared, Taylor feared for his safety, being
so stridently pro-Union yet living a stone's throw from two slave states.
All he had for protection at home, he mused, were scimitars, an African
spear and war club, and a rhinoceros-hide shield from his adventurous
trips abroad.

Later the author of the most famous novel of the Brandywine region,
The Story of Kennett (1866), Taylor enthusiastically played up the history of the creek, along which his Quaker ancestors had settled in Penn's
day. Among his earliest poems was "To the Brandywine," published in
the *Saturday Evening Post*. And a youthful letter Taylor sent as a farm boy
to his father about a ramble with friends down the creek from Unionville
to Chadds Ford on April 5, 1840, was reprinted in the *West Chester
Register* as "A Visit to the Battle-ground of Brandywine." It was his first
publication, albeit one riddled with embarrassing printer's errors. (Later
as editor of *Union Magazine*, Taylor accidentally inserted a typo of his

own into Thoreau's essay, "Ktaadn," which made the transcendentalist angry.)[11]

Taylor's 1840 letter gives a good sense of what tourists were shown, back in those days. The teenager stood on the bridge at Chadds Ford and looked "a few yards above" to where the old ford had crossed the "turbid and crimsoned stream." In a nearby meadow, Hessians were said to be buried. West of the bridge, the road ascended alongside a wooded knoll; the cutaway road-bank had yielded cannonballs. At Chadds Ford Tavern in the village, they looked out on the meadow where General Wayne was stationed, and, on the brow in back of the tavern, saw a semicircular ridge that had once been Procter's breastwork ("now hardly distinguishable"). On a wooded rise near Brinton's Mill they admired a tulip poplar tree with seven American cannonballs embedded in it. At Sandy Hollow, the supposed site of Lafayette's wounding was pointed out, marked by the decaying stump of a walnut tree.

Taylor later wrote a celebrated account of a Brandywine picnic in June 1865, a happy postwar occasion he shared with fellow writer Edmund C. Steadman. "Camping" in a meadow, they waded barefoot into the creek, fished, and drank a pail of milk punch. Their wives and children wove wreaths and garlands of oak leaves and wildflowers. When a herd of one hundred cattle trundled along, Taylor put a wreath around the horns of a steer and Steadman rode it, everyone marching in fanciful Arcadian procession. Both writers published sonnets about the cheerful episode.[12]

As its name suggests, Cedarcroft was known for its trees, Taylor landscaping the grounds in the lush tradition of nearby Peirce's Park arboretum. On a visit in 1876, Southern writer Sidney Lanier wrote a poem, "Under the Cedarcroft Chestnut"—he was told it was eight hundred years old. There was even a giant sequoia brought from California, as Emerson mentioned in a letter. Taylor sat on the Cedarcroft veranda (a place draped in ivy, Dutchman's pipe, Virginia creeper, wisteria, and trumpet flower where hummingbirds darted) and admired his extensive woodlands. Appropriately, the tree-loving Taylor is buried at Longwood

Cemetery just outside the gates of today's horticultural paradise, Long-wood Gardens. When a sumptuous Victorian library was built in West Chester in 1888, a glass case in the northwest corner enshrined Taylor's schoolboy collection of wildflowers alongside several of his valuable manuscripts, a heartfelt effort to transmit a local hero's fame to posterity.[13]

And the War Came

Abraham Lincoln crossed the Brandywine by train at Downingtown on his way to be inaugurated, taking a furtive route from Philadelphia westward because an assassination plot was feared. Then the Civil War hit home when someone set fire to barns up and down the creek in September 1861, including James Painter's by the creek and Jesse Seal's near Birmingham Meeting, all "blazing almost at one and the same time," a pro-Lincoln newspaper noted. "All the owners of these barns are Republicans in politics with strong anti-slavery tendencies! . . . We believe these barns to have been burned by the instigation of the sympathizers with Jeff Davis."[14]

Even during this era of crisis, tourists continued to visit Brandywine Battlefield. For many their excursion began at Jefferis's Ford—now spanned by a covered bridge popular with artists—where ladies averted their eyes in horror from skinny-dipping boys at Blue Rock Swim Hole just upstream. A newspaper of 1862 described the typical tourist route:

> Parties happening in West Chester—desirous of a pleasant excursion in a fine agricultural district—and curious to survey grounds now become classical,—may accomplish their object, by proceeding to JEFFERIS'S FORD, thence along the road by STRODE'S MILL, over OSBORN'S HEIGHTS, and by Birmingham Meeting house to DILWORTHSTOWN; from that ancient Village, take the Wilmington road to Smith lane, and thence by the farm house late of George Gilpin (where

Famous crossing. In a bucolic setting, Jefferis's Bridge (1833) leapt over the East Branch right where the armies of Cornwallis and Howe had waded across in 1777. Even 106 years after the battle, in a photograph taken during flood-time, the agricultural setting was little-changed.

Howe quartered after the battle), down to the Birmingham Valley, formerly called Bottom, thence by the former residences of Gideon Gilpin and Benjamin Ring,—once the Quarters, respectively, of LAFAYETTE and WASHINGTON, to Chadsford; thence along the left bank of the stream, up again to Jefferisford, and so back to West Chester.—The circuit, here designated, affords a good view of the whole battle ground,—and, in pleasant weather, a very agreeable Drive of about 15 miles.[15]

The Civil War would ultimately touch the lives of everyone along the Brandywine. When the conflict began, the same Chadds Ford meadow that saw the 1860 Lincoln rally (and earlier political meetings in 1840 and 1844) now hosted Union soldiers. Captain Chapman Biddle's Company A, First Regiment Pennsylvania Artillery, drilled here in July 1861. A lawyer and scion of a patriotic family—his father and grandfather had fought in the War of 1812 and the Revolution—Biddle was responsible for protecting his native city of Philadelphia, choosing, as George Washington had done before him, the Brandywine as his chief line of defense. A newspaper called his regiment a vibrant spectacle for day-trippers:

> The company is said to be composed of good material, and presented a fine appearance previous to leaving Philadelphia. The West Chester and Philadelphia Railroad Company are running excursion trains to the encampment, at reduced rates from the usual fare. The ride is a pleasant one, through a beautiful country, studded with finely cultivated farms. Many will visit the camp to see one of the Revolutionary battle grounds.[16]

Down at Wilmington, the war quickly made the PW&B railroad over the Brandywine "the greatest military highway in history," transporting soldiers and matériel from the North to Virginia battlefields. In April 1861 the Massachusetts and Pennsylvania volunteers who had been stoned by mobs in Baltimore fled back north through Wilmington and over the Brandywine by train. That night, secessionists burned most of the railroad's bridges between there and Baltimore, an attack that helped tilt a wavering New Castle County toward the Union cause. Delaware soldiers from an encampment called Fort Brandywine were sent to secure the Maryland bridges.[17]

Local industry received a big boost in wartime. The celebrated Jackson & Sharp firm opened in 1863 beside Brandywine railroad bridge in Wilmington to meet wartime demand for freight and passenger cars. At work inside this "perfect hive of industry" were woodworkers, car builders, cabinetmakers, carvers, turners, blacksmiths, spring makers, upholsterers, painters, tinners, plumbers, and gas-and-steam fitters. Standing at the river's mouth, one could have watched the new U.S. Navy monitors *Patapsco*, *Saugus*, and *Napa* float down from Harlan and Hollingsworth shipyards toward the Delaware River. Local doctor and literary man S. Weir Mitchell reported how drinkable Brandywine water was carried down in tugs to the island prison camp for Confederates at Fort Delaware, the construction of which Wilmingtonians had observed with spyglasses from the highlands above the city.[18]

Valley in Wartime

But some of the most feverish activity was happening upstream at the powder yards. Their importance to the Union effort cannot be overstated. By 1860, about half of the national output of explosives came from the three DuPont plants along the creek: Upper Yard, Hagley Yard, and Lower Yard. These were collectively regarded as the largest powder works in the world, producing a product used heavily for quarrying, mining, and railroad construction. But military purchases were always welcome: DuPont had supplied both sides in the recent Crimean War.

The company's head, "Boss Henry" du Pont, was opposed to Lincoln—of whose election he learned while sitting at the telegraph in First Office near his home at Eleutherian Mills. But once war began, he demonstrated his patriotism by refusing to fulfill Southern orders. Soon, the Brandywine yards became vital to the entire federal war effort, supplying four million pounds of military powder, some 42 percent of the total used by the North in battle or at sea—the cannons of USS *Monitor*, for example, would fire Brandywine "Mammoth" powder against the *Merrimack*.

The Sunday after Fort Sumter was cannonaded, a special "in time of war and tumults" prayer was recited at Christ Church Christiana Hundred, recently founded on a hill overlooking the creek by pious family members Alexis du Pont and Captain Samuel Francis Du Pont—soon to be a legendary Civil War admiral. The church's cellar had been dug in an oak grove in August 1854, "all the handsome blue stones" being laid by for use on the buttressed outside walls. The founders were high church in their leanings, and debates arose about the chancel arrangement and having a cross on the soaring steeple, which was hoisted—sans cross—in November 1855.

On opening day the following spring, "the forest trees (in the midst of which the church stands) were arrayed in tender and budding green," a member of the congregation wrote. The handsome edifice lay amid "hills, sloping down to the water's edge, so bright in summer; and the creek itself, flowing with a gentle and soothing murmur over the stones." The first funeral here was Alexis's, after he died in a powder-yard blast, two thousand mourners trudging behind the casket up to the family burial ground in Sand Hole Woods, where Alexis was interred with a prayer book under his head. When war came, two young men of the congregation "sang the old hymns of the Christ Church choir" in their tent during the Union occupation of Yorktown in 1862.[19]

After Fort Sumter, a big flag was raised on the flagpole at Henry Clay Mill downhill from the church, which began turning out wool and cotton goods for the U.S. Army. The powder yards ran night and day; as seen from the bedroom windows at Eleutherian Mills, the refinery below was brightly spangled with kerosene lamps. To protect the yards against attack or sabotage, Camp Brandywine was established in summer 1861 and again in September 1862 for Delaware and Pennsylvania troops, across from old Buck Tavern on Kennett Pike, where an historical marker commemorates the spot today. One of Howard Pyle's earliest childhood memories was of seeing the blue-coated soldiers tramping through.[20]

When General Lee twice invaded the North, it was assumed that Hagley was among his most tempting targets. As Confederates pushed into Pennsylvania in 1863, Admiral Du Pont (who had lived at Lower Louviers along the creek since 1837) wrote of "not expecting to find the Powder Mills, nor my home standing" when he next returned. Possibly owing to sabotage, there were eleven blasts in the powder yards during the war, wrecking thirty mills and killing forty-two workmen. The explosion of ten thousand pounds of cannon powder in the Hagley pack house in February 1863 killed thirteen and caused a tremor felt at Philadelphia (where houses shook "frightfully") and Baltimore. Blasts were so common, people at a distance began to notice a warning sign that instantly preceded them: one's windows rattled.[21]

After Lee was narrowly turned back at Gettysburg in July 1863, robust plans were made to defend Philadelphia against future attack. A survey of the lands to its west was carried out in December 1863 under the direction of prominent resident Alexander Dallas Bache, superintendent of the United States Coast Survey and a noted scientist and engineer. The result was *Map of Reconnaissance of the Valley of Brandywine Creek*, an invaluable record of topographic and landscape conditions at that time. It shows the terrain in detail between Jefferis's Ford and Smith's Bridge and even includes woodlots, making it a good indicator of deforestation: during that heyday of agriculture, there were far fewer trees throughout the valley than there are now. As during the Revolution, the creek was regarded as a vital defense for Philadelphia, and possible artillery emplacements were marked on the hilltops.

The Brandywine produced a figure who will always be associated with the battlefield of Gettysburg: Emmor B. Cope, who grew up at his father's Brandywine Machine Works at Copetown. When war broke out, he joined the local Brandywine Guards, Company A, First Pennsylvania Reserves. A talented mechanical draftsman, he served as a sergeant at Gettysburg under engineer General G. K. Warren, who gave him the job of surveying the battleground the following October, producing the famous "Cope Map." When a national military park was established at Gettysburg in 1895, Cope returned as topographical engineer, placing tablets, laying out avenues, and designing steel observation towers. At the end of his long life he served as the first superintendent of the park.

The conclusion of the Civil War saw operations slow at the DuPont works, but explosions remained a threat. One of the best-documented blasts came in July 1869 at Hagley, killing two, whose pitiful remains were slopped into kegs. "The scene after the disaster was terrible, women and children crying and screaming, and begging for admittance through the gates of the yard, which had to be kept closed and guarded," a witness reported. "All along the creek the roofs of the buildings were to be seen floating down the stream, thrown there by the terrible shock." Buildings nearby were devastated, their doors, windows, and roofs blown

Across the crick. DuPont powder mills were designed with explosions in mind: massive walls topped by flimsy roofs aimed concussions over the river. These rolling mills in Lower Yard (below Rising Sun Bridge) blew up in July 1889.

hundreds of yards and their furniture "torn into thousands of fragments." There were freakish results: a spring that went suddenly dry. Cornfields uprooted. A package of sugar blown open on a windowsill a mile away. On distant Concord Pike, leaves were torn from the trees and fluttered as if it were a hurricane. At Henry Clay Factory, every door and window was punched in. "The girls employed in the building were terribly cut up by the glass from the windows, and came rushing out covered with blood."

There were close calls, too: far away, stones fell on people from the sky. An injured man jumped into the Brandywine for safety and nearly drowned. "A huge hinge from one of the doors of the mill passed within a few inches of the head of a woman and a child she was carrying in her arms, and buried itself in a hen coop." Hearing the blast, hysterical relatives ran across fields all the way from Wilmington, trying to rejoin their husbands and fathers at the damaged powder yards along the river banks.[22]

Such spectacular explosions made national headlines. None was more damaging to property than that of October 1890, caused by one William Green while soldering wooden boxes of black powder to make them airtight. A little mistake of some kind triggered what contemporaries called the biggest man-made explosion ever seen in history. Thirteen men died, including Green; most were "blown to atoms." Scraps were gathered in a basket; one human head was found across the creek. The blast devastated 150 acres, in a scene of crumbled buildings that reminded responders of the recent Charleston earthquake. Five hundred workers were left homeless. The series of detonations could be heard in Trenton, New Jersey; sounded like an approaching cyclone in Bucks County, Pennsylvania; and caused mirrors to drop from the walls in Philadelphia, where panicked residents rushed into the streets. Careful study of old photographs allows a sizeable crater to be identified even today, indenting the hillside southeast of the Soda House at Hagley.[23]

The yards were soon back in operation, and by the time of the Spanish-American War, Alfred I. du Pont had them churning out a record twenty thousand pounds of gunpowder every day, loaded onto the Wilmington & Northern Railroad and supplying virtually all the U.S. military's needs during that brief conflict.[24]

These historic yards continued to operate until just after World War I. Oral histories conducted with old-timers shed light on how the Irish powdermen and their families experienced the Brandywine in late Victorian times and into the twentieth century: skating behind the dams, swimming in the raceways, picking blackberries, climbing Indian Rock below Rockford Tower, stumbling over sleeping cows in the covered bridge at Rising Sun at midnight. Mothers and children peeled willow shoots for charcoal (pollarded trees long stood in rows along the creek banks). In winter they cut ice on the river—sometimes packing it around the body of a deceased relative "killed in the powder." They all admired the fancy du Ponts who jogged in pony carts up and down the creek, or drove nifty electric automobiles.[25]

Money No Object

World War I brought phenomenal profitability for DuPont, allowing lavish improvements to many of the family estates along the Brandywine, in what we today call "Chateau Country." At Nemours, on the creek above Alapocas Woods, the company's second-largest shareholder, Alfred I. du Pont, built formal gardens emulating Versailles. Today's visitors still admire his grand forecourt terrace, Tapis Vert, and one-acre Grand Basin, all forming a stunning vista. Antique garden features were imported from abroad, including two marble sphinxes once belonging to French minister Jean-Baptiste Colbert and wrought-iron gates owned by Catherine the Great.

The heavy French emphasis reflected du Pont's pride in family history. An orphan, he had grown up on Breck's Mill Lane, living a free, out-of-doors boyhood: building miniature waterwheels he put to work in Thundergust Run and playing ice hockey on the river with his Down-the-Crick Gang, fierce rivals of the Up-the-Crickers. "Boss Henry" du Pont collected relics of the Battle of the Brandywine, so Alfred and pals concocted rusty bullets to sell to the old man for ten cents each. Decades later, Alfred's will would create the Alfred I. duPont Hospital for Children on his vast acreage; today the Nemours Foundation uses his trust, worth billions, to run one of the largest pediatric health care organizations in the U.S. Having been an orphan, he cared about youngsters, and he was medically minded owing to premature deafness—caused, his doctors said, by an old childhood injury, a broken nose from diving onto a hidden rock in the Brandywine.[26]

Likewise enriched in wartime was Irénée du Pont, Alfred's cousin who presided over the family company from 1919 to 1926. In creating the estate called Granogue, near Smith's Bridge, Irénée bought four contiguous farms comprising more than five hundred acres and erected a brick colonial revival house (1923) spacious enough for his family of nine children plus six live-in servants. The site was a lofty hilltop with spectacular views across the Brandywine. Floors were reinforced concrete covered in teak; walls were paneled in oak, carved by American Car and Foundry; master forgeman Samuel Yellin provided iron hardware. A garage housed twelve cars. Du Pont collected minerals, and his wife, Irene Sophie, was a horticulturist, so the architect included a museum, solarium, and conservatory. A Maxfield Parrish mural hung above a large organ. The basement contained a chemical laboratory and milk-testing facility for the estate's dairy operations. As the twenty-first century began, Granogue remained occupied by Irénée du Pont's son, an unostentatious man who lives surrounded by reminders of the grand lifestyles of long ago.

To celebrate the 150th anniversary of the DuPont Company, Hagley Museum was founded at the ruined powder yards in the 1950s. The late Joe Monigle worked for the museum in its earliest years, driving there in his Chevy station wagon each morning. In an interview, he told me he had hoped to retain the wide floorboards in Henry Clay Mill (to be transformed into the visitor center), but they were so oil-soaked, the entire building had to be gutted. At one point a careless welder almost set the place on fire. Monigle found old glass from Wilmington trolley barns for use in the rebuilt windows. "Money was no object" at Hagley: it had the largest staff of any private museum in the country, with six model-builders on hand, creating intricate working models of mills (with real running water). The "talking map" of the Brandywine Valley was originally narrated by English actor Charles Laughton, but visitors were too focused on his celebrated identity, not the story. That display was high-tech for its era, with internal lights that illuminated in sequence. The map with its sonorous recording is still in daily use, having gained, after almost sixty years, considerable period interest in itself: a faithful workhorse for teaching generations of visitors from around the world about the importance of the Brandywine, a place that du Pont creativity and profitability helped make legendary.

Plate 1, Preface. **Summer idyll.** Prosperous Quaker farms form the backdrop to a happy Brandywine boyhood in N. C. Wyeth's classic depiction *Two Boys in a Punt* (1915).

Plate 2, Preface. **Beauty and utility.** Romantics noted the Brandywine's blend of industry with nature's wild splendor. Below the dam is Gilpin's pioneering paper mill; Wilmington in distance. Painting by Thomas Doughty (ca. 1825-1830)

Plate 3, Chapter 2. **Penn's vision.** For Quakers, Pennsylvania and the Brandywine country formed a glorious antithesis to crowded London, at right. N. C. Wyeth, *William Penn, Man of Vision-Courage-Action* (1933)

Plate 4, Chapters 3 and 9. **Eyewitness.** The battle haunted the imagination of N. C. Wyeth, who once dreamed he watched it from his painter's scaffold as young Andy sketched nearby. Washington narrates as Lafayette rides up from the left. *In a Dream I Meet General Washington* (1930)

Plate 5, Chapter 4. **World-famous mills.** Oceangoing ships pulled right up to the heart of Piedmont industry in this uniquely favorable setting along the Fall Line. Market Street Bridge at center, Wilmington at left. Bass Otis, *Brandywine Mills* (ca. 1838)

Plate 6, Chapter 4. **Print revolution.** Gilpin's Mill on the Brandywine above Wilmington witnessed the first paper-milling on the creek, then the first use of a machine to make paper anywhere in the United States. Painting by Thomas Doughty (1830)

Plate 7, Chapter 5. **Cope's Bridge.** For more than two hundred years, east–west traffic has crossed the river on this stone-arched span on the East Branch, historic gateway between Philadelphia and pioneering settlements westward. The two willow trees have been pollarded for making charcoal for industry. Painting by George Cope (1897)

Plate 8, Chapter 7. **The stonemason's craft.** Another superb house of the colonial era, this one at Marshallton was built and occupied by Humphry Marshall, who trained as a stonecutter in his youth. His famous arboretum once surrounded it. Watercolor, 1870s

Plate 9, Chapter 7. **Trout in the Brandywine.** West Chester folk artist George Cope marketed paintings (like this one of 1904) toward local sportsmen who had grown up fishing on the creek. But catches were declining as industry polluted the once-clear water.

Plate 10, Chapter 7. **Old Home Day.** John McPhee rediscovers the Palmer homestead where his great-grandfather lived along the Doe Run tributary of the Brandywine's West Branch. Ruinous in 2013, these well-built schist walls have stood nearly two centuries.

Plate 11, Chapters 7 and 9. **Summer freshet.** Shown by Andrew Wyeth in a painting of 1942, this centuries-old sycamore below historic Chadds Ford bears the scars of countless floods— and still overhangs the creek today.

Plate 12, Chapter 7. **Last of the chestnuts.** As a disastrous blight killed off these handsome forest trees, N. C. Wyeth recorded their demise at Chadds Ford (ca. 1916).

Plate 13, Chapter 8. **Birmingham Meeting.** Nineteenth-century poets and novelists savored the dramatic irony: a sleepy place of Quaker piety scarred by bullets, stained with blood. Famous self-taught painter Horace Pippin visited in 1941.

Plate 14, Chapter 8. **Haymaking.** As the twentieth century began, the Brandywine lay just twenty-two miles from America's third-largest city but retained its traditional scenery and folkways, as antimodernist N. C. Wyeth constantly stressed. Cover art for *Country Gentleman* magazine (1944)

Plate 15, Chapter 9. **At Lafayette's Headquarters.** This timeless sycamore, still thriving today, has witnessed the history of the valley since Indian times. In an iconic work, Andrew Wyeth showed it sheltering the Gideon Gilpin House: *Pennsylvania Landscape* (1942)

Chapter 7

❧✿

River of Nature

Americans' nature-loving habit got a boost from romanticism and made good use of the Brandywine as a center for ecological inquiry and as a wellspring for effusive poetry and prose. The region's proximity to Philadelphia, scientific capital of the early republic, made it a notable laboratory for the study of natural history.

It was fortuitous, too, that West Chester proved a small but lively center for scientific investigation; in the 1820s it had only a thousand residents, its streets were full of mud, and you could only grope your way down sidewalks at night by "a tallow dip in a tin lantern," but nonetheless it boasted an Athenaeum and Cabinet of Natural Sciences: "To the votaries of natural science, this is particularly interesting ground." The study of plants was a fitting adjunct to the area's long-standing commitment to intelligent improvements in agriculture; the mowing machine and revolving horse rake were invented in Chester County, for example, and the place was, to the nation's farmers, always renowned for its enlightened approaches.[1]

In 1848, Horticultural Hall was built in West Chester of green serpentine stone by architect Thomas U. Walter, only the second edifice in the nation dedicated to the study of plant life. Still today, the Brandywine Valley is especially famous for gardening and the study of plants and horticulture—from the great sweep of Longwood and Winterthur to the small-scale charms of Bill and Nancy Frederick's Ashland Hollow, which the *Washington Post* has called "one of the most admired private gardens on the East Coast," and the Dan Kiley-designed layout at Patterns, home of Governor Pete and Elise du Pont, right on the Brandywine's banks. (Pete du Pont became nationally known by running for U.S. president in 1988.) Even the DuPont powder yards, after their abandonment, were transformed into an appealing garden; when Henry Seidel Canby walked from Christ Church down to the industrial ruins in the 1930s he found sheets of colorful bulbs pushing up in "one of the most serene and natural parks in the world"—preserved today at Hagley. "The Brandywine has such a longstanding history of gardening, going back to the Quakers" says Winterthur historian Maggie Lidz, "and it's still a living culture here. Longwood and Winterthur have set a standard—you have world-class gardens that people become intimate with, then develop their own places." She lists a half-dozen outstanding private gardens on the Brandywine, then adds, "Elise du Pont's is one of the best in the country."[2]

Quaker Horticulturists

Even before Wordsworth made the out-of-doors fashionable, Quakers appreciated natural beauty as a gracious manifestation of the Divine. "The country life is to be preferred for there we see the works of God," William Penn said as he founded his "Green Country Town" of Philadelphia. In his very first months in America he urged that Delaware Valley plants be sent to England to improve horticulture there. "The woods are adorned with lovely flowers, for colour, greatness, figure, and variety," he said. "I have seen the gardens of London best stored with that sort of beauty, but think they may be improved by our woods: I have sent a few to a person of quality this year for a tryal."[3]

Penn's followers included some of the most avid botanists of the colonial period, men who, by shipping plants abroad, helped revolutionize horticulture in the mother country, even as they laid the foundations for today's garden excellence locally. Most famous was John Bartram, born in the village of Darby near Philadelphia, then in Chester County.

Later he turned his farm on the Schuylkill into America's premier botanical garden. It is said that he died from anxiety that the British would wreck the place as they invaded Philadelphia after the Battle of the Brandywine.

Bartram's passion for plants came to be shared by his cousin on the Brandywine, Humphry Marshall. A stonemason by training—and uneducated beyond age twelve—the grave and reserved Marshall farmed and ran a gristmill on the West Branch. He began collecting plant specimens, and from 1767 to 1775 he shipped boxes of plants to fellow Quaker John Fothergill in England. Upon erecting his Marshallton house (still extant) from native stone in 1773, he made the grounds into only the second botanical garden in the colonies, copying the famous one of his cousin Bartram (see Plate 8). Magnolia, stuartia, fothergilla, and larch vied with other showy specimens. After the Revolution, Marshall became the leading American exporter of trees and flowering shrubs to England and France, a profitable trade. He sent plants to Sir Joseph Banks from 1786 to 1793, including snakeroot and martagon lily for the gardens of George III. His pioneering book on American trees, *Arbustrum Americanum* (1785), encouraged scientific study in the spirit of his friend Franklin, plus doubled as a sales catalog.[4]

West Chester botanist William Darlington wrote Marshall's biography and catalogued the trees that survived in his overgrown Marshallton garden in 1849. Several gnarled specimens lived well into the twentieth century. Marshall's arboreal collection inspired nearby Peirce's Park, core of today's Longwood Gardens. And it encouraged the plantings in West Chester's Marshall Park, which pioneering forester and plant collector Joseph T. Rothrock, a distinguished resident of that town in late Victorian days, would call the nation's best for the "selection of its noble trees." The five-and-a-half-acre square was laid out in concentric circles in 1848 under the guidance of Darlington; its official authorization called for it to be filled with "various ornamental trees and shrubbery" in memory of Marshall, "one of the earliest and most distinguished horticulturists and botanists of our country, having established the second botanic garden in this Republic." Marshall Park was replanted in 1878 with the ambitious goal of growing "specimens of every kind of tree which will live in this climate," including a rare turkey oak that found its northern verge here. As late as the 1980s, two dozen trees and shrubs shown on an 1853 map still grew in the park, including a big osage orange.[5]

At the head of Pocopson Creek, four miles west of its junction with the Brandywine at Painter's Bridge, lies Longwood, where Quaker Joshua Peirce built an extant brick house in 1730. His wife, Rachel Gilpin, had been "born in the cave" at Chadds Ford where Joseph Gilpin made his first hardscrabble home in America. Joshua Peirce's twin grandsons, Joshua and Samuel, began a fifteen-acre arboretum at Peirce's Park in 1798. In emulation of Bartram, Samuel traveled as far as the Catskills, western Pennsylvania, and the cypress swamps of Maryland to find rare specimens such as Kentucky coffee-tree. The Peirce's Park ginkgo is enormous today, rubbing limbs with a yellow cucumber magnolia, largest in the United States.

After a century of affording pleasure to visitors, Peirce's Park was threatened with destruction by a rapacious new owner in 1906, who had a sawmill ready. Hearing of this impending calamity, wealthy industrialist Pierre S. du Pont of Wilmington bought the 202 acres and gave strict instructions against removing any "branch, dead or alive, unless I specify it to be done." This was the genesis of today's Longwood Gardens, 1,050 acres that comprise one of the premier horticultural attractions in the world, with an incredible eleven thousand types of plants on display.

Pierre du Pont had enjoyed youthful trips to World's Fairs in Philadelphia, Chicago, and Paris, where greenhouses and fountains impressed him deeply. In 1907 he laid out Flower Garden Walk at Longwood, with a central fountain, intending this as a focus for garden parties every June—a setting enhanced by a nearby outdoor theater in 1914, the year he enlarged the Peirce farmhouse into a proper country estate. The new house design featured a conservatory, prequel to much larger ones to come: hand-over-fist profits during World War I allowed an enormous greenhouse complex to arise nearby, where du Pont hoped "to exploit the sentiments and ideas associated with plants and flowers in a large way."

Large indeed: the new greenhouse facility was modeled on the orangeries of Versailles, but in modern steel and concrete, today expanded to four-and-a-half acres. It required three men just to run the huge basement boilers, another eight to tend the indoor flowers. President Calvin Coolidge was invited to visit, offering, as was typical of him, no comment except once to point out something he recognized amid the infinite abundance of the hothouses: "Bananas." For Coolidge, the business of America was business, and few men had been more successful in this line than Pierre du Pont; yet paradoxically, what he created at Longwood was the very antithesis of the industrialization and pollution that chemical and explosives companies typically brought to mind. Surrounded by flowers and birdsong in the gardens, the 1920s visitor could hardly have guessed that all this was made possible by roaring factories in distant states churning out some of the most lucrative products of the age: Duco paint for automobiles, cellophane, and rayon, with nylon soon to follow.[6]

Flora Cestrica

The Peirces were amateur botanists, but in their day the banks of the Brandywine produced two serious professionals, William Baldwin and William Darlington. Baldwin grew up on the West Branch and was inspired by Marshall's garden. As a ship's surgeon he collected specimens around the world. Living in Wilmington at the end of his life—he died young of tuberculosis—he botanized along the Brandywine and compared findings with his friend Darlington. Interesting specimens included ground cherry near Concord Meeting, shining pondweed at the Forks, and smooth rockcress beside the creek at one spot only in 1811.[7]

Great-grandson of a Quaker who came over with Penn and settled near Brinton's Ford, William Darlington grew up on a farm that lay, as he put it, halfway between the two main parts of the battlefield. (Later in life he would assist the Historical Society of Pennsylvania in their researches into the events of 1777.) Detesting agricultural toil, he studied medicine with a doctor in Wilmington and helped his teacher save lives in the 1802 yellow fever outbreak there. That same year he read Englishman Erasmus Darwin's *The Botanic Garden* and got hooked on plants.

Darlington enrolled in medical classes at the University of Pennsylvania and studied botany with the prominent William Barton, who often took his students to Bartram's Garden—pharmaceuticals in those days forming a branch of horticulture. Having earned his degree, he returned to his father's house and spent two dull years as a country doctor, riding rounds through the hills above the Brandywine. Upon marrying in 1808 he settled in West Chester and became involved in every conceivable civic initiative, eventually running the local bank as well as serving two terms in the U.S. Congress. Starting in 1813, Darlington combed his native county for plant specimens, eventually amassing a huge herbarium. His *Flora Cestrica* (1837)—"Cestrica" meaning "of Chester County"—earned the admiration of leading American scientists, including John Torrey, who named a California pitcher plant *Darlingtonia*.

Always lively, *Flora Cestrica* refers to contemporary uses for many plants: basswood for ladles, kalmia for knife handles, arrowwood for fuse sticks "for blowing rocks," sumach for "tanning morocco leather." Horse chestnut, mulberry, and buttonwood were favorite shade trees in yards, Darlington says. Lombardy poplar was losing its appeal. He refers to Lenape folklore: "I well recollect the last Indian Doctress," he wrote of Indian Hannah, for whom gentian was "a sort of Panacea."[8]

Chester County forms a hinge between flora north and south, and among Darlington's observations was that some northern species of trees grew in cool places along steep, shady slopes beside the Brandywine: sugar maple on the East Branch above the Forks, Carolina hemlock on cliffs above Painter's Bridge. The northernmost fringe tree in the United States was said to grow in Brandywine woods near West Chester.[9]

Darlington noted that some plants were increasingly rare: turk's-cap lily could be found only in one alluvial spot along the road to Wilmington; ginseng "is now becoming rather scarce,—and, together with some of our other coy native vegetables, will doubtless ere long totally disappear from this vicinity." At the same time, exotic species like ten o'clock and horse nettle, escaped from gardens, were proving a serious agricultural nuisance.[10]

With Philadelphia so near, many other botanists frequented the Brandywine, including English-born David Landreth, Sr., and Thomas Nuttall. Born in Brandywine Village, botanist Edward Tatnall ran a nursery there and collected extensively in the valley starting in 1831. He found smooth rock skullcap in what was thought to be its only Eastern Seaboard locality, in rocky woods above Bancroft's Mill. He was also the first person to find the water plant *Potamogeton crispus* in the United States, near Wilmington. His 1860 catalogue of plants of New Castle County mentions Brandywine Creek fifty-eight times, so rich in plant specimens had it proven. A fellow amateur botanist, James Canby, planted a rare cedar of Lebanon tree at the entrance to Wilmington and Brandywine Cemetery on the river's west bank, which still thrives today. That 1843 establishment is a fine example of the rural cemetery movement then popular, creating verdant surroundings for the memorialization of the dead and pointing the way to the nationwide city-park movement to come.[11]

Mergansers on the Milldam

Even as the Brandywine offered fertile ground for botanists, so too did ornithologists appear, making this region one of the most-investigated locales in the country: "Few like sections have been more carefully worked," an expert noted in 1919. The Cabinet of Natural Sciences (founded 1826 in West Chester) had an early collection of bird skins and eggs, and by the Civil War a list of nearly two hundred species had been compiled in the county. The first Townsend's warbler ever found in the eastern United States was at Coatesville (1868); the first nest ever described of the elusive worm-eating warbler was near West Chester (1869). The place was especially productive, given its "hinge" location halfway between north and south; the mockingbird, blue-gray gnatcatcher, Carolina chickadee, and Carolina wren all found their upper limits here, for example.[12]

The ornithological tradition in the area began with Alexander Wilson, a penniless Scottish weaver who arrived by ship with his nephew in New Castle, Delaware, on a hot day, July 14, 1794, and proceeded toward Wilmington, seeking work in a mill. "We set out on foot through a flat woody country, that looked in every respect like a new world to us," Wilson wrote, "from the great profusion of fine fruit that everywhere overhung our heads, the strange birds, shrubs, &c, and came at length to Wilmington." Here at the Brandywine he "saw two silk looms going, and some jennies preparing for establishing some little manufactory of cotton cloth," but there were no jobs. So the pair trudged across the bridge toward Philadelphia. "Very little of the ground is cleared," Wilson marveled as he walked, and the only houses he saw were of "large logs of wood" amid fields of corn, potatoes, and oats. In Philadelphia he finally got a position in a weaving mill on Pennypack Creek but soon became a schoolteacher instead.[13]

Wilson's greatest achievement, however, had its roots during his initial walk toward the Brandywine: he saw a red-headed woodpecker and was astonished by its beauty. He shot it, along with a brilliantly red cardinal north of the river. Soon he was collecting bird specimens and drawing them for a landmark book he called *American Ornithology*. In it he mentions the abundance of mockingbirds near Wilmington, which were caught for sale as cage birds in the markets of Philadelphia. His beautifully illustrated opus became the standard text on birds in the years before John James Audubon, and, along the Brandywine, nature-loving du Pont daughters copied pictures from it.

In 1810 came a chance meeting between Wilson and Audubon himself, a French émigré who had spent some youthful years at Mill Grove on Perkiomen Creek outside Philadelphia, fifteen miles northeast of the Brandywine. It was one of the most fateful encounters in the history of ornithology. Neither man had heard of the other when Wilson pushed open the door of Audubon's general store in Lexington, Kentucky. He showed Audubon the just-published second volume of *American Ornithology*. Now, he explained in his Scottish brogue, he was traveling the country trying to round up subscriptions for the next volume—having walked all the way to Pittsburgh in midwinter, then descended the Ohio River 720 miles to Louisville in an open rowboat.

Audubon was profoundly impressed by Wilson's book, and he agreed to subscribe. But then his business partner, Ferdinand Rozier, whispered to him in their native French that money was not available for such a splurge: the general store was teetering on the edge of bankruptcy, as all of Audubon's enterprises seemed to do. Moreover, Rozier said, "You are a much better artist yourself." It was true that Audubon let Rozier run the store while he wandered the countryside shooting birds for his amateur watercolor illustrations.

Audubon showed some of his own pictures to Wilson before declining to subscribe to *American Ornithology*. Bitterly disappointed, Wilson wrote in his diary as he left Louisville, "Science or literature had not one friend in the place." Meanwhile Audubon was suddenly fired up to write a book of his own. Fourteen years later, long after the frail Wilson's premature death, Audubon arrived in Philadelphia seeking a publisher. But his bragging that his artistic ability was superior to Wilson's earned him many enemies in the city that cherished his rival's memory, and he was forced to sail for London to publish his masterpiece, *Birds of America*.[14]

Audubon was well aware of the Brandywine, either from personal experience or from his correspondents there. His account of the hooded merganser mentions its fondness for the dams of the millers along the creek, and he noted how his own personal diary (now mostly lost) was written on paper from Gilpin's Mills. He often depended on correspondents, as a local example shows: Ezra Michener of the farm Sylvania near Avondale, some miles west of the Brandywine, collected birds for science. On a visit to him in May 1833, Philadelphia ornithologist John K. Townsend shot a strange finch in a grove of cedars at New Garden meetinghouse. He sent this "white-throated bunting" to Audubon, who published it in *Birds of America* as Townsend's bunting—one of five mystery birds that tantalize readers of that book to this day. Recent investigation of the tattered specimen, now at the Smithsonian, suggests it was not a new species at all, just a pale dickcissel.

Many of the younger generation of American ornithologists indebted to Audubon had close ties to the Brandywine. The Quaker institution, Westtown School near West Chester, emphasized natural history, and bird experts Townsend, Thomas Say, and John Cassin all studied there. Philadelphian Samuel Washington Woodhouse farmed for a time near Marshallton and collected birds for the Academy of Natural Sciences in his native city in the 1840s. Publisher Willis P. Hazard lived near the creek outside West Chester for decades and reprinted Wilson's *American Ornithology*. Another local was Charles J. Pennock, active in the late nineteenth century—by which time some species of birds had precipitously declined. Ruffed grouse were gone in the area, he noted, as were passenger pigeons (still occasionally abundant as late as the early 1870s). He had heard of someone finding a bald eagle nest along the Brandywine, but that was long ago.

To compare Pennock's list to the situation today is to find that many species have continued to wane, and some are entirely gone, including, most famously, the extinct passenger pigeon (the last sighting along the Brandywine was near Birmingham Meeting in 1886). But some have rebounded with the end of hunting: bald eagles are back, as are the once-rare wood duck, pileated woodpecker, and kingfisher. Conserved land throughout the Brandywine Valley provides vital habitat for birds; for example, the Laurels, a Brandywine Conservancy preserve on two West Branch tributaries, hosts 178 species, including rare Henslow's sparrows, bobolinks, and blue grosbeaks. Many birds are found in higher numbers at the unspoiled Laurels than anywhere else in southeastern Pennsylvania.[15]

Blue Rocks

Other types of scientists were nurtured by the Brandywine, too. Born on the battlefield at the foot of Osborne Hill in 1848, Isaac Sharpless pored over books in the library of Birmingham Meeting and went on to become an astronomer and then president of Haverford College. And one of the greatest paleontologists in history, Edward Drinker Cope, likewise had a Brandywine connection.

Cope was the great-grandson of an early settler near West Chester. His grandfather told stories of having heard the Battle of the Brandywine raging from his schoolroom, its violent sounds distinguishable "even to the small arms." "Eddie" Cope would grow up amid antebellum affluence on an estate outside Philadelphia. To toughen up a precocious but runty boy, his father sent him to Westtown School and insisted he work on cousins' farms in summertime. Here his love of natural history blossomed.[16]

In 1855, when Eddie was fifteen, he worked in East Bradford along the Brandywine, taking a break by swimming and fishing with friends, eating dinner from a basket on the banks and catching a big mess of sunfish for breakfast next day (see Plate 9). He studied "the birds & snakes & fishes that abound here" with books his dad sent him, and he caught a "water wampum" snake. By 1858–1859 he was collecting Chester County bird specimens. Defying his father's wishes that he become a gentleman farmer, Cope eventually gravitated toward the scientific community in Philadelphia and, along with his implacable rival O. C. Marsh—their feud is legendary—dominated the American study of paleontology in the post-Civil War period, blending intellectual prowess with pugnaciousness.[17]

Geology also became a subject of inquiry along the Brandywine, in part because of the constant need for stones for building. The lower creek cuts through dark-gray gneiss ("Brandywine blue rock") of the so-called Wilmington Complex, which forms rounded boulders, often of great size. As the creek flows seaward through mica-rich and crinkled Wissahickon schist, it makes a great lurch westward upon first hitting the hard gneiss at Brandywine Creek State Park. First formed 570 million years ago, this gneiss underwent metamorphosis in the Ordovician Period unusually deep in the earth (thirteen miles) and was heated to nearly the highest temperature of any Appalachian rock (1,600 degrees Fahrenheit), which accounts for what pioneering Delaware geologist James C. Booth called in 1841 its "superior gravity, hardness and toughness" for building. No rock in eastern America is harder.[18]

Passing through Wilmington when the town was only fifteen years old, traveler Peter Kalm reported that its houses were frequently made of stone. This blue rock gets its name from the blue sheen of the quartz that, along with feldspar, distinctively bands it. So much blue rock was consumed in building Wilmington, it can be difficult to find places today where the huge round boulders still strew the ground; but there are jumbles of elephantine boulders in the untouched woodlands at Nemours and across the creek from Hagley. No wonder travelers in search of the picturesque admired the Brandywine so much. Such scenes recall Alexander Pope's impressions of Windsor Forest along the Thames, almost like "the groves of Eden, vanish'd now so long":

> Here hills and vales, the woodland and the plain.
> Here earth and water seem to strive again;
> Not chaos-like together crush'd and bruised,
> But, as the world, harmoniously confused.[19]

Blue rock was obtained from countless small quarries, including one that is today fitted up with restored apparatus at Hagley Museum, and in vast quantities at Brandywine Granite Quarry. Now part of Alapocas Run State Park, that place was especially busy in the 1880s, when a 180-foot-high aerial cable system was installed to swing blocks of stone to waiting Pennsylvania Railroad freight cars across the creek. Thus did Brandywine stone go to build breakwaters on the Delaware Bay at Lewes, the railroad viaduct through Wilmington, and Walnut Street Bridge in Philadelphia. By 1900 the immense quarry was three thousand feet long, with walls 180 feet high, and 150 men were employed in cutting 350,000 Belgian blocks for paving the streets of Camden, New Jersey. As a boy, Henry Seidel Canby watched the quarry teams of three massive horses, jingling with brass ornaments, hauling bluestone that was suspended by chains from a long truck.[20]

Green Rocks

As geologists would gradually discover, many interesting types of rock appear along the Brandywine. At Chadds Ford and a little north, the stream cuts through a belt of Baltimore gneiss, at 1.1 billion years old some of the most venerable rocks on the continent. Some Cockeysville marble occurs near the historic Chads's Lower Ford. Botanist Thomas Nuttall found fibrolite along the creek (a type of sillimanite, which was later named the state mineral of Delaware). Rarer stones were a subject of interest very early, including fire-resistant asbestos mentioned in an 1698 account: "Besides here are load-stones, ising-glass, and (that wonder of stones) the salamander-stone, found near Brandy-Wine River, having cotton in veins within it, which will not consume in the fire, though held there a long time."[21]

It became almost as popular to collect rocks as it was to dig up Revolutionary cannonballs. West Chester bank cashier W. W. Jefferis assembled a huge collection of local minerals. Drawn to the area by Nuttall's accounts, Philadelphians G. W. Carpenter and George Spackman went up and down the creek in 1825 hunting rock specimens, guided by pioneering Chester County geologist Joel Baily. They explored Joseph Taylor's serpentine quarry north of West Chester; elsewhere, they identified dozens of curious rocks and minerals, including graphite on the Strasburg Road, zircon at Jefferis's Ford, diopside below Painter's Bridge, tourmaline on Street Road, and fibrolite on Kennett Pike.[22]

The striking, green-colored stone called serpentine occurs in scattered places running down the American Piedmont, with concentrations around West Chester, along the Mason-Dixon Line, and west of Baltimore. Originally a deeply buried rock of the earth's mantle, it has been metamorphosed and oxidized by contact with seawater. Full of toxic metals, the stone sometimes forms "barrens" where rare plants grow.

Unusual birds were found on West Chester barrens, too, including, it is said, the now-extinct heath hen. Serpentine can be found near the Brandywine in patches from Sconnelltown and Strode's Mill running eastward to Street Road. At today's Serpentine Drive is Brinton's Quarry, opened very early, in 1730. At first, stone quarried here was used to build the distinctive green farmhouses in the immediate vicinity; later, when High Victorian Gothic style made colorful architecture popular nationwide, it provided half a million cubic yards of stone for public buildings in Baltimore, Wilmington, and Philadelphia, before final exhaustion of the supply in 1888.

Because the serpentine craze coincided with the most profligate phase of Victorianism, a great many of these buildings have subsequently been demolished, including the New Castle County Courthouse on Rodney Square and Greenstone Hall elsewhere in Wilmington. Happily, Grace United Methodist Church survives in that city, for which ground was broken a month after Appomattox. Leading citizens visited Birmingham Meeting to study the appearance of serpentine before choosing it for this huge edifice. The trim was Connecticut brownstone and a paler stone from New Brunswick, Nova Scotia, giving a colorful effect, although today the serpentine is fast crumbling away.[23]

Laced with nickel, chromium, and cobalt, serpentine is essentially poisonous. Flora from the Ice Age tundras, forced to retreat everywhere else, hung on in serpentine barrens. Darlington studied serpentine flora on the Barren Ridge north of West Chester, where he saw the rare fameflower. His friend William Baldwin collected specimens of plants on those barrens as early as 1811. Continued interest by scientists has made the serpentine barrens of Pennsylvania and Maryland some of the most intensively studied botanical locales on the continent.

Serpentine and other stones were a subject of discussion during a recent trip up the West Branch with *New Yorker* writer John McPhee, famous for his many popular books on geology. Far into the hills of horse country, muted by October mists, we got out of the car and walked a dirt track along Doe Run, hopping over a red-painted gate with a rusty chain, to discover the millrace of Joseph Palmer, McPhee's ancestor who ran a sawmill here, supplying boards for book covers in the Philadelphia publishing trade (see Plate 10). Photographs from the 1940s show a couple of houses and barns along the lane, but forest has reclaimed everything, and after thrashing through underbrush we were soon clambering down into the original homestead: stone walls towering, dangerously unstable, with the roof having long since caved into the cellar. McPhee stopped himself just before grabbing a certain protruding stone, which if he had pulled it loose might have brought the three-story wall above it down on our heads. "I would've ended up in a cairn," he quipped. Winner of the Pulitzer Prize for his geology book *Annals of the Former World* and known for his literary craftsmanship, McPhee seemed to quietly contemplate the sturdy workmanship of his ancestors, who piled stone on stone with interlocking care, an edifice of schist and quartz so well wrought, it endures even in this perilously ruinous state—its mortar gently weathered away by ten thousand rains, so that only rocks remain.

Riparian Phenomena

Researchers have continuously investigated all aspects of the ecology of the Brandywine for generations, making it, according to some accounts, the best-recorded small river in the country. West Chester doctor William D. Hartman collected freshwater shells and was quoted by Charles Darwin on the subject of cicadas in *The Descent of Man*. Benjamin Everhart, owner of a general store in town, became one of the top mushroom experts anywhere. As early as 1907, biologists had catalogued the species of fish in the creek, including lamprey, trout, gudgeon, sunfish, and darter, and hydrological studies began as early as 1920. Johns Hopkins scientist Gordon "Reds" Wolman wrote his 1953 dissertation on the geomorphology of the Brandywine, a paper that was subsequently much cited. Building on this work, he later coauthored a classic book, *Fluvial Processes in Geomorphology*, with Luna Leopold—son of Aldo Leopold, the renowned conservationist—who undertook a Brandywine study of his own in 1967. Recent investigations have ranged from bank erosion to the historic droughts of the period from 1995 to 2002, which caused the creek to go dry at its mouth—the worst such spell in at least a century.[24]

Amateur naturalists sometimes explore the creek, one recently describing insect life in summer in Delaware:

> *June 10.* Down to the Brandywine past the old house site at Garden of Eden, honeysuckle vines blooming white and yellow. Wide mown fields, sun-sparkling water; rough-winged swallows rise and plunge over the creek, their mouths filled with insect wings. They are trying to feed their young in a hole in the bank below my feet. They nest solitarily in such places, or in the crannied walls of an old stone mill. A huge gang of fearsome waterstriders all facing upstream where the tributary forms a glassy pool. These gerrids do not bite, but the backswimmer does—like a lozenge with long oars, propelling himself with albatross-like motion through the depths.
>
> Beneath a 300-year-old sycamore, the tributary has scoured a deep hole for fish, clear in the afternoon light all the way to the rocky tumble at the bottom in the shadows, powdered with olive-yellow silt. As the creek falls in summer, sunlit shallow flats are tufted with clumps of green shrub like a Western desert, only these by some miracle of adaptation are completely submerged. Seen dimly from above, they wave in the steady current, blurry in the dusty depths. Scattered logs, a tire. Big wagon-wheel of a fish nest, the bream tirelessly patrolling, hovering near the middle but now darting out fiercely to meet some threat. It's so shallow and clear, you can count the pebbles on the bottom or read the word BUDWEISER on a crushed can, its red stripes fading to yellow in the aquatic sun.

The Brandywine is capricious, its mood quickly turning from quietly meandering to savagely raging (see Plate 11). It can go from placid to violent in hours, when heavy rains happen upstream. During one storm around 1860, the river rose so high it washed the iron rails off the trestle of the Penn Central Bridge at Chadds Ford. Since 1911, that bridge has housed a U.S. Geological Survey stream-gaging station, providing a long database of the life of a river, its risings and fallings over time. Once recorded manually or on tape, the data are now electronic, transmitted hourly to a satellite and made available to everyone on the Internet. An unusually extensive network of stations on the creek in Chester County record a variety of information, from dissolved-oxygen content to water quality, useful for numerous local and regional agencies, municipalities, academics, and even transportation departments and police responding to dangerous flooding.

As it flows under the bridge at Chadds Ford, the creek is 150 feet above sea level and drains 287 square miles upstream. In record flooding after Hurricane Agnes in 1972, this gaging station recorded a flood crest of 16.56 feet above normal; after Hurricane Floyd in 1999, the crest hit 17.15 feet. Development in the valley—ever more asphalt, less grass—means rainwater drains off quicker, floods become more common: five of the twelve greatest "annual peak streamflows" have happened since 2000.

Technology to study these floods has become very sophisticated lately. Kirk White of the U.S. Geological Survey described to me how he stood on the U.S. 1 bridge after Hurricane Irene in August 2011—exactly a century after the USGS first came to Chadds Ford— and created a computerized cross section of the tumultuous creek using $40,000 worth of equipment mounted to a floating boogie-board. "It shoots a beam to the bottom, recording incremental velocities across the whole channel," he explains. "The creek was probably cranking ten feet per second. There were huge trees coming down it, and we'd have to pull the boogie-board out of the way." Every second, 18,300 cubic feet of water was passing beneath his feet, the third-highest total ever witnessed here.

Back in the days when winters were truly severe, ice that melted in a time of thaw would sometimes surge downstream like a battering ram, piling up against dams and bridges in "ice gorges" that burst explosively from the weight of impounded snowmelt in the rising river. These phenomena fascinated and terrified locals. February 1893 was typical:

> All day yesterday the ice came down the Brandywine and by noon the Sager Dam, just above Lenape, was one mass of huge ice cakes gorged in a solid body from the breast up nearly to the forks of the stream. There were hundreds of thousands of tons of ice in the huge mass and the water was backed up back of it and spread out over the meadows for a long distance on each side of the stream. It was about 1:30 when the gorge gave way under the enormous pressure. . . . Down the stream came at first a few scattered cakes and back of these an almost solid wall of ice extending from bank to bank of the stream. . . . The huge cakes tumbled and crashed against one another with a steady grinding noise and rushed over the breast of the dam with awful force. Intermixed with the mass were huge trees, stumps, planks, and two boats were noticed, both badly crushed.

The Electric Railway bridge at Lenape was threatened: "A force of men armed with long ice hooks stood along the trestle and warded off the huge cakes while the full force of the rush lasted." Panicked fishermen fled the wall of water, one in Painter's Meadow narrowly finding safety in a treetop. At Chadds Ford bridge, a herd of swine was washed away.[25]

Camping Out

As peace returned to a war-torn nation after 1865, the Brandywine became ever more popular as a recreational venue. Nearby towns were steadily growing; West Chester went from five thousand people in wartime to eight thousand in 1890, the year Philadelphia topped one million. At the same time, the expansion of industries threatened the creek with a new and very modern problem—pollution.

These phenomena on the Brandywine reflected, in a small-scale way, the story of the Thames, which found itself after 1880 in a "blaze of publicity," a contemporary marveled: suddenly everybody was taking excursions up the river (including the famous one chronicled in Jerome K. Jerome's novel-guidebook *Three Men in a Boat*) and "camping out." This was great fun, but at the same time these sojourns had deep resonance: moderns were escaping into an antimodern realm filled with rich associations. Historian-photographer Eric de Mare has called the Thames "an open-air museum of English culture, history and tradition—a microcosm from which a general impression of the whole country can be gained. . . . It is the most English of English rivers and the most English of English regions." To explore the Thames was to get back in touch with the bygone virtues of a seemingly vanishing world.[26]

The same was true on the Brandywine, which so closely resembles de Mare's description: "Its country is always quiet and modest, with its rich meadowland, its deciduous woods, its gentle hills and its tranquil, though never turgid, stream. Its homely villages, towns and structures . . . epitomize the history of England." The Brandywine offered an American Arcadian alternative that could feed the imagination and the soul: it nurtured the "upward tendency of thought" toward the spiritual and the good that a writer reported experiencing along a pastoral stretch of the Thames in 1853, where "rural sights and sounds" contrasted with London's "city odours and city dust."[27]

A Londoner of 1876, similarly "choked with the dust of streets, and deafened by the noise of traffic" longed for just such flight: "We look up the stream, and pine for the atmosphere of old-world tranquility which yet hangs about the villas and villages upon its banks." He yearned to "get into the unprogressive country"—a good term for the mythical Brandywine, too, an *unprogressive* realm surrounded by a bourgeoning nation devoted to material progress. Such visions were inherently paradoxical, however: the Thames was even less wild, in actuality, than the Brandywine. Although Jerome called it a "fairyland," the Thames "is not a natural stream," one historian cautions—"For centuries man has interfered with it." De Mare agrees: its character was "created partly by nature working on her own but mostly by man working with nature." Both Thames and Brandywine present that Janus-faced quality, under increasing pressure from modern growth and development yet increasingly lauded for being soothingly old-fashioned and natural.[28]

Visitors to the scenic Brandywine took advantage of improving railroad connections. In 1869, a new, tin-roofed covered bridge was built over the creek at Chadds Ford by the Philadelphia & Baltimore Central— replacing the original span there—just as hundreds of workmen were laying tracks for the du Pont-financed Wilmington & Northern Railroad, which followed the creek's west bank and was meant to haul Pennsylvania anthracite coal to seaboard. These railways became the gushing pipelines of the tourist trade. By the 1880s, the Wilmington & Northern station at the mouth of Pocopson Creek, stylishly built of serpentine stone and still extant today, was the jumping-off place for picnickers headed for a pleasant grove on the creek bank, Birmingham Park. Pocopson Creek with its swimming holes formed the backdrop for Arcadian summers in the childhood of Henry Seidel Canby, who canoed the river and pondered the clever strategy by which the British outflanked General Washington.[29]

Upstream still stands a leafy picnic spot called Lenape Park, established beside an eighteenth-century mill site in 1892 by the West Chester Street Railway, an electric trolley service that connected to the Wilmington & Northern and gave convenient access to the creek, replacing the bumpy stage line long offered by S. Alphonso Kirk. It made the Brandywine more accessible for tourists even as it introduced a discordant note of modernity into the shadowy woods and lanes through which it buzzed. A dam served Sager's Mill and, when Lenape Park came, offered a pond for sailing in summer, skating in winter. Hundreds of people could be seen on the lake on warm days, and there were fifty canoes to rent. A "cabin colony" sprouted upstream and still thrives today.

Many other riparian picnic sites were popular, too—drawing summertime visitors from Philadelphia and indeed much of Pennsylvania. Brinton's Bridge was a favorite spot, as was Point Lookout. In a grove of oaks near the Delaware state line still stands Brandywine Summit

Camp Meeting, one of the oldest Methodist camp meetings in the country. The first prayer session was held here in Johnson's Woods in July 1865. Canvas tents came two years later, with pots of pitch and resin for illumination. Later, frame cottages were built; there are sixty-six of them today, crowded up alongside each other and rubbing against the forest trees which, by rule, cannot be cut. At the center of the meeting is a covered tabernacle for song and worship, a milieu thoroughly Victorian.

"Camping out" first became a nationwide craze about a decade after Appomattox. A West Chester newspaper marveled at the phenomenon in 1886, witnessing a scene that hinted at that on the Thames, then becoming fully exploited for leisure:

> *The Brandywine as a Summer Resort.*—It has come to be a very popular thing with West Chester people to resort to the Brandywine and spend days and even weeks along its banks during the warm weather. With a common army tent, two or three rude cots and a few necessary articles for housekeeping whole families live in comfort and happiness. A gentleman who came in by the stage from Lenape this morning says the banks of the creek are lined with tents, and some of them have stood there for a long time.... The hills and undulating land that surround the stream make the scenery attractive to the eye. The part of the stream nearest to West Chester is several hundred feet above tide water, and consequently free from any danger of malaria.[30]

Camping was so popular, groups jockeyed for the best sites. In 1908, the whimsically named Camp Sambo of Philadelphia boys hoped to occupy the meadow above Lenape, but the farmer wouldn't allow it. They tried the Forks instead, only to be driven up to above Shaw's Bridge by some "city folks" who had rented the place already.

Cope's Bridge and Deborah's Rock were perennial favorites with picnickers. A Saturday in April 1910 proved "an ideal day for strolling

by the Brandywine. . . . Violets, hepaticas and bloodroots were blooming. . . . It was a great day for young women to be out riding, unat-
tended. A town resident noticed first a road cart with three, then a
buggy with two."[31]

The Orchards

The very lowest reaches of the Brandywine, flat and muddy at the margins of a growing city, enjoyed a recreational heyday with the coming of
the Orchards, a favorite spot for fishermen that evolved, before World
War I, into a colorful yacht basin and picnic park. But in the sluggish
Coastal Plain section of the creek the Brandywine paradox (industrializing, yet natural) balanced on a knife edge, and the forces of modernization eventually won out.

Busy Wilmington was quintessentially a town of mechanics and shipyard workers, men who spent weekends building their own recreational
motor-craft with names like *Pioneer, Swastika, Nimrod,* and *Liberty.* The
nautical variety at the Orchards was endless: dories, yawls, naphtha
launches with gleaming brass stacks, converted sturgeon skiffs, big power
launches owned by du Ponts. A fantail boat called *Sunshine* was built by a
blacksmith from Eastern Malleable Iron, who powered it with a French
automobile engine. A ship jointer from Harlan and Hollingsworth yards
built *The A* from oak and cedar—trimmed with mahogany, with a can-
opy top and shiny stanchions of brass and copper. It could outrun any
local boat except the Wilson Line ferry to New Jersey, the *Brandywine.*

The Orchards was famous for its many houseboats. Recreational
fishermen spent summer nights there so they could be out on the Delaware River early next morning. But things eventually degenerated, an
old-timer noting in 1929 how "machinery has taken the place of natural
freedom and beauty along the river," which was now "polluted with gar-
bage and refuse from factories, killing all the fish." The Orchards finally
became a shantytown of grounded boats and flimsy homes that resem-
bled chicken shacks, up on stilts to avoid the floods that tore through.
The setting retained a quirky charm, however, and when the Depart-

ment of Health razed it in 1957, one resident complained, "Of all the slums in Wilmington, why do they have to pick this place to tear down?"[32]

The Mills Go Silent

Not only the Orchards seemed threatened by eventual despoliation. Human activity was everywhere: newspaper accounts show a remarkable variety of nineteenth-century uses for the creek, in addition to recreation and milling, that ranged from ice-cutting in winter to the gathering of sand to use for mortar. With all the bustle, a regular theme was the Brandywine in decline. Old-timers complained how certain types of native fish had disappeared, even as the Wilmington & Northern regularly stocked the creek for the enjoyment of excursionists. As early as 1865, fishing with seines was outlawed from Brinton's Bridge down to Smith's Bridge as catches waned. And John Russell Hayes wrote a wistful poem:

> O, I think I could linger forever beside that beautiful stream,
> Linger and loaf with my fishing-pole in dream on happy
>   dream;—
> 'Tis very easy dreaming when you fish in the Brandywine,
> For old Marsh Preston caught the last bass back in eighteen
>   ninety-nine.[33]

The trees that shaded the banks were increasingly cut by farmers seeking to cultivate every available bit of land; woodlots on the hillsides, never large, were dwindling further. And starting about 1880 there came a dramatic shrinking of the water supply, which hastened the demise of milling in the valley, a fate earlier generations could hardly have imagined. "Quietude reigns about the neighborhood of Hawley's Mill," an observer noted in Chester County in 1895. "Long since have the mill wheels ceased to turn, and the tearing teeth of the buzz saws no longer rip through logs which are cut in the neighborhood. The portable sawmill, operated by steam, has given those old-time plants the go-by in many places." At Bowers Paper Mill below Copetown, local antiquarian

Wilmer MacElree found that "the doors stand open on their hinges, and the shattered windows freely now admit the sunlight. . . . There are no secrets now, no signs that bar admittance—historian, tramp, school boy and coon hunter, alike are welcome."[34]

In 1904 a gentleman farmer gave his opinion of why the river was steadily contracting and, at the same time, why efforts to plant new trees along the creek only resulted in their getting washed away:

> That, I think, is due to the fact that the floods are greater and more frequent than they were fifty or one hundred years ago. The general volume of the Brandywine has decreased, but the floods, after heavy rains, are larger. There are fewer forests in Chester County and the water runs off in the streams. The rains dry up more quickly and the streams grow smaller. But the big floods wash out the banks and the trees. That is my theory.[35]

One of the most shocking changes along the creek came with the death of nearly all the chestnut trees in the great national blight, as recorded by N. C. Wyeth in his elegiac painting, *The Last of the Chestnuts* (ca. 1916): "It makes me sick to think of it," he wrote (see Plate 12). Forests along the creek in Delaware had been heavily chestnut; the concussion from the 1890 explosion at the DuPont works memorably blackened the ground with innumerable chestnut balls. Now billions of chestnut trees nationwide all died from a disease that came over with nursery stock imported from Japan. We can hardly conceive what it must have been like to have all these magnificent trees perish at once. A few crumbling rail fences at Winterthur are about all the trace that now remains.[36]

Pollution and Preservation

Even as the Brandywine was visited by thousands in summertime—it was said to offer some of the best canoeing in Pennsylvania—concern was mounting about pollution. Upstream in the industrial town of Coatesville, the metal-plate manufacturer Lukens Steel Company, founded in 1810 as Brandywine Iron Works and Nail Factory, grew to cover six hundred acres, one of the largest steelworks in the country (site of today's National Iron and Steel Heritage Museum). There were paper mills at Modena; four paper mills at Downingtown; and hideous piggeries at Chadds Ford and Cossart that dumped offal right into the creek. Frequent floods washed through factory yards, overflowed waste reservoirs. Paper-making dyes stained the creek blood-red. Newspapers reported a never-ending assortment of ills: a "repulsive greening scum" on the river (1886), a spate of piggery waste (1891), crude-oil slicks (1912), and oil and grease (1928). Recreation was increasingly spoiled, as when "bad water" annoyed fishermen in 1908, who blamed the paper mills at Downingtown: "A man might as well cast his line into a swill barrel."[37]

A West Chester newspaper complained that summer,

> Boys who went swimming in the Brandywine at Mortonville said the water stung and burned their bodies, as though it contained acid. This condition is considered with much seriousness by the fishermen and pleasure seekers. They admire the stream of which poets have sung and where artists have been pleased to locate their easels. They are fond of telling their friends about the "beauteous Brandywine," "the picturesque Brandywine," etc. They say they dislike seeing this stream turned into a sewer.[38]

The coming of the automobile brought ever more tourists "to visit the old revolutionary battlefields and see the wonderful stream which history has made famous," a West Chester resident noted. "What must be their feelings when, instead of a beautiful flow of sparkling water winding its course . . . they see only an open sewer, bearing its burden of discolored, polluted, ill-smelling filth onward through miles of verdant pastures? . . . The city of Wilmington drinks this stuff."[39]

In fact, Wilmington was worried. In 1827, its authorities first installed a water-powered pump below Market Street Bridge to feed a reservoir at today's Rodney Square, supplying citizens with a reliable drinking supply. A steam pump was added in 1861 and several handsome buildings were built, including City Mill Pumping Station, in High Victorian Gothic style (1872). As the Brandywine grew more polluted early in the twentieth century, however, Wilmington was said to use more alum and chlorine gas to purify its water than any other city in the country.

Growing concern led to calls for the creation of a big park on the banks of the creek above Wilmington, keeping industry at bay and offering healthful recreation. A proposal for the city to buy acreage was rejected in an 1865 town meeting, however. Three years later, the threat of houses going up between Wilmington and Brandywine Cemetery and Rattlesnake Run led to an outcry: the banks "must belong to the whole people, rich and poor." A committee was established in 1868 and recommended a "Brandywine Park," the fast-flowing rocky stream being a scenic amenity such as few other American cities could boast.

Still, nothing was done. Without a park, "there is danger that the beauties of the Brandywine, near Wilmington, may in time be sacrificed to the greed of 'enterprising' citizens," warned the popular 1872 book *Picturesque America*. In 1881, textile magnate William P. Bancroft complained that Wilmington was growing fast yet had "scarcely any provision for parks or open spaces of any kind—except cemeteries." Two years later he pushed the state legislature to set up the Wilmington Board of Park Commissioners, to which his cousin, banker William M. Canby, was appointed. Canby wrote to Frederick Law Olmsted, the legendary Boston landscape designer, who accepted an invitation to visit Wilmington. Olmsted reported in December 1883 that the city should move quickly to purchase both banks of the river, which it finally did, buying 115 acres in 1886–1887.[40]

Bancroft himself provided land for Rockford Park farther up the creek in 1889 and 1895, totaling some two hundred acres—about the time that visiting President Cleveland took a pleasure drive along the "romantic Brandywine." Then the DuPont company donated the rugged slope overlooking today's Experimental Station—where no one dared to live, lest Lower Yards blew up. Rapid urban growth (Wilmington reached 70,000 in the 1890s) demanded a water tank on this hilltop, so Rockford Tower was begun in 1899, attractively faced with huge blue-rock boulders pried from old stone fences. Inside was a metal tank through which ten million gallons of Brandywine water flowed annually; today's rate is four million gallons *daily*, so greatly has water demand increased. The 115-foot tower has an observation deck atop, allowing spectacular views of the Brandywine Valley.

In its shadow, the William M. Canby Memorial, a granite bench looking up the gorge, was installed in 1905. An amateur botanist who once owned a farm at Chadds Ford, Canby had explored Alaska with naturalist John Muir, who now attended the dedication, hearing a speaker extol "the wild and natural beauty of the new park, along the banks of the Brandywine."[41]

Son of the founder of Bancroft Mills, William P. Bancroft started Woodlawn Trustees in 1901, a nonprofit with the goals of protecting open space along the creek and building workers' housing in town. Eventually it came to control thousands of acres on Concord Pike, which it sold or leased for commercial and residential development, using the income to purchase riparian land. As development pressures increased after World War II, Woodlawn Trustees played key roles in the establishment of parkland, donating land and money for part of Brandywine Creek State Park (founded 1964) and, in the 1980s, spending $5 million in outbidding developers for two miles of river frontage. In 2012, eleven hundred acres of Woodlawn Trustees land, newly dubbed "Woodlawn," became the focus of intensive planning toward possibly creating that national park in Delaware. In March of the following year, President Barack Obama created First State National Monument in part "to preserve Woodlawn consistent with William Poole Bancroft's vision of a rural landscape accessible to the public for their health and well-being."[42]

Abutting the national monument on the south, Brandywine Creek State Park embraces one of the finest mature Piedmont forests in all the

Mid-Atlantic; moreover, it offers Delaware's best inland locale for bird-watching. Originally it formed part of the Winterthur estate. For many years the du Pont family held land in a kind of communistic arrangement, but "Boss Henry" du Pont eventually broke with tradition, seizing for himself huge tracts out of the common holdings, to the dismay of some of his kin. As if forever to mark the landscape as his own, he (and later his son, Colonel Henry A. du Pont) had Italian masons—the "Never-Sweats"—build extensive stone fences around this far-flung Winterthur estate, using rock from Brandywine Granite Quarry, which the family partly controlled. The section that later became the park was bought by landscape architect Robert Wheelwright in 1951 and auctioned after his death, at which time developers proposed a housing tract for the 433 acres. Concerned citizens pushed the reluctant State Park Commission to buy the property instead, and today it is cherished open space along the Brandywine.[43]

"I love the landscape here," park naturalist Jessica Turner told me. "We have so many habitats from streams to meadows to old growth. In Tulip Tree Woods I tell the kids to put their hands on the trunk and look up—they are always mesmerized." Turner leads countless activities, including canoeing, kite-flying, and orienteering, all to show "that nature and the public can mingle" in this surprisingly wild-seeming park surrounded by suburbia. Exotic plants are constantly pressing in; one recent summer, the park borrowed two 800-pound Asian water buffalo to eat invasive grasses in a marsh along the Brandywine that had nearly been choked by the infestation. "Water buffalo eat almost anything," Turner explains. "We do a lot of interesting things to help preserve this place."

With the Coming of Sprawl

By 1938 a headline read, "Wilmington a Leader in Municipal Parks," with 928 acres set aside. But there was still much to be done. In that decade, Clayton M. Hoff, a stocky DuPont chemist with a clipped black moustache, took long hikes along the creek and was appalled by what he found: "It was the stench, not the sight" that worked him up, he later recalled. Hoff founded Brandywine Valley Association in 1945, which some have called the very beginning of the "small watershed" conservation movement that soon spread nationwide.[44]

One concern of the association was the mud that was allowed to wash from farmers' fields—seventy suspended tons went through Wilmington daily, a study showed, and this skyrocketed to thirteen thousand in flood time. By 1957 the group had built 175 farm ponds, terraced or contoured twenty thousand acres, and planted 1.5 million trees. "We need a long range comprehensive plan, not only for the Brandywine, but in all streams," Hoff said four years later. "With the demands of an increasing population, the cries for more highways, more schools, more housing developments, you have too many people who are prone to grab the instant dollar rather than taking the economic long view." The Brandywine Valley Association remains active today, its 800 members supporting efforts aimed at water protection and environmental education.[45]

New Castle County nearly doubled its population in the 1950s, and the population of Brandywine Hundred grew by an incredible 142 percent. The nation's leading advocate for land preservation in those years of headlong expansion was William H. "Holly" Whyte, who grew up around West Chester and became dismayed at the bulldozing of scenic Brandywine landscapes—which he thought some of the loveliest in the entire country—for housing and commercial developments. Often the changes were piecemeal, death by a thousand cuts: he rued "the couple who opened a frozen-custard stand by the old covered bridge; the local officials who had the bridge torn down and a concrete one put up," the brutal Philadelphia Electric Company transmission towers that marched "through the most historic and beautiful stretch of the Brandywine" despite "bitter protests." Already famous for his book decrying societal conformity, *The Organization Man*, Whyte now began to write about the evils of urban sprawl and urge the use of "conservation easements" to save farmland. A mid-1960s plan that he drew up with Ann Louise Strong of the University of Pennsylvania called for preservation of unspoiled parts of the Brandywine Valley; it was not adopted, but it had a great influence on planners nationwide. Then the Brandywine Conservancy joined the fray in 1967. In the words of associate director of the land stewardship program David Shields, it "has been a pioneer for the whole country in the use of conservation easements by land trusts," an inspirational model for preservationists everywhere, who look to the Brandywine for the most sophisticated new approaches.[46]

Chapter 8

❧ ✿ ❧

Literary Pastoral

Beneath a little bridge over Ramsey Run, where sunlight sparkles on the current, children have built a dam of stones, and the water splashes as it finds its way around the obstacles, flowing out of the shadowy coolness of the tunnel and into the broad mudflats where deer have scored the brown banks with their hoofs. It's a good place to sit on a boulder, eat a sandwich, and read an old book about the Brandywine.

For all the scientific attention focused on the valley over the years, the place has become even more famous for its cultural legacy, including the inspiration it has provided to writers. If today we believe the Brandywine is a place worth preserving, well, that is because it has developed a mystique; and this mystique originated with the written word, patiently burnished over many generations through enthusiastic productions in poetry and prose. The Brandywine writers, now mostly forgotten, deserve some homage.

For one thing, we cannot understand the art of the Wyeths without appreciating their literary forebears. Wyeth paintings are saturated with narrative affinities, as art critic Brian O'Doherty has noted, and need to be seen as the culmination of a long tradition of viewing the Brandywine through a lens of antimodern thought:

> The whole Brandywine Valley is sign-posted by Andrew Wyeth's paintings. Here is the [Barns-Brinton] house off Route #1

where the dead deer hung. That became *Tenant Farmer*. . . . A place is altered because a picture happened there. A landscape becomes a stage for a crisis of thought, a dilemma of action, an event, an interior soliloquy. His real Chester County has—artistically—a lot in common with Faulkner's imaginary Yoknapatawpha County. Going through Wyeth country is like walking into a novel in progress.[1]

River of America

For many years, the best-known book about the creek was *The Brandywine* in the Rivers of America series (1941). Son of a prominent banker, Henry Seidel Canby grew up in a fashionable part of Wilmington, at 1212 Delaware Avenue; at age five he would have watched construction of the Howard Pyle Studio across the street. Later he became a noted Yale professor and man of letters who presided over the Book-of-the-Month Club, dictating the reading habits of millions in those halcyon days of literacy.

His family had lived on the river for six generations: he was descended from Oliver Canby, who began the flour-milling boom, and he owned a cherrywood table from the home of ancestor Joseph Tatnall on which Washington wrote dispatches before the battle. As a boy he canoed the creek, searched for the ruins of old mills, followed supposed Indian trails along the banks, watched in awe as thousands of herring and alewives thrashed the eddying water trying to get past the dams. "The loveliest wild flowers in Brandywine," he recalled, were on the South Race beside the Canby gardens at the estate called Bishopstead.[2]

Launched in 1937, Rivers of America achieved legendary status as one of the noblest endeavors in twentieth-century publishing history: sixty-five books that tell the stories of many regions of the country through the life and culture of their waterways, written in a pleasingly literary style and embellished by professional artists (as we saw, Andrew Wyeth illustrated *The Brandywine*). Canby was chosen on the basis of his family background and erudition: he was a biographer of Whitman and Thoreau. In researching *The Brandywine*, Canby immersed himself in the collections of the Delaware Historical Society and produced a book that, if it had a fault, was in discouraging any attempt at imitation for decades to come. His was the definitive twentieth-century treatment of the Brandywine.

A Vision of Pastoral Loveliness

But long before Canby, the Brandywine had found its literary voice. As American letters began to flourish, they needed a place in the New World they could liken to Arcadia. Long-settled, peaceable, and domesticated, the Brandywine filled the bill perfectly—generations before a quarter-scale model of the Parthenon was erected at the creek edge in Eleutherian Mills gardens around 1930, in a highly literal evocation of the Arcadian theme. In the 1860s, Bayard Taylor hailed "our idyllic Brandywine" as a place for "wild Arcadian pomp." And novelist George Lippard wrote decisively,

> When you seek a vision of that pastoral loveliness, which fired
> the poets of Greece and Rome,—that loveliness which presents
> in one view, the ripeness of the orchard, the green slope of the
> meadow, the mirror-like beauty of tranquil waters,—then
> come with me to the shades of Brandywine! . . . Here indeed,
> the verdure seems richer, the skies more serene; here the hills
> arise with a more undulating grandeur, than in any other valley
> throughout the Continent.[3]

In a similar vein, in the early twentieth century, novelist Joseph Hergesheimer found in Chester County's "green and slumberous peace" that "far idyllic country" of his dreams, "a land with little towns and farmhouses of stone and wood, barnyards within stone walls and barns filled to their high roofs with hay"—again, a perfect Arcadia.[4]

The growth of publishing that accompanied the steam press, much of it centered in Philadelphia, made the Brandywine a regular subject of literary attention in the early Republic. Wilmington was an erudite place, too; by 1796 there was a printing shop and bookstore "at the sign of Shakespeare, at No. 5 High Street, opposite the Upper Market," just one of several in town. And West Chester was not far behind: by 1841, seven newspapers had been established in a village of only 2,100 souls (Wilmington's population had by then reached 8,300).[5]

Novels exploited the Brandywine's historical and picturesque possibilities as early as John Neal's *Seventy-Six* (1823). And poetry about the creek got under way well before that, initially in the form of patriotic effusions. Erudite Delaware officer John Parke wrote odes in the manner of Horace while in his headquarters tent on the "Heights of Brandywine" before the battle and later, on Perkiomen Creek not far east, penned a gruesome elegy excoriating General Howe:

> *Witness, O Brandywine, thy purple wave,*
> *Thy fields deep-furrow'd by the whist'ling ore;*
> *Thy mountains spread with many a yellow grave,*
> *Thy trees bespatter'd round with human gore!*[6]

And in Boston in 1793, George Richards praised the late General Nathanael Greene, who fought on the Pennsylvania battlefield, now sacred turf:

> *Array'd in tears and garb of sable hue,*
> *See Brandywine the chieftan's hearse attend . . .*
> *Immortal grounds! the theme of every age,*
> *Your meanest dust shall speak the hero's praise.*[7]

In the newly popular vein of topographic poetry, some verses called "The Brandywine" appeared in the *American Museum* magazine in 1788. With the stated aim of emulating the lyrical excellence of Alexander Pope, the anonymous author sought "to sing the beauties" of the creek, "this crystal stream" with steep and rocky banks. Especially lovely was a point of woods "a little below Brandywine bridge," meaning Market Street in Wilmington. As customary with the picturesque imagination, the watercourse here was seen to be both scenic and functional, "taught to turn full many an useful mill."[8]

Daughter of a physician-farmer, the poet Elizabeth Margaret Chandler was born in 1807 on a 167-acre farm in a bend in the Brandywine near Centerville—doubtless Point Lookout. (This is on the state line, so both Delaware and Pennsylvania now claim her as a famous native.) The child's mother passed away almost immediately. At nine, Elizabeth moved to Philadelphia, her father died, and she began writing poetry. Her best-known offering, "The Slave Ship," appeared when she was eighteen, establishing her as America's first female Abolitionist poet. She moved to Michigan not long before her untimely death at age twenty-six.

Chandler's *Poetical Works* opens with "The Brandywine," a nostalgic look at "my native hills." "My foot has climbed the rocky summit's height," she writes—apparently thinking of Point Lookout's crags. She also recalls the long-ago Revolutionary battle: "Where the share, in passing o'er the scene, / Turns up some rusted ball." She thrilled to the historic associations at Birmingham Meeting: "On its floor warm life-blood was poured out," the stone walls ringing with "the convulsive groans of mortal agony" (see Plate 13). And outside she gazed upon the hallowed vista:

> This valley, that now looks so lovely in its slumbering tranquility, once rang with all the wild turmoil of battle. Behind yonder hills, you may hear the murmurs of the shaded Brandywine, and here, where you now stand, the earth was red with slaughter, on the day of that fight. On that height Lafayette received his first wound in the service of our country—these fields, where the luxuriant corn is now bending so gracefully to the breeze, were then the death-couch to many men.[9]

Horrible, Shrieking, Bloody Plots

Thomas Buchanan Read grew up on a farm at Corner Ketch near Downingtown and, even after he moved to Europe and became a best-selling writer and artist, retained his love for Chester County scenery—as shown in his melodrama *Paul Redding: A Tale of the Brandywine* (1845), which sings the praises of "the bright, the laughing Brandywine, / That dallies with its hundred mills." Read is best known for his Civil War poem, "Sheridan's Ride," and later that old Corner Ketch farmhouse became a place of literary pilgrimage.

George Lippard's 1846 novel *Blanche of Brandywine: Or, September the Eleventh, 1777* mushroomed into a runaway commercial hit. Descended on his mother's side from early settlers in Brandywine Hundred, Lippard was born along the stream in Chester County but moved to Germantown near Philadelphia at age two when his father was crippled in a wagon accident. A sickly and eccentric boy, Lippard liked to wander along Wissahickon Creek, which later figured prominently in his writings. Abandoning his plans to become a minister, he found himself a penniless author in the city, often essaying Revolutionary themes, as in his story "The Battle-Day of Brandywine" in the *Citizen Soldier* newspaper (1843), written in the torrid romantic vein that became his signature. Lippard wanted to give Pennsylvania its due as a place of stirring military actions: his great-uncle had fought at Brandywine.

His magnum opus, *Blanche of Brandywine*, first appeared in the *Saturday Courier* and combined his favorite themes, patriotic drama and Gothic sex and horror—"gory, horrible, shrieking, bloody plots," one reviewer said. Lippard describes "heaps of dying and dead, the blaze of burning houses . . . the smell of human blood." In one hideous scene (which he invented), a Chadds Ford schoolmaster is burned alive in a haystack by Redcoats.

Lippard visited all the key places associated with the battle and described them meticulously: the dark gray stone of Birmingham Meeting with its burial-yard wall and mounded graves where "carnage [raised] his fiery hymns of cries and groans"; the brick inn at Dilworth Corner; a knoll with five oaks where, he was told, Washington once prayed. Brandywine scenery was splendid, Lippard found—"A sight as lovely, as ever burst on mortal eye." But everywhere he imagined blood and havoc, even at the delightful creek where soldiers "standing in mid-stream . . .

poured the rifle-blaze into each other's faces, when they fought foot to foot, and hand to hand, when the death-groan bubbled up to the water's surface, as the mangled victim was trodden down into the yellow sands of the rivulet's bed."[10]

Some of Lippard's literary episodes were based on interviews conducted with elderly men as he went house to house along the creek, seeking stories. At Birmingham Meeting a grizzled Quaker approached him as he stood and "looked upon the mounds of the graveyard, and examined with a reverential glance, the most minute details of the old fabric. . . . And while the silence of evening gathered round us, the old man told me stories of the battle-field that thrilled my blood." He conjured up a vision of the graveyard "choked with ghastly heaps of dead—broken limbs, torn corpses, all crowded together in the graveyard of Peace! Cold glassy eyeballs—shattered limbs—mangled bodies— crushed skulls—all glowing in the warm light of the setting sun."[11]

Above all, the creek itself was irresistible. Often Lippard stopped to admire "the silvery waves of the Brandywine glistening and trembling with radiance." Long ago, he thrilled to imagine, this place saw savage warfare: "The charge was terrible. Every tiny wavelet of that fair stream turned to blood [and] the faces of the dying, contorted with the spasm of violent death, thrust from beneath the waters."[12]

Lippard became wildly popular. Known for his dashing, Byronic appearance, he married his wife by moonlight on a rock high above the Wissahickon. Later, devastated by her death from tuberculosis, he is said to have tried to jump off Niagara Falls, except that a friend pulled him back from the brink. Lippard once rescued his associate Edgar Allan Poe from starvation. He himself died of consumption at age thirty-one, and his writings were soon forgotten—but not the myths he spun. It was Lippard who single-handedly concocted (for another *Saturday Courier* piece) the story of the Liberty Bell.[13]

Blanche of Brandywine was turned into a popular play for Mrs. H. M. Ward in Philadelphia in 1847, advertised as "the first domestic drama on the Revolution ever played in this country." Later it was adapted again by James G. Burnett in 1858 for performance at Laura Keene's

Theater, New York, with the famous actor Joseph Jefferson starring. Years later, poet Paul Laurence Dunbar borrowed the character "Black Samson of Brandywine"—a giant man armed with a scythe—from Lippard.

A Lippard biographer notes that the stories in *Blanche of Brandywine* were accepted as truth by generations of schoolchildren, including the one about Washington kneeling to pray between opposing lines on the battlefield. And "as recently as 1919 historians were still digging up turf in the Brandywine area searching for the remains of Lord Percy of Monthermer, unaware that Percy was merely a creation of Lippard's fancy."[14]

Awful Grandeur

Another romantic writer closely linked with the Brandywine was John Lofland, Delaware-born (the "Milford Bard") and a poet from the age of ten. In 1846, Lofland, then forty-eight, moved to Wilmington from Baltimore to edit a local newspaper, *The Blue Hen's Chicken*. He was a deeply troubled intellectual: his friends took him on long walks along the Brandywine, lest he stay home and indulge his opium habit. Dissipation steadily destroyed his health, and Lofland died after just three years in Wilmington. But during his short time there, the creek inspired him to write a series of romantic poems and stories, including "Fatima, or the Fairy Queen of the Brandywine," "Manitoo, the Indian Beauty of the Brandywine," and "Ono-Keo-Co; or, the Bandit of the Brandywine."[15]

Lofland's collected works reveal the full extent of his preoccupation with the historic creek: he imagines seeing a ghost in the graveyard of Old Swedes Church, for example, and longs to have glimpsed the native tribes: "When I wander the romantic banks of the Brandywine, I fancy that I see their dusky forms and bark canoes. . . . But alas! they are not there—those sublime solitudes have been silent, and unbroken by the voice of the Indian, for ages."[16]

Lofland often returned to a youthful theme, the Battle of the Brandy-wine—as early as 1826 he had written a poem about it. In July 1847 he traveled up the river and then to Valley Forge, hoping to "pick up incidents among the old residenters, on which to found a Revolutionary Tale." From the high balcony of the Mansion House hotel in West Chester he surveyed the bucolic region, renowned for its rich fertility, its tall waving corn. On another occasion, he and "a party of literary gentlemen" visited Chadds Ford to see "the lofty hill on which General Washington took his stand, and poured down a deadly fire on the enemy in the valley." His poetry about September 11 waxed gruesome: "It cleft his skull, and blood and brain / Came spouting forth upon the plain."[17]

In true romantic form, Lofland routinely eulogized the vanished past. As he stood on the hill above the Chad House he mused, "No mementoes are left of the battle. A calm sunshine and solitary silence now rest on those fields, those hills and valleys, which have been drenched with American and British blood." At Wilmington, even the boulders were fewer nowadays, Lofland recalling Indian times and "the innumerable rocks, which were then piled in awful grandeur on the steep banks of the Brandywine, the most of which have since been removed by the hands of civilized art and industry."[18]

This Historic Ground

As the fame of the Brandywine spread widely, literary references appeared in far-flung places. "I wandered for amusement on the banks of Brandywine," a poet wrote in 1836, among "many rough and cragged rocks [and] lofty ancient trees." That work was published as far away as Boston. Most writers were closer to home, however, including Delaware playwright Robert Montgomery Bird, who visited "the Brandywine Battle Ground" in 1828 and gained new resolution to finish a Revolutionary-themed work; it "furnished me with many hints and clues for my story." Another local enthusiast was a U.S. congressman from West Chester,

James B. Everhart. His "The Brandywine" may not rank among the most felicitous examples of Victorian lyric ("where sunbeams illume / With changeable gleams arboreous gloom"), but it occasionally succeeds in out-Lipparding Lippard, whose trope of bloody waters now gives way to whole slaughtered armies bobbing seaward:

> Heroes and horses, distorted and torn,
> Bloated and dead, on its surface upborne,
> Wounded ones writhing and wailing for aid,
> Fragments and missles o'er hillock and glade,
> Havoc and horror, disaster and night
> Palling the scenery, and quenching the fight.[19]

Eager writers continued to come throughout the nineteenth century. Medical doctor S. Weir Mitchell summered near Sconneltown at Reculver Farm (near today's Bala Farms Road), earning fame for his novel of the Revolution, *Hugh Wynne, Free Quaker* (1896), with illustrations by Howard Pyle. Destitute and suffering from tuberculosis, Southern poet Sidney Lanier spent summers at boarding houses in Chester County in 1876 and 1877, the second one on the north side of today's Brinton Bridge Road uphill from the future Andrew Wyeth estate. He described its "vista running for miles along the Brandywine. . . . A long green hill in front of the house slopes down to the river, and within a few feet is a wild ravine [behind the house] through which a stream runs down to the great rock-built milldam. . . . All this loveliness of wood, earth, and water makes me feel as if I could do the whole Universe into poetry." In the vale of "yon dreaming Brandywine" Lanier wrote such poems as "The Dove" and "Chadd's Ford."[20]

A then-obscure journalist named Theodore Dreiser visited in 1897, three years before he published his bombshell novel, *Sister Carrie*. "There is no more lovely vale in all Pennsylvania than this historic ground through which the Brandywine river wends its peaceful way," he wrote, where spotted cattle stand in pools under the trees and delight the easel-painters. He found the crumbling remains of an earthen breastworks from the battle, on a knoll overlooking the creek.[21]

Old Days and Old Ways

The great nineteenth-century tradition of the Brandywine pastoral culminated with John Russell Hayes, one of the most passionate of the river's Anglophile admirers. He and his wife and three daughters lived at 517 Elm Avenue in Swarthmore, where he was long the college librarian (1906–1935); but whenever possible they escaped to the Brandywine, his native country. His ancestors had lived along the creek for generations, and Hayes constantly returned to the home of his elderly grandmother—the still-extant Green Lawn, at the foot of Harvey's Bridge Road, Embreeville, next to the farm where Mason and Dixon lived. There stand two houses, apparently the family hearth since Revolutionary times: a low, "red-roofed" colonial dwelling of 1774 and a stone mansion of 1841. Hayes's seldom-studied diaries, preserved at Swarthmore, show how completely the place captivated him.

A slender, contemplative-looking man with spectacles and a neat black beard and moustache, Hayes wrote in the cool parlor at Green Lawn or out in the garden amid hollyhocks, roses, petunias, and nasturtiums (his 1895 debut book of poetry was called *The Old-Fashioned Garden*), listening to the sound of tinkling cowbells in the meadows across the creek. He enjoyed riding "Topsy" over the hills, or drifting down the quiet waterway in his cloth canoe, reading Isaac Walton's *The Compleat Angler*, or paddling by moonlight. He visited nearby villages looking for the birthplaces of famous authors, brushing the dirt off the gravestones of early settlers.

A highlight was the visit of fabled naturalist John Burroughs, then age sixty-five, to the Brandywine in October 1902—he caught his first glimpse of the stream from a carriage right at Green Lawn. Accompanying the kindly, bearded man on a woodland stroll, Hayes piously recorded many utterances of this great American popularizer of nature.

The burrs seemed "delighted to get hold of him" as they passed through a thicket. On crows noisy in flight: "They're just having a little political CAW-cus." He averred that Whitman was no atheist, but "always steadfast" in faith. "I do not read him every day, only in my best moods, and then it is like climbing a great mountain." About his own writing, Burroughs said that it "took hard work for him to work out the *musk* from his style."

One year, Hayes's cherished Christmas present was an illustrated book by noted West Chester trial lawyer Wilmer MacElree called *Down the Eastern and Up the Black Brandywine*, a compendium of local scenery and lore. The author was an enthusiastic amateur historian who gave chalkboard lectures in which he showed the locations of the historic fords on the Brandywine at the time of the battle to audiences occasionally lost in confusion. Hayes admired the book as "full of reverie & landscape & old folks & old houses & old farms."[22]

Having long written pastoral poetry about the creek, such as "In Meadows by the Brandywine," published in *Lippincott's* magazine, Hayes began to develop a series of stories about the region, "with local color, sentiment and humor. Reading [Thomas] Hardy's rural scenes started me on the idea." There were numerous British currents in his thinking, including Thomas Herrick, William and Dorothy Wordsworth, Charles Lamb, Richard Jefferies, and Eden Phillpott's *My Devon Year*. In 1910, Hayes published *Brandywine Days: Or, The Shepherd's Hour-Glass*, a lyrical account of his old house and the surrounding countryside, arranged as a diary, with plenty of digressions concerning his favorite reading.

In the now-forgotten writings of Hayes, one slips back into a bygone world in the valley, before asphalt roads and suburbanization, before the general demise of agriculture and the return of cloaking woodlands. Gone today are his ruddy farmers whetting their scythes, cows lowing in the meadows, rows of sweet-smelling hay, creaking wagons going down dusty roads and rumbling through dark covered bridges (see Plate 14). Even in his time, one could feel nostalgia for rural virtues beginning to leave the land: every page celebrates the heritage of "this antique Brandywine," declaring that "the old days and the old ways have their natural home in these tranquil valleys; quietude and conservatism are seated here by ancient right."[23]

From an Old House

The automobile was coming, and everything would change. During the years right after World War I, the valley became home to Joseph Hergesheimer, who brought nationwide attention to the region through his books set in colonial times, including *The Foolscap Rose*, sited on the Brandywine. A Philadelphian who liked to stress how little schooling he had received, Hergesheimer married a West Chester belle and, as we saw, settled down in an historic house on the edge of town (at the foot of Goshen Road facing the golf course), the Dower House of 1712. In the early 1920s, top critics considered Hergesheimer one of the most important living writers. Today he is only remembered—if at all—for his speedy, headlong tumble into obscurity.

Outspoken and deliberately unconventional—"I'm just a natural boor"—Hergesheimer was a fixture of the *Saturday Evening Post* and a subject of public fascination. He churned out eleven novels in eight years, writing (and exhaustively revising, over and over in red ink) in every room of the Dower House—on bridge tables or wherever he could find a spot, carrying a little electric fan along with him. His method was to lay down 2,500 words a day in a blue book that would hold no more. His meteoric success amazed him, he told a reporter: "This is like a dream. I am so damn dumb, you know, that it's like being possessed by a spirit to find that I can make money by pushing a pen over a piece of paper."

Hergesheimer adopted the lifestyle of the country squire, strolling the property accompanied by barking Airedales, puffing a huge cigar, admiring the golf links: "I love the green when it takes these long shadows." But he complained that the automobile was ruining the bucolic countryside: "The hum of motors down the concrete road past his West Chester estate annoys him, awakes his indignation," a visitor noted. Once a country lane through meadows and orchards leading to the headwaters of the Brandywine in the Welsh Mountains, it was now "a thoroughfare of concrete," and all night Hergesheimer was bothered by the sound of motors roaring down the hill, then pounding up the farther rise. He longed for the days when he first moved there, when evenings brought the sound of farmers driving down the sleepy lane whose steep banks were dark with violets in April: their inebriated songs, the clatter of hoofs.

But paradoxically, Hergesheimer relished the society of the wealthy who now invaded the Brandywine region and brought horse shows, fox hunting, antiquing. His luxury automobile sported a Lalique glass ornament on the radiator cap that, he bragged, cost more than the car itself. At the Dower House he entertained a long list of celebrity visitors. Then writing a novel called *Main Street*, Sinclair Lewis briefly moved to town in summer 1919, renting a house next to the library. Two titanic egos were too much for one small town, and Lewis soon fled—although his wife would always cherish Joe's recipe for succotash. Actress Lillian Gish spent four days in 1921, enjoying steaming plates of scrapple for breakfast. F. Scott Fitzgerald's visit was infamous: he got characteristically drunk at a dinner party and pulled down his pants, H. L. Mencken reported, exposing his "gospel-pipe" to stunned fellow guests.[24]

Hergesheimer himself often seemed at war with local society. Once he took off his dinner jacket at a party, to which the indignant hostess said, "Joe, why don't you take off your shirt, too?" So he did. Famously misogynist, he lectured on "The Feminine Nuisance in American Literature." Invited to address a gathering of Radcliff College alumnae, he said that beauty is all that women have going for them: "If your nose is shiny you might as well be dead!"

For all his sociability mingled with combativeness, Hergesheimer craved privacy and solitude, complaining of "the loud disrupting pressure of the present" and wishing to retreat into "pastoral quiet." The timeless Brandywine paradox was, with him, a subject of unresolved anxiety as he vacillated between the urge to be fully contemporary and the urge to escape the modern. Increasingly consumed with nostalgia for the superior virtues of a bygone past—"the conviction that things had been better then"—Hergesheimer immortalized the Dower House

The antiquer. This *Saturday Evening Post* cartoon of 1928 was captioned, "We have with us today—a celebrity! Joseph Hergesheimer, having taken a day off from the strenuous task of writing, returns after wandering among the hills of Chester County, Pa., seeking recreation."

in his 1926 book called *From an Old House,* which attracted a wide audience during this heyday of fascination with "Americana." "Before the blackened fireplace" he could feel, at last, "the accumulated decades of stillness."

Hergesheimer's ever-increasing traditionalism owed much to his worry about what was happening to the United States in that age of immigrant influx: he pitied tenement dwellers with no rootedness in the land and lamented "there were so many people in America now to whom its past meant nothing." As so often with writers of the nineteenth century, the Brandywine served as a counterpoise, a bulwark of heritage and true values buffeted by the tempests of change. Hergesheimer called his beloved Chester County "peculiarly, in an older sense, American; the heritage of the soil, of the long establishment in Pennsylvania, was articulate and undiluted by later arrival."[25]

From an Old House helped turn antiques collecting into a great contemporary mania: as Hergesheimer himself complained, it ended the days when you could find a colonial ladder-back chair for fifteen cents, sitting cobwebby on some farmhouse porch. There followed a national explosion of collecting, driven by the newly rich who were beginning to flee the cities for a suburban life in automobile suburbs. As Henry Seidel Canby noted, suddenly "'colonial' furniture came down from the attic." Wilmington-born novelist John Marquand satirized the Roaring-Twenties types who bought an old farm dreaming of reviving

> the atmosphere of those dear old people who had lived on it and who had made things with their hands, such as pail yokes and wooden scoops and sap buckets, and those dear little cobblers' benches that you could stand in front of the fireplace to put things on, such as cigarettes and cocktail glasses and what have you.[26]

Muckraker Sinclair Lewis, who had lived for a time in Arden, Delaware, savagely attacked the genteel lifestyle Hergesheimer promoted at the Dower House, pointing up the contradictions long inherent in the Brandywine mythologies: a gentle Arcadia inhabited by chemical company directors and corporation lawyers. Hergesheimer pretended to embrace the simple and colonial but in fact lived ostentatiously in chic West Chester,

> an ultra-fashionable suburb of the opulent city of Philadelphia.... In this tallest of ivory towers in America our artist lives, surrounded by lowboys and highboys, field beds and hunting boards, Chippendale sofas and Windsor chairs, rat-tailed spoons and a Philadelphia silver tea-set. He tells us how he sits and gazes upon these objects, and dreams stories that are not stories, but merely characters to "hold together" the cupboards and pewter, the William and Mary chairs and Phyfe tables.[27]

Hergesheimer's literary reputation collapsed with the coming of the Depression and a preference for tough realism, instead of escapism into the colonial past. Unable to afford his luxurious lifestyle any longer, he sold the Dower House and moved to, of all places, the Jersey Shore. Mencken's diary, when unsealed twenty-five years after the Sage of Baltimore's death, offered a close-up view of the full tragedy of "Joe's" last years, marked by poverty and writers' block. But Hergesheimer left a legacy: the Americana craze that he helped trigger would become indelibly associated with the Brandywine Valley. In fact, some grumpy critics would place the art of Andrew Wyeth within this great mid-twentieth-century commodification of Americana, charging him too with the creation of "characters to 'hold together' the cupboards and pewter" (or to assemble like actors and dance around a quaint maypole in his late painting, *Snow Hill*). Regard it however we will, the collecting movement found its perfect milieu along the Brandywine, as today's grand house museums attest—Nemours, Eleutherian Mills, and especially Winterthur—and this has become the essential place in the nation for cultural tourism around the theme of Early American antiques.

When Henry Francis du Pont became master of Winterthur upon his father's death in 1926—an enormous estate of 2,400 acres, rolling down to the verdant banks of the Brandywine—he undertook a multimillion-dollar expansion of the house, building a gigantic addition to showcase his growing collections of classic Americana. The existing thirty-two-room mansion was supplemented by a wing with more than a hundred rooms, designed for good natural light and standing fully nine stories high on the downhill end. Eventually there were to be more than 175 period rooms in all, purchased from historic buildings in the thirteen original colonies. In picturesque Brandywine tradition, the house was surrounded by spectacular, naturalistic gardens sprawling across sixty acres; when the Garden Club of America honored du Pont with a 1956 prize, it called him perhaps "the best gardener this country has ever produced." By then, Winterthur Museum had been opened to an admiring public—130,000 tourists would eventually come every year, admiring some ninety thousand decorative objects from the seventeenth century to the early nineteenth. "At that point he becomes a national figure," says Winterthur historian Maggie Lidz, "and it focuses attention to the Brandywine in a whole new way."[28]

Eccentric Earl of Ellerslie

It was the inimitable lifestyles of these du Ponts that led editor Maxwell Perkins to suggest to F. Scott Fitzgerald that he move to Wilmington in spring 1927—surely he would find novelistic inspiration amid this larger-than-life clan. There would have been plenty of room for satire, playing up the Brandywine paradox: Henry Francis du Pont, for example, was simultaneously a farmer tending three hundred Holstein dairy cows, a gardener who lovingly coordinated the colors of his dinner plates and bouquets of table flowers . . . and a shrewd director of General Motors, biggest automaker on the planet.

Young Fitzgerald had achieved, with remarkable swiftness, fame and riches for his novels of society life but had then floundered in Hollywood, trying to become a screenwriter. He had burned through the money earned from *The Great Gatsby* and needed another hit. His Princeton roommate, Wilmingtonian John Biggs, found a house, Ellerslie, for Scott and his Alabamian wife, Zelda. A Greek Revival showpiece of 1842, it sat empty on the Delaware riverbank a mile and a half from the Brandywine in a zone gradually becoming industrial—later it was torn down to build a DuPont factory. Here was the best deal in town: thirty rooms but only $150 a month. There were other costs, however: the place required two maids, and Zelda designed oversized furniture, constructed in Philadelphia, to fill immense rooms. Fitzgerald fell in love with the mansion—it could hold a candle to Douglas Fairbanks's Pickfair and other Hollywood showplaces—and he took to calling himself the "Eccentric Earl of Ellerslie."[29]

Zelda planted white roses; she painted maps of France on the garden furniture and stars and flowers on wooden lawn chairs. Inside, she decorated six-year-old daughter Scottie's bedroom with painted fairytale scenes and cut out paper dolls of historical subjects. Amid this outpouring of creative energy, she completed her first oil-on-canvas painting, too: a view of the historic home. Her industry, occasionally unstoppable, was tinged with mania, prequel to the mental illness that would soon find her committed to an asylum.

Fitzgerald made an attempt to write a novel—later called *Tender Is the Night*—sequestering himself on the third floor. And he briefly hobnobbed with the du Ponts, perhaps at Granogue on the Brandywine: "A friend took us to tea in the mahogany recesses of an almost feudal estate where the sun gleamed apologetically in the silver tea-service and there were four kinds of buns and four indistinguishable daughters in riding clothes and a mistress of the house too busily preserving the charm of another era to separate out the children."[30]

But distractions were constant, including trips to New York, or to Philadelphia where Zelda took ballet lessons. With frenzied energy she danced in front of an enormous mirror in the Ellerslie parlor while, upstairs, Scott littered the floor with crumpled paper as he struggled with writer's block. And then there was the drinking that would kill the unfortunate novelist little more than a decade later—he guzzled gin and kept "a very wet house in Delaware," writer Carl Van Vechten told Mencken. Biggs, a lawyer, had to get the Fitzgeralds out of trouble when they were arrested by local police for drunkenness in a tough section of town called "Bloodfield."

Visitors came in droves to see the famous author in the picturesque setting of his antebellum mansion. Ernest Hemingway arrived after the Princeton-Yale football game. Parties were legendary—moonlit cocktails under the huge horse chestnuts to the sounds of a black jazz band. One such soiree celebrated Lindbergh's flight. Partygoers used the dinnerware for skeet-shooting and borrowed huge plow horses from the neighboring farm to play a zany polo match with croquet mallets, which today has made the word "Ellerslie" almost synonymous with 1920s decadence.

"Wilmington has turned out to be the black hole of Calcutta," Zelda wrote in discouragement at the end of their inebriated stay, which had lasted, with a hiatus in Paris during summer 1928, from March 1927 to March 1929. The Fitzgeralds again left for France and embarked on a downward spiral that concluded in two premature deaths. Little survives from their time in Delaware, except for Scott's touching story "Outside the Cabinet-Maker's," which portrays his tender love for Scottie. The action—such as it is—happens while Fitzgerald's automobile is pulled up outside a shop in Wilmington. Zelda goes inside to buy a doll's house while Scott waits in the car, telling make-believe stories to an enthralled child. The scene lay "at the corner of Sixteenth and some dingy-looking street" a little ways off Market, which would place it at the edge of downtown—right along the Brandywine.[31]

Chapter 9

❧ ❦

"Painters of True American Art"

Looking downstream near Granogue on a May morning, the artist finds a dozen subjects for a painting: the green and undulating floodplain carpeted with flowers, contorted black boxelder trees half-horizontal over the water, red canoes in a swale, the shimmering reflections of forest and sky as the river, high from winter rains, courses down toward Thompson's Bridge. The easel sinks in the brown mud, the canvas shakes in the wind, but the artist perseveres, hoping to win a place in the great tradition of the Brandywine painters.

The man to emulate, of course, is Andrew Wyeth. We think we know him well, but there were many contradictions and complexities in a career that stretched from Herbert Hoover nearly to Barack Obama. In 1975, a *New York Times* reporter marveled at how Wyeth, ostensibly an artist of simple rural scenes, in fact formed the figurehead of an opulent local gentry, King Arthur to an American Camelot:

> Wyeth's presence has spawned an almost manic obsession for his person and his painting. . . . The Brandywine Creek, or river—it is called both—has created a valley here that is as close to a pastoral idyll as any region in the nation. . . . Scattered throughout are huge estates with dozens of graystone mansions studding the land—and barns and stables and servants quarters and coach houses and sleek-looking horses in

the pastures and large handsome dogs running on the grounds. It is old money from old families, and in the evenings the twilight silence is broken only by the soft sounds of laughter and the ringing of fine silver on good china drifting out from the verandas.[1]

Here arose once more the Brandywine paradox: pastoral values coexisting alongside the vast wealth produced by manufactures. The ironies seem inescapable. It is strange to think that Andrew Wyeth's own brother, Nat, was a top DuPont engineer who invented the plastic soda bottle—billions of which are discarded annually, a major source of pollution in rivers everywhere, the Brandywine included.

The "good china" crowd that embraced Andrew Wyeth, including several U.S. presidents, made the artist an even more tempting target for the barbs of the art critics. On every level they stood apart from him, ideologically: they were New Yorkers, he was mud-spattered and rural; they had rejected prewar American Scene values in painting in favor of internationalism; being good modernists, they loathed representational art. For them it was almost a cardinal sin, in the troubled modern world, for an intellectual to turn his back on contemporary problems and instead to revel in a bygone age of coverlets, Windsor chairs, and hay-scented barns. They had left Wordsworthian escapism far behind.

Those who charge Wyeth with sentimentalism would argue that he did not depict the actual Chadds Ford or Brandywine Valley; instead, a quasi-imaginary realm in which those places were scrubbed of modern-day intrusions. But this was, as we have seen, a very old intellectual tradition along the Brandywine. Although his unconventional compositions show awareness of modernism in painting ("I like abstractions up to a point"), Wyeth's mentality was not unlike that of poet John Russell Hayes of an earlier generation, stressing the pleasures of "reverie & landscape & old folks & old houses & old farms." Whenever possible, he favored garbing his models in archaic (and often colonial-era) clothing, positioning them alongside early American furniture in old-fashioned settings. As much as the automobile has transformed the landscape, it is striking that Andrew Wyeth never shows a Buick peeking from around the corner of a crumbling barn, a Chevy nosing up to a rusty watering trough. In reality, cars are everywhere; in Wyeth's art, they are virtually nowhere. Modernity is excluded almost as ruthlessly as it was from The Homestead—N. C. Wyeth's custom-designed, theater-set environment of ye olde colonial chairs and spinning wheels and candles—when Andy was a boy there. This kind of antiquarianism is extinct among American intellectuals today and has been for sixty years or more; to the disgust of critics, Andrew Wyeth continued in an antiquarian vein even when few others still dared (see Plate 15). But he had good warrant: he was the heir of what has come to be called the Brandywine Tradition.[2]

En Plein Air

This valley beloved of romantic poets became, following the Civil War, perhaps best known for the many artists who haunted its banks, who painted in its sunny meadows and among its upland fields. When Howard Pyle established a summer art academy at Chadds Ford with the lofty goal of launching a movement of "painters of true American Art," he showed the way for the Wyeths, father and son, who collectively painted along the Brandywine for a century and garnered extraordinary fame both for themselves and for this great American place.

In selecting the Brandywine as a nursery for "true" Americanness, Pyle chose well: its pedigree was unimpeachable. Already the Battle of Brandywine had been depicted in historical canvases by several nineteenth-century painters, including Alonzo Chappel and John Vanderlyn (who showed Washington and Lafayette riding spirited horses). Charles Willson Peale, Thomas Doughty, and Bass Otis sketched or painted along the creek, concentrating on early American industry amid nature's romantic splendor. Thomas Birch produced a print of the Brandywine as early as 1805. Later the attention shifted upstream into Pennsylvania, especially once the easy railroad connections were established with Center City Philadelphia. Portraitist John Neagle depicted a local farming village "on the spot" in 1839. Thomas Anshutz painted here, as did Edward Moran; apparently so did leading Hudson River School painter Jasper Cropsey. Artists frequently appeared in West Chester on their way to the creek; by 1898 that suburbanizing town was linked to Philadelphia by trolleys that ran every fifteen minutes.[3]

Illustrator Granville Perkins sketched the Brandywine for wood engravings to accompany an essay by Oliver B. Bunce in the landmark 1872 book, *Picturesque America*. "No minor stream in our country enjoys a wider reputation," Bunce declared. "Its rare beauties have been delineated by painters, praised by poets, and described by tourists, until few of us have not some pleasant recollection or anticipation connected with its wooded shores." Arguably the stream was picturesque not in spite of its industry but because of it: "Too often labor mars the landscape it enters, but the mill seems to partake of the spirit of its surrounds, to gain a charm from woods and waters, and to give one. This is particularly true of the factories along the Brandywine."[4]

Philadelphia's greatest-ever artist, Thomas Eakins, spent holidays and summers at his sister's farm in Avondale, west of the Brandywine Valley, which meant that he regularly took the train through Chadds Ford. Among his many doctor friends in Philadelphia was John Hill Brinton, who asked Eakins, about the time of the 1876 U.S. Centennial, to paint a little picture of the Brinton 1704 House near Dilworthtown as it had looked in its colonial prime, before Victorian alterations.[5]

Poet and painter Lloyd Mifflin grew up on the Susquehanna, taking long youthful rambles with a copy of Tennyson under his arm. In 1871 he went up and down its valley, making sketches from a railroad train or steamer, contemplating an illustrated book. The next year found him painting on the Rhine. In 1874 Mifflin strolled down the Brandywine, making 145 sketches for another book he had in mind, *The Mystic Stream from Source to Sea*—ultimately never published. "And sylvan Brandywine has in her keeping / Some whom death glorified," he once wrote of the battleground.[6]

William Trost Richards's *Valley of the Brandywine*, depicting haymowing one hazy September day, is an unforgettable highlight of today's Brandywine River Museum of Art. Famous as a painter of marine subjects, Richards produced a lyrical body of rural-themed work at a farm near Coatesville between 1884 and 1889. A Philadelphian, he had grown up fishing on the Wissahickon and, as a teenager, undertook an expedition out to the Brandywine in August 1851. "I was down on the Brandywine last Monday week," he wrote a friend, "the farthest I have ever been from home! It is a beautiful place, very much of the same character as the Wissahickon, but without the pine and such height of hill."

Six years later, the Historical Society of Pennsylvania commissioned Richards to paint a scene of Brandywine Battlefield, as he had recently done of Mount Vernon for a local art society; unfortunately, the painting is lost. Richards returned to the valley later in life when he bought Oldmixon Farm for his daughter's family, setting them up as poultry farmers. In summer months he painted en plein air, for example depicting the *Head-Water of the Brandywine, Near Coatesville* (1884). He might have painted longer, but the poultry operation was destroyed by fire and the farm was subsequently sold.[7]

Many other Philadelphia artists hopped the train to Chadds Ford on summer weekends, including watercolorist Carl Weber, who painted a riparian scene for a gentleman in faraway London in 1881. It was executed, a West Chester newspaper reported, "about two miles this side of Downingtown and represents a pretty meadow, with the Brandywine taking its zigzag course under drooping trees, which adorn its banks. In the distance the spires of Downingtown appear with the north valley hills in hazy softness, forming a grand background to the whole." Weber's *Dungeon Bottom* depicted a swamp just above Painter's Bridge. In *Deborah's Rock*, picnickers relaxed beneath the trees on an Indian Summer day.[8]

Working alongside Weber in 1881 were Wilmington painter Henry Lea Tatnall and Philadelphian James Brade Sword; all appear to have made sketches outdoors, then painted finished pictures in their studios over the winter. Sword sketched Cope's Bridge and Deborah's Rock. In *Painter's Bridge*, Tatnall showed "the famous drive along the Brandywine, a few miles above Chadds Ford. . . . The lights and shadows of the road as it curves around the bluff and loses itself in the grove beyond are reproduced with singular accuracy and a high artistic sense; and the familiar and quaint forest flowers at the foot of the bluff are remarkably fine." When it hung alongside his *Deborah's Rock* in a showing at West Chester, the exhibitor noted that "dozens of our prominent men have pointed out to us in these art productions points where they in their boyhood days swam, fished, boated and had a jolly good time with the girls."[9]

Newspapers noticed the influx of artists. "The 'forks' of the Brandywine have long been a paradise for the marksman, the angler and the artist, while at the same time the lowing herds browse upon its green pastures and the husbandmen gather the rich harvests from the neighboring hillsides," a journalist wrote in 1901. Around that same time, E. Taylor Snow painted *Brandywine Willows* at Brinton's Bridge and said that his most popular pictures were always Brandywine scenes.[10]

With Camera and Brush

Among the artists were photographers, too. Probably the first ever were the pioneering Langenheim brothers of Philadelphia, who took three daguerreotypes of the battlefield for a publication of the Historical Society of Pennsylvania in 1846; they showed Birmingham Meeting, Washington's Headquarters, and the Chads House.[11]

Later the Philadelphia firm of George O. Bartlett and William French (in business from 1867 to 1869) produced an intriguing series of stereo views of the creek in Delaware, called *Beauties of the Brandywine*. At least one of the pictures shows a man "playing dead" amid piles of boulders in homage to those famous Civil War pictures of Gettysburg. Many of the views appear to have been taken in the wild woods and jumbled rocks ("Featherbed Lane") across from DuPont Lower Yards; access to this area was facilitated by the Wilmington City Horse Railroad of 1864, which made Riddle's Woods and nearby locales popular for picnicking. Many of the stereo views show rocky banks and hillsides that no longer exist—blasted into oblivion by road and railroad construction, quarrying, and sewer work. Not for nothing did DuPont, starting in the 1880s, entirely dominate U.S. production of dynamite.[12]

Other photographers soon came as well. The famous William Henry Jackson photographed the B&O iron-trestle bridge at Wilmington, rising high above the forested gorge. French immigrant and powder-yard worker Pierre Gentieu painted a view of Lower Yards in 1878 and then spent the rest of his life taking more than three hundred glass plate photographs of DuPont holdings, offering us a window back in time. Upstream in Pennsylvania, forestry expert Joseph T. Rothrock set up his tripod to take an attractive print he called *Brandywine Banks: Above the Ford* in 1889. A decade later, Douglass E. Brinton exhibited numerous photos of the battlefield. A newspaper reported in October 1904, "William H. Jones and Lee Scarlett, of Philadelphia, are taking photographs in the meadows along the Brandywine today. They met on a trolley car coming out from the city this morning."[13]

Among photographers and painters alike, the liveliest activity was at Chadds Ford. "Chadds Ford hotel is filled to its utmost capacity, the majority of the visitors being artists from New York and Brooklyn, who may be seen sketching along the Brandywine during all hours of the day," a newspaper reported in June 1898.[14]

But the artists who cherished the Brandywine most were the local painters, serving the fine art markets in West Chester, Wilmington, and Philadelphia. Foremost among these was George Cope. A cousin of the artistically inclined Emmor Cope, who drew the topography of Gettysburg, George Cope grew up hunting and fishing along the Brandywine, which flowed west of their farm (on today's Copeland School Road). He did sketches on his slate in lieu of classroom assignments, for which his teacher sternly rebuked him. In 1875 he began painting landscapes that he offered for sale in store windows in West Chester. Lessons with Philadelphia artist Herman Herzog led to a friendship in which the two men took camping trips to northeastern Pennsylvania, painting as they went.[15]

Cope's more than four hundred pictures in folk-art style, including many trompe l'oeils of dead game, have mostly disappeared over the years. His bucolic Brandywine scenes still surviving include *Pyle's Ford* (1896), *Trout in the Brandywine* (1904), and *Birmingham Meeting* (1909). As a penniless old man, Cope was reduced to peddling baskets of wild-flowers on the streets of West Chester for a dime. His last work was a pencil sketch of the creek in 1928.[16]

Frail and infirm, Wilmingtonian Robert Shaw was a prolific water-colorist and etcher who, as a child, had delighted his little friends by drawing animals on their gray slates in the schoolroom. He produced scores of etchings of scenes along the Brandywine between 1890 and 1904, with an emphasis on colonial landmarks like *The Old Barley Mill*. His views illustrated John Russell Hayes's book, *The Brandywine* (1898)— his artistic skills having been bolstered by a year he spent sketching along the rivers of England and Wales. For a period of four years, Shaw went blind from so much close work, then recovered his sight, marveling to Hayes about "the wonder of seeing again the birds and flowers." He died suddenly in midlife while at work on a watercolor of a colonial house along the creek, part of his admirable effort to, as he put it, "pre-serve some of the old landmarks about our city." "I didn't begin soon enough," he lamented, so many places having already been obliterated by progress.[17]

Numerous other artists were active on the Brandywine before and during Shaw's time. Rockland, Delaware, was a favorite spot: London-born John Rubens Smith painted the covered bridge twice in 1835, before it washed away; Young's Mill on the east bank and Kirk's on the west also appeared. The long stone Jessup and Moore paper mill was shown in a wood engraving as "Scenes on the Brandywine" in *Picturesque America*: "All lovers of the picturesque delight in brook-side mills. . . . There is always a strange pleasure in this combination of the beautiful and the useful." Jefferson D. Chalfant (a decorative painter at Jackson and Sharp Car Works in Wilmington) painted the mill as *The Brandy-wine Below Rockland* about 1885.[18]

The Brandywine's covered bridges delighted countless artists, but with the coming of automobile and truck traffic in the twentieth century they were virtually all dismantled. An exception is Smith's Bridge, near Delaware's northernmost point and in sight of the Pennsylvania state line. The first covered span here (1839) suffered damage from traffic and was eventually burned by an arsonist. Smith's Bridge was recently rebuilt using Bongossi, a fire-resistant African hardwood of rock-hard resinousness, and it again welcomes the Sunday painter.

What have all these artists, generation after generation, taken from the Brandywine? Again, it is surely a New World equivalent to the Thames, which one historian calls "an open-air museum of English culture, history and tradition—a microcosm from which a general impression of the whole country can be gained." By averting their eye from industry, these artists have found an idyllic place where quaint surroundings recall those of the colonial era, full of colorful incident and suggestion. They have discovered a Sleepy Hollow like the famous one of Washington Irving, one of those "little retired" valleys where "population, manners, and customs remain fixed, while the great torrent of migration and improvement, which is making such incessant changes in other parts of this restless country, sweeps by them unobserved. They are like those little nooks of still water which border a rapid stream where we may see the straw and bubble riding quietly at anchor or slowly revolving in their mimic harbor, undisturbed by the rush of the passing current."[19]

River valleys have long served such a beneficial function for artists, ever since Claude and Poussin roamed up the muddy banks of the Tiber. Historian Jonathan Schneer has described how the painter J. M. W. Turner spent the summer of 1805 on the Thames, sketching its banks from a boat and reading Ovid and Virgil. There he found "the antithesis of London . . . an Arcadia by contrast, a countryside in which Greek gods and goddesses, and the people who worshipped them, might have felt at home, but where also were preserved England's truest values and virtues: the purity of nature, the slow rhythm of country labour, man's organic connection with the countryside. . . . He was painting England as he thought it had been and should always be." This exposure invigorated Turner's art, for "in his mind the river and surrounding countryside stood for the national verities, for England's essential character, indeed for the nation itself." For countless artists, the Brandywine has worked a similar magic, one tinged with patriotism and moral virtues. As Schneer says, Turner "shows us a river that was many-sided, contradictory, complex and . . . quintessentially English"—so too was the Brandywine quintessentially Early American. But we should never forget that, like the Thames, the Brandywine has "both the real and the ideal" facets, often greatly at variance.[20]

Young Artists at Turner's Mill

The Brandywine school of art, so-called, was founded by a tall, stern, and square-jawed Wilmington native, Howard Pyle—the most successful American magazine and book illustrator of the late nineteenth century, legendary for *King Arthur* and other classics. Pyle gave us our modern conception of knights and pirates, vivid images that Hollywood later appropriated, and his reputation continues to grow. He had a passion for Revolutionary history, as countless paintings and illustrations attest—for example, the stirring depiction of Continental troops advancing in *The Nation Makers* (1906), now at the Brandywine River Museum of Art. Between 1877 and 1909, he illustrated no fewer than eighty-seven magazine articles on colonial and Revolutionary subjects, playing a significant role in that bourgeoning cultural movement of the day, the Colonial Revival.[21]

From earliest youth, Howard Pyle knew the Brandywine intimately. His ancestors had grown up near its banks—his mother at Painter's Crossroads on Concord Pike east of Chadds Ford—and his venerable great-grandmother told him firsthand stories about the tragic aftermath of the battle. The son of a leather manufacturer, Pyle spent his early childhood at the house now called Goodstay (c. 1740), at today's 2600 Pennsylvania Avenue, Wilmington. The "choicest ornamental trees" occupied the grounds, perhaps including the huge gingko that still stands. At what he called "the quaintest, dearest old place you can imagine," young Howard pored over picture books while lying on a rug in the library by the fire, had fun rolling down the "terraced bank" in front of the house, shooed poultry from big Turkey Rock in the garden, and watched Conestoga wagons rumble by on the turnpike.[22]

By 1872, when he was nineteen, he was taking art lessons in Philadelphia and exhibiting a *Brandywine Scene* painting in a jewelry store window in Wilmington. After a stint in New York he returned to his native surroundings, married, and began writing and illustrating articles for popular journals. "Old-Time Life in a Quaker Town," which describes Old Swedes Church, appeared in *Harper's* (and, by some circuitous route, came into the hands of a struggling painter overseas named Vincent van Gogh, who said its artwork "struck me dumb with admiration.") Pyle built his famous studio, still used by local artists today, in 1883 in Queen Anne style, with big fireplaces, heavy ceiling beams, and rustic-shingled interior walls.[23]

Eventually Pyle commuted to Philadelphia to teach at Drexel Institute, from which school he brought his most talented students to Chadds Ford in 1898 and 1899 for summer sessions. Male pupils (including Stanley Arthurs and John Schoonover, both later illustrators of note) boarded at Washington's Headquarters; female students stayed at Lafayette's. As we saw, these historic surroundings were fitting: Pyle's ambition was to found a great artistic movement for the nation, an approach to oil painting that would be rooted in love of indigenous rural landscapes, building on those "painters of true American Art" like Winslow Homer and George Inness, whom he deeply admired. It would be the New World equivalent of the Barbizon School of Corot, Millet, and others who escaped Paris to paint amid wildflowers, boulders, and venerable oaks in the forest of Fontainebleau.[24]

All-day painting sessions took place in Turner's Mill across the road, shaded by an immense sycamore. The students enjoyed hearing water gurgling over the millwheel beneath the floorboards while they worked in the "grain-scented rooms." Often they painted in the fields and meadows, occasionally fleeing from ornery bulls. For a pirate-themed illustration for *Harper's*, Pyle had the students build a tilted platform like a ship's sloping deck, slosh it with water, and then pose on it in costume,

Turner's Mill. At Chadds Ford, Howard Pyle gathered his best art students, including N. C. Wyeth, for immersion in the American rural scene. For five summers they painted upstairs in the historic mill.

under the spreading buttonwood tree, which still shelters the former mill more than a century later.[25]

Pyle constantly led his students on nature walks and told them all about the battle. Afternoons regularly featured a swim in the Brandy-wine for the young men—with soap used on Saturdays. For fun there were baseball games in the meadow by Brinton's Mill or bike rides to Wilmington for lemonade at Anscow's Restaurant and Oyster House.[26]

Sessions resumed from 1901 to 1903, after Pyle left Drexel and established his own school in Wilmington. Among Pyle's students this round was a young man from Needham, Massachusetts, named Newell Convers Wyeth, who quickly fell in love with "The Ford," sometimes walking sandy roads all the way from Wilmington. His first such walk came in October 1902, the morning after the twenty-year-old arrived by train from New England: The landlady at his boarding house at Tenth and Adams fixed him a sandwich, which he ate at Adams Dam (a pond along Montchanin Road, belonging to Winterthur estate). He had brought a trout-line in his pocket and fished a while before strolling on to Chadds Ford and, fatefully, first meeting Howard Pyle. Decades later, Wyeth could recall every detail of that life-changing day.[27]

Pyle was famously obsessed with historical accuracy. To take but one example, Andrew Wyeth long owned an oil sketch by Pyle that shows almost microscopically precise details of a fire crackling in a colonial fireplace, complete with real eighteenth-century andirons and tongs—all a study for an illustration concerning the life of Washington. At the same time, Pyle could discourse endlessly about the Revolutionary past. At Chadds Ford, he wove an historical spell for his young protégés, telling them those tales he had heard from his great-grandmother, who had watched the beaten Continentals retreating past the family farm, "trailing their muskets over the dry fields of September, their shoeless feet wrapped in gunnysack, and bleeding."[28]

No student seemed more receptive to these thrilling stories than N. C. Wyeth. In July 1903, Pyle had Wyeth drive him on a twenty-five-mile carriage tour of the battlefield. That evening, master treated student to a vivid discourse on the events of September 11, 1777. Wyeth was awed by this lesson in history and later searched for earthworks and relics on the creek banks.[29]

Pyle and his big family rented Lafayette Hall, a stately mansion beside the famous wartime headquarters. Also called Painter's Folly, it had been built by Samuel Painter around 1857; later owner Joseph Pyle leased it to Howard Pyle. (In our time, the brush of Andrew Wyeth has brought it renewed fame.) Letters of N. C. Wyeth's, written when he was a student at Lafayette Hall, contain appealing accounts of summertime life with his fellow pupils, including tennis, ping-pong, and long talks on the spacious veranda overlooking hallowed ground.

On August 23, 1904, Wyeth and Arthurs paddled from Wilmington to Chadds Ford during high water, then back, shooting over dams and rapids; once the canoe overturned, and Arthurs nearly drowned. The following summer, N. C. courted shy Wilmingtonian Carolyn Bockius by taking her on trips in his birch bark canoe each weekend, sometimes from Chadds Ford clear down to Wilmington. By now the valley had captivated him utterly, and in later life he sometimes threw out his arms and exclaimed nostalgically, "Those glorious days!"[30]

N. C. Wyeth spent some months painting in the West but longed for a return to familiar scenes, to the kinds of verdant farms he remembered from boyhood in New England—he had grown up on the old-timey banks of the Charles River in Massachusetts, to which he constantly compared the Brandywine. In summer 1907, the newly married Wyeth rented the tower of Windtryst, a vine-covered, serpentine-stone Italianate villa built by wealthy Philadelphia lawyer Joseph C. Turner (c. 1864) on a knoll uphill from Washington's Headquarters. Turner had met his poetical wife, Eliza, after the battle of Gettysburg, where both were serving in hospitals; later she invited poor city kids to spend weeklong summer vacations with them at Chadds Ford.

From Windtryst, Wyeth daily strolled down to his studio in Turner's Mill. By now it had fallen permanently silent—no more of its sonorous rattlings nor the splash of water over its wheel. Wyeth worked to the sound of horned larks in Hoffman's Valley outside the windows as he painted his celebrated "farm series" for *Scribner's*, including *Scythers* and *Mowing*, which Pyle warmly praised.[31]

One day in early 1908, Wyeth and his visiting brother Ed took a morning walk out of Wilmington, climbing Rockford Tower with its view across the Brandywine Valley; then they scrambled down through big boulders to the river and along its banks back to town, talking about trees and nature. Later that spring, Wyeth rented the Eli Harvey homestead (General Green Headquarters) on the eastern edge of Chadds Ford village and set up his studio in the carriage house. He undertook much illustration work—he was nearing the height of his powers in that field, already perhaps excelling the abilities of any other American practitioner, ever. But his dream was eventually to quit illustration and become a landscape painter, part of that "true American Art" crusade Pyle had preached. Living close to nature along the Brandywine seemed essential for his future progress, it being an unspoiled realm equivalent to the Barbizon region for Millet, whom Wyeth passionately admired.[32]

Genius of The Homestead

In 1911, Wyeth earned an immense $2,500 commission from *Scribner's* to illustrate that classic British novel, *Treasure Island*. Local people posed in costume for him as he completed the canvases at his Harvey-place studio. With the proceeds, N. C. bought eighteen acres on the slopes of Rocky Hill overlooking Chadds Ford and built a colonial revival house and studio, which he called The Homestead. The heights were thoroughly historic, having been occupied by Pennsylvania militiamen during the battle.

In designing this house, Wyeth insisted the architect keep everything "practical, picturesque, and indigenous to the country"—befitting his deep-seated antiquarianism and with a nod to another author's home, Cedarcroft: "With white trimmings and green shutters and big chimneys, I shall perpetuate Bayard Taylor's spirit in architecture!" The eighteenth-century flavor extended to the uphill studio, as well, with its capacious fireplace fitted with a spinning wheel, tin lantern, musket, and powder horn. Once the studio's inside walls were painted "gray pearl," Wyeth would never paint them again, preferring to watch as they gradually became mellow and antiqued with time.[33]

In glowing letters, Wyeth described The Homestead in terms that stressed its cottagey, archaic flavor: "quaint," "homey," "simple," "very colonial, harmonizing with the country," "with the atmosphere of a much older house." Modern comforts were few: there was a telephone (one of the first callers said that Howard Pyle, then living in Italy, had died), but for years there were no electric lights, all five Wyeth children huddling around a lamp at night to draw. Nature lay right at hand, as seen from comfortable chairs on the front porch: fields spangled with dandelions, a stream flowing left toward the Brandywine, Sugar Loaf hill in the distance—his favorite walk.[34]

The Wyeth kids virtually lived outdoors; sometimes N. C. took them to Brinton's Bridge for ice cream under the trees, and they swam or picked strawberries while he fished. "My grandfather never went to the Caribbean, never to Europe," Jamie Wyeth says today. Instead, the Brandywine was his beloved home turf and formed "all the physical background" to his art—local woodlands serving, for example, as Sherwood Forest in his famous illustrations for *Robin Hood*.[35]

N. C.'s copious letters reveal the depth of his antimodern mindset, rooted in New England transcendentalism and near-worship of Thoreau. Cities were evil, he believed; commercialism inevitably corrupted. He was horrified when automobiles first came snarling through the quiet valley, describing how one pulled unexpectedly up his lane one May night in 1909: he was aghast at "the great trembling car that throbbed with suppressed power, and the rank nauseating odor of gasoline which it emitted." The paving of the dirt road through the village as part of the main artery between Philadelphia and Washington, DC (U.S. 1) brought far more tourists and cars. Wyeth even considered abandoning Chadds Ford once the du Ponts and their associates, made fabulously rich by World War I profits, started buying up old farms along the creek, blowing up the historic barns and colonial houses, then erecting modern mansions ("Babylonian brothels!"). Increasingly Wyeth's moody nostalgia was tinged with depression, which had long run in his family.[36]

As it turned out, N. C. Wyeth could never afford to free himself from his career as an illustrator, but he indulged in landscape painting whenever possible, immortalizing the rolling countryside as seen from Rocky Hill in such classic pictures as *Fence Builders* (1915) and *Corn*

Harvest on the Brandywine (1936). Harvey's Run was a favorite subject—the little stream that twisted through the meadow below his front door before flowing into the Brandywine right where the British had waded across. In *Road to McVey's House* (1917) he depicted the lane that approached his home, showing big twin oaks—still there today, only one fell recently. Wyeth's passion for Revolutionary history never abated; his most whimsical commission may have been a sign for the barber in town, with the inscription, "This is the Place Where Washington & Lafayette Had a Very Close Shave." And the painting he was working on when he died suddenly in 1945 showed George Washington as *First Farmer of the Land*.

Wyeth was friends with the writer Joseph Hergesheimer, whose flashy guests of literature and screen often visited The Homestead—including Lillian Gish (who admired the children's big dollhouse), H. L. Mencken, and F. Scott and Zelda Fitzgerald. According to legend, after one high-spirited party at Wyeth's, Zelda decided her car needed a washing and drove it right into the Brandywine.[37]

On the Harry Bennett farm north of Chadds Ford, the 150th anniversary of the Battle of the Brandywine was celebrated on September 11, 1927. A crowd of seventy-five thousand watched five hundred reenactors refight the battle as airplanes and the dirigibles *TC-5* and *Los Angeles* droned overhead. Wyeth brought along his ten-year-old son, Andy, and described the scene in an ecstatic letter to his father back in Massachusetts:

> The sham battle was superbly done, in a setting unsurpassed in the world! Not far from the Birmingham Meeting House, in a rolling field and amongst the towering woodlots, between which the distances of the marvelous valley spread out for six or eight miles, the advance of the Redcoats and the retreat of the bedraggled Continentals took place. As the "company fronts" emerged from a woods, halting to fire, the rattle of musketry echoing across the hills, the moving forward, the halt to load again and then another volley from 200 rifled barrels!—was a sight and

sound that made me tingle to the point of tears. . . . Nothing has
changed in the surroundings. Perhaps a few less woods, perhaps
a few new farms in sight since that old day, but almost all the
original farms in that vicinity are still there! The worm fences are
there, and the swaybacked farm wagons. . . . Well, you can imagine Andy's reactions. The boy is lost today in drawings of cocked
hats, guns with bayonets, Hessian miter helmets![38]

Three years later, N. C. had a dream: he was standing on his painter's
scaffold overlooking the valley when suddenly the Battle of the Brandywine erupted before him. General Washington rode up and, in a Virginia
drawl, narrated the whole show—he wanted, he explained, for a modern
generation to know "what kind of a fuss was kicked up in these hills in '77."
So extraordinarily vivid and moving was this dream, N. C. pushed aside
other, more lucrative commitments and painted a big canvas of it in 1930
(see Plate 4), summarizing many years of his own personal daydreaming
about the Battle of the Brandywine and the rich resonance of Revolutionary history—not a subject dry and distant but instead crackling with life,
always ready to spill over into our contemporary world—as we have seen,
a very "Brandywine" idea, this pungent immediacy of the past.[39]

All Stirred Up About the Landscape

In 1932, fifteen-year-old Andy Wyeth began a painter's apprenticeship
in his father's studio. The nostalgic tenor of his entire artistic career would
owe much to a childhood immersed in historic Brandywine scenes, hearing constant talk of historical events. And it was right along the river
that Andy first flexed his remarkable talents in drawing and painting. A
1933 drawing of Turner's Grist Mill was his first published artwork, in
a Scribner's pamphlet promoting the new Brandywine edition of the
works of Howard Pyle. Among his earliest book illustrations were those
for Wilmer MacElree's topographic history *Around the Boundaries of
Chester County* (1934) and historical sketches for Christopher Ward's
Delaware Tercentenary Almanack (1938). Andy also did a dozen draw-

Apprentice to history. In 1932, Andrew Wyeth, age fifteen, began learning the painter's craft from his father, with an emphasis on Brandywine landscapes. Nearly seventy-five years later he was still painting such scenes.

ings for Henry Seidel Canby's *The Brandywine* (1941), earning $350. N. C. Wyeth was delighted that this last project had gotten his son "all stirred up about the landscape here, which is as it should be." All these commissions had a strongly historical-antiquarian flavor; all offered the young artist a saturation in the antimodernism that had for so long tinged the cultural thought of the region.[40]

As a boy, the sometimes sickly Andy was deliberately kept free of formal schooling by his unconventional parents, who left him to his own devices. So he played make-believe amid the dark boulders of Rocky Hill, which he was sure were pockmarked with bullet holes from the battle: "I used to search around the base of these rocks and find the bullets, too." And he wandered over the hills, visiting adjacent Kuerner's Farm almost daily. As early as 1932 he was painting there. In decades to come, this became his major artistic locus in the Brandywine area; he was free to go anywhere on Kuerner property, and no one bothered him. Few books on American art have ever been so popular as *Wyeth at Kuerners* (1976); a Kuerners scene was among many Wyeth prints on the walls of television's Partridge family; and, in secrecy there, he painted the Helga pictures, an international sensation when these nudes were finally revealed in 1986. Kuerner's has recently been called, rather sweepingly, "the most famous farm in the world."[41]

Only ruins survive today of Mother Archie's Church near Kuerner's, an octagonal Quaker meetinghouse that had later become home to a black congregation. Andrew Wyeth painted the vicinity countless times, starting with one of his few oil paintings, before he switched to tempera: *Burial at Archie's* (1933). Both *Road Cut* (1939) and the much later *Ring Road* (1985) show the church from the steep lane he liked to call "the entrance to my valley" and down which he tobogganed as a child. On a rise nearby lived his black friend Adam Johnson in a spot the painter showed from a vulture-eye view in *Soaring* (1942–1950); ornithologists had long noted the abundance of turkey vultures locally, and legend said they had first proliferated feeding on corpses after the 1777 battle. Raggedly attired, Johnson was one of many quirky local characters that Wyeth immortalized, an effort that strongly calls to mind his dad's hero, Thoreau. Like the New England writer, Andy (following his father before him) put great stock in taking rambling walks, during which he would chat with the outcasts who lived at the periphery of the village. Andy's constant revisiting of the Johnson locale—eventually painting the old church in ruins—seemingly echoes the "Former Inhabitants" section of *Walden*, where the author meditates on the history to be found about humble old cellar holes, some of them once home to former slaves.[42]

Patriarchs of the Brandywine landscape, sycamore trees with their mottled, scaly bark formed one of Andy's earliest artistic themes, rendered in a hyperrealistic, tempera-painting mode (likewise his father had made an artistic breakthrough in youth by carefully depicting the trunk of an apple tree). In 1942, N. C. praised his son's latest panel, *Summer Freshet* (see Plate 11): "A stunning and vivid thing it is too, a very intimate glimpse of a fragment of a Brandywine bank: a leaning tree trunk, great fronds of leaves hanging over the water. . . . For two weeks Andy has been perched on a tall stool in the middle of the stream." That was near today's Brandywine River Museum of Art, where the huge sycamore is still to be seen, leaning over the rushing creek.[43]

Sycamores live for centuries. One that grows beside Lafayette's Headquarters was already enormous when the historian Lossing sketched it in 1848; today it measures an extraordinary twenty-three feet around and 136 feet in magnificent spread. N. C. showed it bursting forth in springtime in *Buttonwood Farm* (1919), and later it became the centerpiece of Andrew Wyeth's iconic *Pennsylvania Landscape* (1942), with the Brandywine wending by just beyond—instead of the busy highway that actually lies there. "I think of it as the whole Pennsylvania landscape in one picture," he later said, "with that marvelous buttonwood tree in the middle. . . . The mystery of that nearly five-hundred-year-old tree." (Still today, Jamie Wyeth is in awe of this sycamore, "A tree that heard the battle.") Andrew Wyeth first gained wide public notice with one of these sycamore paintings, *The Hunter* (now in the Toledo Museum), an autumnal scene that appeared on the cover of the *Saturday Evening Post* in October 1943.[44]

From Chris to Andrew

The 1777 battle had a "huge impact" on young Andrew, says James Duff, for thirty-nine years the director of the Brandywine River Museum of Art. "He just loved history; in fact, he literally grew up on the battlefield. Those vestiges of the eighteenth century were all around him and just fascinated him," Duff told me. "He painted those vestiges. He didn't paint history—but its *remnants*." Jamie Wyeth agrees: "My father felt such a strong connection to that past, probably even more than *his* father." The Revolutionary War haunted him in particular: "He was fascinated; he could never read enough about it."

Wyeth's passion for Brandywine history received a great boost from N. C.'s eccentric friend, Christian Sanderson, whose packrat-style museum remains an attraction in Chadds Ford to this day. Sanderson moved to the village in 1906 to teach school, renting Washington's Headquarters as his home, which he shared with his mother. Through his irrepressible habits of artifact collecting and lecturing, Chris helped draw renewed public attention to the battlefield. N. C. (who considered Sanderson a modern-day Ichabod Crane) exhibited some of his own and Sanderson's battlefield relics at Birmingham Meeting in September 1915, when six thousand people gathered for the dedication of historical plaques around the battlefield, installed by the new Pennsylvania Historical Commission and the Chester County Historical Society. The French ambassador spoke—Lafayette's republic was then fighting for its life—and President Woodrow Wilson sent a message saying "how thoroughly worthwhile it seems to me to do things of this sort." N. C. Wyeth was awed by the dark bloodstains he was shown on the oaken floor of the meetinghouse, where the operating table had stood.[45]

Although for a time he moved away from Chadds Ford, Sanderson always intended that "Lover of the Brandywine" be carved on his tombstone in testament to his deep affection. In the 1930s, he gave weekly historical talks over the radio in Wilmington. Eventually renewing his ties to Chadds Ford, Chris befriended Andrew, whom he gruffly called "boy"; they worked together on the 1936 *Map of Historical Chester County*, for which Andrew supplied thumbnail sketches of local scenes and landmarks. In 1937, N. C. Wyeth arranged to have the destitute former teacher occupy part of the house that is now the Sanderson Museum, telling the landlord that if Chris couldn't pay the rent, "I will; I just want him back here in Chadds Ford."

That same year, Andrew painted a portrait of "Sandy," among the first for the budding artist. Pointing the way toward the tenor of Andy's whole future career, it strips the Brandywine valley of all modern intrusions—although it does not yet show the sepia tones of Wyeth's maturity; the vibrant colors of this fascinating early work exactly recall N. C.'s palette. Sanderson holds a big map of Chester County, pointing out historical sites; behind him spreads the valley from Washington's Headquarters to the Brandywine and beyond, and it is pointedly shown in its colonial condition. The portrait is a very literal evocation of Sanderson's antiquarian mindset—and young Andrew's, too.

In 1940 Sanderson went "hunting scenery" with Andrew, who was about to illustrate Canby's *The Brandywine*, and the older man helpfully read over the manuscript for the author. Sanderson's aged mother died at their home three years later, a scene that Andrew depicted in a haunting picture, *Christmas Morning*, her body merging with the wintry Brandywine landscape. The "Brandywine Museum" grew with the years, overflowing throughout the house ("Chris hoarded before hoarding was cool," a modern visitor quips). In 1959 he opened the front rooms to the public, and after his death in 1966, Andrew Wyeth assured the permanence of the Christian Sanderson Museum. After immersing himself in this curious place that reveals so much about the antimodern origins of Wyeth's thinking, one recent guest said he learned more about the famous painter here than by touring his actual studio.[46]

Nourished by the kindred passions of N. C. Wyeth and Chris Sanderson, Andrew Wyeth's own love for the remains of the Revolutionary past never dimmed. He explained his 1980 depiction of an old military jacket, *French Connection*, by saying, "The painting is all about my strong feelings for the American Revolutionary War, the aura of which surrounds me here and which I feel from my constant wandering around these hills in the Brandywine Valley." In his studio, opened to the public after his death, stand rows of toy soldiers, many of them in Revolutionary garb—like his father's friend F. Scott Fitzgerald, he collected these avidly.

N. C. Wyeth's oil paintings are vibrant with color and often thick with impasto. As if in reaction, his son eventually chose to paint thinly,

Shrine to the Brandywine. Andrew Wyeth's portrait of Christian Sanderson (1937) presides over the varied antiquarian collections of the Sanderson Museum. Tommy Thompson, left, began the museum after Chris died in 1966.

in egg tempera, and with severely muted color. (Devotees of his art insist that there is much color there, but the overall impression is surely closer to tonalism, what was traditionally called grisaille.) N. C. deplored this brownish palette and urged the fledgling artist to change course—as Jamie Wyeth recalls today, "N. C. was first appalled and thought his son wouldn't support himself." Perhaps the limitation of color heightens the historical sense, the feeling that things are happening in a bygone time—much as Hollywood occasionally reverted to sepia for moments of historical suggestiveness once color movies took hold in exactly this era (Andrew enjoyed films and kept a motion-picture projector right at hand in his studio). In an interview, Wyeth linked his brown motif to the tragic fate of Washington's army after the Battle of the Brandywine. Comparing Chadds Ford to Maine as a subject for the painter, he said, "The Brandywine's sort of ugly, looking like what George Washington must have felt when he camped at Valley Forge. I like the difference between New England and this tough place."[47]

Catching the Heart of America

An astonishingly productive career ended abruptly when N. C. Wyeth (along with young grandson Newell) was killed in a car accident. By some freak chance, his station wagon was struck by a train as he was crossing the Central Railroad tracks at Kuerner's Farm in October 1945, forty-three years to the day after he had first arrived in Wilmington. To the last, his mindset was antiquarian: just before reaching the tracks, he pulled the car to the side of the road in the stillness of the morning to show Newell how farmers were husking corn, a vanishing folkway. The laborers heard him tell the boy, "You won't see this again. Remember this."[48]

"When he died," Andrew recalled, "I had this terrific urge to prove that what he had started in me was not in vain—to really do something serious. . . . Fortunately, I had always had this great emotion toward the landscape and so, with his death, I seemed to—well—the landscape took on a meaning—the quality of him."[49]

As we have seen, N. C. had been an illustrator with a longing to turn his attentions entirely to painting the Brandywine landscape as "true American Art." Andrew took up the latter cause entirely, as if to finish his father's heartfelt project. He would never move away from his ancestral ground, never abandon the scenes of his childhood. Although he was already praised as an artist in his own right, doubtless he expected to struggle financially. But by a turn of fate, these humble scenes were about to help make him the most famous American painter in the world.

As Jamie Wyeth told me, "It was quite a daring thing to do at the time. He consciously decided to focus on this little valley. He barely traveled. His whole world revolved around this small area. It all relates back to the battle of the Brandywine and Washington. The fact that he could hold in his hands a bowl associated with Washington—all that just thrilled him."

"That ominous child," Joseph Hergesheimer had called Andy during his frequent visits to The Homestead. In fact the two men turned out to be kindred spirits, a generation apart. Published when Andy was nine, *From an Old House* constantly refers to Hergesheimer's primitivistic attachment to the soil: to "the mood, the earth, of the Dower House," that bulwark against "all the inroads of the doubtful present, and the positively threatening future," with its "stone foundations set so deeply in the earth"; his role as homeowner that makes him "a proprietor in the earth of Pennsylvania." Walking up a hill, "I stamped a foot into the earth," Hergesheimer writes—and instantly discovers a profound connection with "my own place. This slope, the weeds, the earth, were mine; it was my ground." Andrew Wyeth, with his brown palette, would come to share this preoccupation with the color of bare earth and almost seems to illustrate Hergesheimer in his painting *Trodden Weed* (1951), in which the artist himself strides across a brown Chadds Ford slope wearing old costume boots of Howard Pyle's.[50]

By its habit of looking back, Wyeth's work struck a nerve: within a decade of his father's death, Andrew had paintings on display in the White House. *Roasted Chestnuts*, set along Concord Pike east of Chadds Ford, was a special favorite of President Eisenhower's, who famously called Wyeth's art—in sharp contrast to modernism—"what America likes." John F. Kennedy invited Wyeth to his inaugural, but the artist started a picture of the Barns-Brinton House the day he was supposed to leave and telephoned Washington to say he couldn't attend—the art always came first, even if that meant snubbing the leader of the free world. "I'm glad you worked on that picture when you did," Kennedy later told him upon seeing *Tenant Farmer*. "The results were worth it."[51]

In 1963, Wyeth made the cover of *Time* magazine, and JFK honored him with the Presidential Medal of Freedom, the country's highest civilian honor. No artist had ever received it before. The Chadds Ford painter was said to command the highest prices of any artist on the planet, except for Picasso.

How to explain his meteoric ascent? For one thing, the generation of successful Americans who began patronizing "The Rich Man's Norman

Rockwell" in droves had, like Ike, typically grown up in a rural United States, only to see it buried under interstate highways and housing tracts; Wyeth brought back the vanished world of their youth. Nostalgia for bygone days proved a powerful force in the modernizing, superpower America of the 1950s—especially when it paid subtle homage to the Revolutionary era, even as the United States nobly sought to export democracy to the world. Wyeth, who had never traveled abroad, felt a high calling as a leading exponent of American culture, sitting in front of his blazing colonial fireplace with a reporter in 1963 and exclaiming, "This country has the greatest opportunity it has ever had to achieve a dominant position in the arts."[52]

As he suddenly became very wealthy, Andrew and his wife, Betsy—no less avid an historian—settled right on the edge of Brandywine Creek when they bought Brinton's Mill in 1958. His home for the rest of his life, it appears in many of his paintings, including that very popular one of a dozing dog called *Night Sleeper* (1979). Standing alone amid a wide meadow, the stone gristmill and sawmill had been built early in the eighteenth century, or maybe even before that; then Amos Brinton added the house around 1778. As Brinton's Ford, this spot was guarded by General Sullivan on September 11; Andrew's late watercolor painting called *Plundered* (1996) shows British troops—looking not a little like his toy soldiers—whitening their stockings with wheat powder after the battle. In the nineteenth century the locale was popular with tent-camping parties. A covered bridge of 1854 burned the year before the Wyeths bought the property.

N. C. Wyeth had often painted there, for example showing the hills to the west in *Brandywine Meadows* of around 1918. Andy grew up skating on adjacent Hoffman's Slough, and he painted a bird's-eye view of that watery scene in 1947. The whole vicinity was historic: southeast, on a hillside above Creek Road, was Roundelay, the Caleb Brinton House, famous for showing a scar in its gable from a British cannonball shot. Up Brinton's Bridge Road was the Edward Brinton House (1726), later the childhood home of William Darlington. Wyeth would paint a view from the knoll above Brinton's Mill in *Battleground* (1981), explaining,

"This is precisely where Henry Knox fought at the Battle of Brandy-wine."[53]

Living on the creek banks proved a thrill for Wyeth: "There were floods in the night, the sounds of branches breaking, trees going over—and silence as the dam's waterfall sank beneath the high water," a biographer says. "Washington once caught a Tory putting ground glass in the troops' flour at the mill," Wyeth assured a reporter following a tour of the snowy property in the early 1960s. "They shot him over there on the other side of the creek." Mary Landa, who came to work for the Wyeths as collections manager in 1979, told me how Andrew would stand in the doorway listening to the water gushing over the dam and marvel, "Listen—that's the same sound that George Washington heard."[54]

At considerable cost, Brinton's Mill provided an opportunity for tangible restoration of the colonial era: the place was badly run down when they bought it, with half-starved coon dogs chained within its crumbling walls. Showing profound reverence for bygone days, Andrew and Betsy went all out, rebuilding whole dams on the Brandywine, hauling fifteen truckloads of tires out of the millrace, reconstructing the sluice gate, then making the milling apparatus work again—though never expecting to make a dime at grinding grain. Assistants recreated the undershot waterwheel from scratch—lovingly joining it without a single nail—spending four hundred hours on the shaft alone, carved from the trunk of a 260-year-old white oak tree.

Rather than replaster crumbling walls inside the home, imprinted with an early owner's signature and cat footprints, the Wyeths applied a DuPont chemical fixative to keep them up. By the 1980s, after decades of exhaustive and painstaking work, the place struck a visiting academic as an elaborate pastiche assembled from fragments of the past. The garage, for example, was a replica of an old Quaker meetinghouse horse shed; inside the home was a new room imitating one at George Washington's Headquarters—"this makes the room a copy of a copy," the visitor sniffed, since the headquarters had been re-created as a public museum following its 1931 fire.[55]

Andrew Wyeth's fame grew and grew, and with it the reputation of his beloved Brandywine, which seemed the very distillation of Early Americanness for those hungry for a return to patriotic roots. In 1970 he became the first living artist to have an exhibition at the White House. He was feted before a posh crowd in the East Room by President Nixon, who said, "As I ask you to drink to his health tonight, I think we can truly say that Andrew Wyeth, in his paintings, has caught the heart of America, and certainly tonight, the heart of America belongs to him."

Wyeth responded by looking around him at the framed pictures from what he called "the hills of the Brandywine Valley":

> There have lived, and still live, those people who have believed in me enough to pose for long hours and who have let me enter their lives, their houses and barns, their fields and woods . . . without hurry. I wish I could have brought all of them here with me tonight. What is here are a few glimpses of these people, their land, hanging on the panels in the East Room.[56]

Of course Wyeth never tired of painting the Brandywine countryside. The pattern of summers in Maine, winters at Chadds Ford continued until he died in his sleep at the Mill one cold January night in 2009. He was ninety-one. In fact, in his later years he veered back toward the specific subjects he had begun his career with: the creek with its shoals, the flood-gnarled sycamore trees that guard its banks. His granddaughter Victoria spent much time with him during this autumnal phase and tells me, "The Battle of the Brandywine really featured in his imagination. He's not just this 'realist'—his is a reality that reflects memories of times long ago. Andy would nap in the afternoon, and he would tell me about dreams he'd had—'I was a soldier in the battle.'" He would point out ancient buttonwoods to her and exclaim, "This tree once had British troops lying bloodied against it! Think what it's experienced and what it's seen!"

Over the decades he advised other artists to make the Brandywine their recurrent subject, including a young filmmaker he dissuaded from going to Hollywood, painter and Brandywine River Museum of Art founder "Frolic" Weymouth, and Wyeth's own son Jamie. The latter's first extensive body of work depicted farm scenes at the Ball place across the creek from today's museum. Going home, Jamie would walk down the railroad tracks along the edge of the watercourse.

Today, both Weymouth (fourth-great-grandson of Eleuthère Irénée du Pont) and Jamie Wyeth (married to a du Pont) own neighboring estates on the creek, on either side of the Delaware line. They live the old pastoral ideal on a large scale: Jamie Wyeth's driveway is a mile and a half long and partly paved with millstones, Weymouth's two miles, kept gravel for his frequent carriage rides. These painters are superstars of the traditional-art cultural scene in the Brandywine Valley and beyond.[57]

Jamie Wyeth described to me his boyhood at The Mill: "I lived completely on the river. I went inner-tubing, I canoed, I swam. And of course I started drawing and painting very early." The history of the area made a deep impression; he recalls being taken into Lafayette's Headquarters by his father and Christian Sanderson at about age eight: "Sanderson told wonderful anecdotes and made it very, very real, and so immediate—and it finally influenced my work, too."

"My farm is partly in Delaware, partly in Pennsylvania," Jamie Wyeth explains. "There's a confluence of not only history—the Indians, the battle—but also industry, and archaeology, all centered right here. So it's fascinating." Jet travel being so easy nowadays, "There is all the more reason to focus on *this area*. I'm not interested in drawing a tree, but a tree that's been here 100 years, that does interest me. The more you know about the background," he says, the more meaningful the art becomes. This thoroughgoing historical sense also typified his father, for whom, Jamie says, the 1777 battle "was incredibly important. He brought it right up to the contemporary. It was a very strong thing in his work; in all his work it was a touchstone. That largely came from *his* father, and from Howard Pyle, who was such an historian, who insisted on accuracy. And I still carry it on; I am still cognizant of the history around here."

By the time of his death, Andrew Wyeth's tremendous fame had long since made Chadds Ford one of the most beloved small places in

America. As everyone surely knows, for plein air painters and enthusiasts of realism in art, the village became a kind of mecca, a cultural critic of the 1980s noting (with some skepticism) "the endless flow of paintings from the brushes of 'Sunday painters' and of photographs from the cameras of Wyeth-stalking tourists." Desperate for privacy, the artist posted a sign on his studio door: "I AM WORKING SO PLEASE DO NOT DISTURB. I do not sign autographs."

A movement had been spawned: a recent book showcases the current efforts of no fewer than *100 Artists of the Brandywine,* including some ardent Wyeth devotees who have refitted old stone houses into studios where they paint rural-themed pictures that stress "change and decay . . . wood silvering with age, grasses drying and shadows lengthening." So popular are such productions, some of the artists worry that they are participating in an "art-as-commodity art scene." Jamie Wyeth observes that for many would-be painters today, "The 'Brandywine Tradition' is an intimidating label. And then there is an army of copyists who all try to follow the same thing, and that doesn't work." Future art in the region will have to come to terms with the titanic Wyeth legacy, it seems, and somehow find ways of deepening the tradition or moving beyond it.[58]

Brief Encounter

A few years ago, a historian who happened to have brake trouble ended up spotting the elderly Andrew Wyeth at Hank's Restaurant in Chadds Ford, the artist's longtime haunt. He was accompanied by Helga, once his model and now his nurse. For an admirer, it seemed a last chance to lay eyes on an artist-celebrity—and how many more of these will there ever be, men who, like Phidias to the Greeks or Corot to the French, belonged to an entire, grateful nation?

> *April 14, 2005.* With an imperious hand held continually in air and waving, Helga summons a tardy waitress. A Styrofoam clamshell to go, and her drink. Then she rises, an awkward assemblage of items in her rough hands—sky-blue purse matching

her sky-blue, outmoded jacket. So they walk to the cash register. Andrew Wyeth is very old—that is my first thought. Robust and ambulatory, but unsteady on his feet. He wears a brownish tweed jacket. His face is deeply lined, a landscape of furrows and fissures, but softer and more tender than I had been led to expect, and tanned. He radiates kindness and warmth and a quickness-to-smile, as he does at the waitresses who know him, waving to them and grinning, his face crinkling and creasing all the more. He seems wobbly, shrunk under his jacket, as he embraces a woman I take to be the owner— who says to Helga, 'Thanks for bringing him in.' He pays at the register with a wad of one-dollar bills. Think of all the brushes those hands have held! Once they painted *Christina's World*. Then Helga leads him out, infinitely solicitous, making sure he is stable—he concentrates on where he is going and lifts his feet with the deliberation of the old and lame. Other than the waitresses, nobody seemed to recognize him.

Here—entirely transformed by time—was N. C.'s offbeat little boy, Hergesheimer's "ominous child." Here was the classic artist-craftsman who formed his sensibilities in a now-forever-lost, genuinely rural Brandywine Valley. Here was a talent nurtured by his own father, America's greatest illustrator—himself trained by the immortal Howard Pyle. Something of the nineteenth century seemed to linger around Andrew Wyeth, born a century to the day after Thoreau and the inheritor of so many old ways of seeing: of faith in painting as a means of exploring the infinite subtleties of nature, of reverential respect for objects and places that link us back to the Revolutionary age.

Deliberately backward-looking, he seemed to hold the last links of the chain—one recalls Hergesheimer's conviction that "the tradition, the feeling, the affection, must be carried in an unextinguished spark." After Wyeth, can the romantic tradition really continue on into the twenty-first century? Or does it finally fall lifeless to earth in the hands of derivative followers with no actual, lived experience of authentic rural folkways, who live on comfortable suburban cul-de-sacs and unintentionally but unmistakably turn it all into caricature?[59]

Awed by a brief encounter, the historian drove up the creek a half-hour later, dandelions and forsythia painting the roadsides a shrill yellow that Wyeth's muted palette studiously ignores. Buttercups grew on the steep bank at the Chad house, by a stone wall. Grass was green in riparian meadows, and the low woods, not yet leafed, were carpeted with celandine. Idyllic as our American Arcadia seemed that day, its paradoxes were never far from view: fat lily pads tipped up in the slough by the road; horses walked circles around a paddock pond; and huge new houses were rising on Brandywine hillsides in scars of up-churned dirt.

Appendix

❧❧

Bridges of the Brandywine

Much Brandywine history, including the great 1777 battle, has centered on fords and bridges. But with frequent changes in name, these places are often confusing to historian and tourist alike. This is a complete list, in geographical order, of bridges from near West Chester (East Branch of the Brandywine) down to the river's mouth at Wilmington. To supplement references throughout this book, places of nearby interest are noted by compass direction. Ones open to the public are shown thus: *Brandywine River Museum of Art. Many of the bridges are, unfortunately, merely utilitarian modern replacements of fine old covered bridges.

Cope's Bridge (W. Strasburg Rd.) Picturesque 1807 stone bridge of three arches on the historic Old Lancaster Road west from Philadelphia, 152 feet long, restored 2011. Previously Taylor's Ford. S: Deborah's Rock, Abiah Taylor House

Stroud Preserve Bridge (N. Creek Rd.) Pedestrian bridge to 571-acre *Stroud Preserve of Natural Lands Trust. S: wooded Bowers Island; site of Bowers Paper Mill

Jefferis's Bridge (Allerton Rd.) Covered bridge (1833) was burned by an arsonist in 1953 and replaced with the current bridge, an old iron trestle originally on Doe Run. The main body of the British army,

Twin spans. The original, metal-truss Baltimore and Ohio Railroad Bridge (1885) and its huge, masonry-arch replacement (1910) cross the Brandywine downstream from Augustine paper mills. Foreground: Wilmington's Brandywine Park. Photo ca. 1940.

including Cornwallis and Howe, crossed here at undefended Jefferis's Ford in the famous flanking maneuver, September 11, 1777. E: Site of Sconneltown on the Redcoat line of march, at today's Birmingham Road and Sconneltown Road

Shaw's Bridge (S. Bridge Rd.) The southernmost road crossing of the East Branch, right above the Forks. Modern 1952 span replacing 1862 covered bridge. As Buffington's Ford, guarded by half of Col. Hazen's troops on September 11, 1777. In the mid-nineteenth century called, confusingly, Brinton's Ford. S: *Shaw's Bridge Park

Lenape Bridge (Lenape Rd.) Long 1912 stone viaduct of seven arches connecting to a modern highway bridge; replacing Sager's Bridge of 1856; there was also a previous span. As Wistar's Ford, guarded by half of Col. Hazen's troops on September 11, 1777; later called Shunk's Ford. N: *Brandywine Picnic Park. S: Dungeon Bottom, a swamp

Painter's Bridge (W. Street Rd., at Pocopson) Characterless modern replacement of long 1857 covered bridge. As Jones's Ford, guarded by a Delaware regiment, September 11, 1777. S: Pocopson Creek, Hoffman's Slough and much-painted "Wyeth Country." E: Birmingham Meeting; heart of the *battlefield

Site of Brinton's Bridge (Brinton's Bridge Rd., on private estate of Andrew and Betsy Wyeth) As Brinton's Ford, guarded by Gen. Sullivan's troops, 1777. Covered bridge of 1854 burned 1957. Andrew Wyeth lived here at restored Brinton Mill for half a century.

U.S. 1 Bridge at Chadds Ford Busy modern highway bridge replaces a series of older bridges (said to have been built 1828, 1860, 1921, and 1938). In the nineteenth century, these were covered bridges and stood a little ways downstream. A crucial river crossing since the Great Road of colonial times; later part of the first paved Maine-to-Florida route. N: dam marks the approximate site of Chads's Ford, guarded by Wayne's Division and Procter's Artillery and scene of fierce fighting, September 11, 1777; pedestrian *boardwalk through a swamp—the "morass" of 1777 accounts. E: Chadds Ford, including *Sanderson Museum, *Chadds Ford Historical Society and John Chads House, and *Brandywine Battlefield Park

Penn Central Railroad Bridge (abandoned) First railroad span (Philadelphia and Baltimore Central Railroad) built here in 1859, rebuilt 1869 and later. U.S. Geological Survey has maintained a stream-gaging station since 1911. About here was Chads's Lower Ford, where British soldiers waded across, 1777. NE: *Brandywine River Museum of Art, formerly Hoffman's Mill (1864). SE: Harvey's Run, Rocky Hill, *studios of N. C. Wyeth and Andrew Wyeth

Pyle's Bridge (Creek Rd.) Bulky concrete replacement (1925 datestone) of a two-sectioned covered bridge/viaduct, or Twin Bridges (1855). Downstream, around the bend, was Pyle's Ford, said to have seen Washington's Army cross going eastward in 1777 in its race to seize the fords. Guarded on day of battle by Pennsylvania Militia and

Col. Eyre's cannon. S: Haskell Estate at Cossart, Great Bend, Point Lookout

Here we enter Delaware at the circular border:

Smith's Bridge (Smith's Bridge Rd.) Picturesque, 145-foot covered bridge, a 2002 reconstruction of original 1839 Burr arched-truss (copying a Lewis Wernwag design) that burned in 1961. Earlier bridges: 1816, washed away 1822; replacement washed away 1828. N: No. 14 Bound Stone of Delaware circular border. S: Granogue estate, "Chateau Country." E: Beaver Valley Rock Shelter. Eleven hundred acres on the east bank became, in 2013, Woodlawn Tract of *First State National Monument

Thompson's Bridge (Thompson's Bridge Rd., Del. 92) 1990s replacement of a long, slender covered bridge (sources say 1834, rebuilt 1850) that was replaced with a concrete span in 1935. N: Former Hollingsworth's Ford. S: *Brandywine Creek State Park, where a footbridge over Rocky Run on the east bank marks the geological boundary between Wissahickon schist and Wilmington Complex gneiss (blue rock). Premier examples of old Piedmont tulip-tree forests. The dirt road down to Rockland is one of the last unpaved stretches in northern Delaware.

Rockland Bridge (Rockland Rd.) Historic Rockland village was famous for papermaking, beloved of artists. Today's concrete road bridge (1934) replaced a covered span (1818, rebuilt by Louis Wernwag 1823, rebuilt again 1839), which in turn supplanted colonial Kirk's Ford. E: Jessup and Moore paper mill, now reused as condominiums. Uphill, Mount Lebanon Church (1834). N: Rockland Dam, first built 1794 and showing intricate construction, now washing away. Nearby stands a giant sycamore growing atop a boulder, already famous a hundred years ago. Kirk's Mill (1803) was razed a few decades back. N: *Brandywine Creek State Park. W: *Winterthur Museum, Garden, and Library

Wilmington & Northern Rockland Branch Railroad Bridge (abandoned) Apparently built after 1885 to connect to the Wilmington & Northern Railroad of 1869, which still operates along the west bank

Iron Bridge, Hagley (*Hagley Museum and Library) 1877 truss on stone piers, connecting two parts of the DuPont powder works properties; replaced an earlier span. NW: *Eleutherian Mills. SE: scenic rapids below Hagley Dam

Tyler McConnell Bridge (Powder Mill Rd., Del. 141) Access to fast-growing DuPont Experimental Station (east bank) was facilitated by this 1952 bridge with some of the first hammerhead-shaped concrete piers in the United States. N: *Hagley Museum visitor center, untouched Holly Island. S: *Breck's Mill, Walker's Mill

Rising Sun Bridge (New Bridge Rd.) This vicinity was once called Henry Clay Factory. The 123-foot, riveted Pratt through-truss span (1928) rests on abutments from an 1883 predecessor—one of the highest and prettiest of the valley's now-lost covered bridges. The roadway is supported by a stone arch (c. 1830) that once crossed a millrace. NE: DuPont Experimental Station, with some ruins of Lower Yards powder mills. SE: *Rockford Park and *Rockford Tower (1899) with observation platform overlooking the valley; Will's Rock on the creek's craggiest slope

Bancroft Mills Bridges (two iron trusses, both abandoned) Once the largest cotton dyeing and finishing plant in the world, with 250-foot yellow-brick smokestack (1911); now condominiums. E: *Alapocas Run State Park, former Brandywine Granite Quarry. W: *Delaware Art Museum. S: Site of historic early papermaking at Gilpin's Mill dam along Mill Rd., the area formerly called Kentmere or Riddle Banks and popular for nineteenth-century recreation

Augustine Cut-Off Bridge (Augustine Rd.) 1980 highway bridge replicating 1885 pin-connected Pratt-type deck-truss bridge, nearly 1,000 feet long and 110 feet high, that carried the Baltimore and Ohio Railroad; converted to automobile use 1920. Piers of blue rock from Brandywine Granite Quarry. N: Augustine Mills (formerly Jessup and Moore) for papermaking, now condominiums impinging on the view

CSX Bridge One of the nation's great masonry bridges. Immense stone-and-concrete structure (1910) for Baltimore and Ohio Railroad; 650

feet long, 115 feet high; seven arches in all, three of them of 100-foot span

Wire Bridge Little swinging span (1910, restored 1975) gave workers access to Augustine Mills. Popular with Sunday strollers, it originally stood a hundred feet upstream until displaced by CSX Bridge. S: *Brandywine Park; Rattlesnake Run draining Trolley Square; Third or City Dam serving Wilmington's waterworks

I-95 Bridge Steel superstructure on mammoth, leg-like concrete piers, finished 1967; 1,870 feet long

Van Buren Street Bridge 1997 rebuilding of 1906 original, 353-foot bridge of eight arches; early example of reinforced-concrete construction. Doubled as an aqueduct, holding a pipe that carried Brandywine water from Porter Reservoir on Concord Pike to the Wilmington filter station. S: faint line of rocks crossing the creek remains from Second Dam at site of Old Barley Mill (west bank), scene of the first seventeenth-century milling on the Brandywine (Stidham Swedish mill), rebuilt 1720s; a millstone stands as a "lone relic"

Washington Memorial Bridge (N. Washington St.) Handsome civic adornment, the 720-foot structure has five reinforced-concrete arches, the longest of 250-foot span, herculean when seen from below. Dedicated on Memorial Day 1922, honoring World War I and George Washington at the Brandywine battlefield; a parade of 1,200 girls strewed flowers on the water. W: *Wilmington and Brandywine Cemetery (1843); historic downtown Wilmington. SE: First Dam, foot of West Street; there were once two millraces on either side of the creek from here down to Market Street. Old First Presbyterian Church (1740, moved here 1918). NE: Site of Edward Tatnall's Wawaset Nursery. N: Dog's Head Rock with rare 1820s graffiti

North Market Street Bridge Single span (150 feet) of steel disguised by concrete, built for automobiles in 1928. This historic crossing carried the main north–south road in colonial America. The first bridge here went up in 1764. Its replacement was a pioneering chain-link suspension span (1810, washed away 1822), itself followed by two covered bridges (1822, Lewis Wernwag, washed away 1839; its successor, demolished 1887), then a wrought-iron Pratt through truss (demolished 1928). N: historic Brandywine Village. E: Site of America's most famous Federal era mills, now gone; city waterworks. W: scene of 1854 powder wagon explosion by "Bishopstead" estate, foot of Orange St.

Pine Street Bridge 1920s. S: *Kirkwood Park; on the east bank was historic Thatcher's Island, now gone. SW: Site of colonial Stidham House, riverbank at Clifford Brown Walk south of 14th St.

Northeast Boulevard Bridge (U.S. 13) 1932, replacing a mid-nineteenth-century bridge at 11th Street; connected to Gov. Printz Blvd., a suburban highway finished 1937. S: Site of the Orchards, a yacht mooring and shantytown on the east bank at former Delaware Terra Cotta Works

Amtrak Bridge Swing bridge (1903) carries the Eastern Seaboard's main north–south commuter railroad line. The first railroad crossing of the Brandywine was here, as the Philadelphia, Wilmington and Baltimore Railroad Bridge (1837). NE: this bank was Timber Island in earliest times; there was a Swedish settlement nearby, Bochten ("the bend"), and a bluff called Third Hook. S: site of Jackson and Sharp Delaware Car Works—formerly a stream, Black Cat Kill. W: *Old Swedes Church. S: *Fort Christina, *Kalmar Nyckel shipyard, junction of Brandywine and Christina rivers

Notes

❧ ❧

Preface. American Arcadia

1. Goodheart, "History's Backyard."

2. Weslager, *Dutch Explorers*, 225–30. Vincent, *History*, 1:263. Dunlap, *Place-Names*, 19–21, says the first "Brandywine" reference comes in 1665: "A Creeke commonly called Brandywine Kill."

3. West Chester *Daily Local News*, November 2, 1911. Wilmington *Journal Every Evening*, May 23, 1944. Smith, *History of Delaware County*, 274. In past generations, "creek" was typically pronounced "crick." In England, *creek* refers only to the *mouth* of a river—the part of our American waterways that seventeenth-century explorers of the Delaware Valley first observed and named. Soon, by extension, "creek" in America came to refer to the whole tributary.

4. Read, *Paul Redding*, 9–10.

5. Holmes, *Pages*, 51.

6. *Sesqui-Centennial Gathering*. Canby, *Age of Confidence*, 198.

7. Lidz, *Du Ponts*, 23. Taylor, *Story of Kennett*, iv. West Chester *Daily Local News*, August 7, 1909.

8. Clio, "Written at the Retreat."

9. Futhey and Cope, *Chester County*, 246.

10. Pitz, *Brandywine Tradition*, 83.

11. Pyle, "Old-Time Life," 181.

12. Ackroyd, *Thames*, 8–9.

13. Lippard, *Blanche*, 181.

14. Hayes, Diary, January 16, 1903. Hayes, *Brandywine Days*, 120–121. Hergesheimer, *Old House*, 35–37. Corn, *Wyeth*, 60.

15. Ackroyd, *Thames*, 346.

16. West Chester *Daily Local News*, May 20, 1889.

17. Hergesheimer, *Old House*, 28–29.

18. Lemon, *Best Poor Man's Country*, xiii. Marquis James, *Alfred I. du Pont*, 286. Darlington, *Address . . . Horticultural Society*.

19. Klein, *Gardens*, 8. Quimby, "Brandywine Valley Estates."

20. Goldsmith, *Deserted Village*, 21–22.

21. De Mare, *Time on the Thames*, 15.

22. Lemon, *Best Poor Man's Country*, xiii.

23. Connelley, *Doniphan's*, 144–45. Hoch, *Lincoln Trail*, 26–27.

1. Fish Creek in New Sweden

1. Williams, *Man and Nature*, 12.

2. The overhang was long called Wolf Rock; legend says that American soldiers hid loot there when fleeing after the battle. Brooks, "Beaver Valley."

3. Williams, *Man and Nature*, 19.

4. Myers, *Narratives*, 21, 25.

5. Myers, *Narratives*, 48.

6. Myers, *Narratives*, 28, 60–63, 72, 87.

7. Myers, *Narratives*, 96, 72, 103.

8. Maynard, *Buildings of Delaware*, 5–7, 88. Williams, *Man and Nature*, 42.

9. Myers, *Narratives*, 69.

10. Johnson, *Swedes*, 217. Myers, *Narratives*, 122, 127.

11. Myers, *Narratives*, 140–42, 164, 173–75. Vincent, *History*, 1:248–51.

12. Dunlap, *Place-Names*, 51.

13. James and Jameson, *Journal*, 108–9.

14. http://homepages.rootsweb.ancestry.com/~tstiddem/Pages/who.html.   Dates vary from 1671 to 1687 for the Stidham mill. Fox, *Journal*, 2:177.

2. Pride of Penn's Woods

1. Horle, *Papers*, 2:455.

2. Wiley, *Delaware County*, 47.

3. Weslager, *Red Men*. Weslager, *Delaware Indians*. *West Chester, Past and Present*, appendix.

4. Myers, *Narratives*, 228–29. Gurney, *Journey*, 93. Williams, *Man and Nature*, 65–66. Beaver: West Chester *Daily Local News*, January 14, 1878. Darlington, *Address . . . Cabinet of Natural Science*.

5. www.nativetreesociety.org. I counted narrow rings on a white oak that was cut down on the Winterthur lawn in August 1997. Three counts yielded ages of between 310 and 340 years.

6. Myers, *Narratives*, 192, 225–26.

7. Taylor, *Story of Kennett*, 3. Reed, *In Memoriam*.

8. West Chester *Daily Local News*, April 23, 1895.

9. Smith, *History of Delaware County*, 246.

10. McWilliams, *Revolution*, 177–78.

11. Stetson, "1704 House," 14–15.

12. Jordan, *Colonial and Revolutionary Families*, 1:425–27.

13. Richie, *Stone Houses*, 22.

14. Hergesheimer, *Old House*, 20–22, 34, 58, 68.

15. *Pennsylvania Gazette*, April 25, 1765.

16. Obama, *Presidential Proclamation*.

17. Kalm, *Travels*, 1:83. Craig, *1693 Census*.

18. Abbott, *Pyle*, 153. Maynard, *Buildings of Delaware*, 88–90.

19. Pyle, "Old-Time Life," 183.

20. Obama, *Presidential Proclamation*.

21. Williams, *Man and Nature*, 100–101.

22. Scharf, *Delaware*, 2:632.

23. Williams, *Man and Nature*, 105.

24. Myers, *Narratives*, 265.

25. Williams, *Man and Nature*, 107–8. Smith, *History of Delaware County*, 237.

26. McGuire, *Philadelphia Campaign*, 2–3.

27. Danson, *Drawing the Line*, 4.

28. Rush, *Medical Inquiries*, 1:92.

29. Danson, *Drawing the Line*, 163–64, 184, 204.

3. A River Red with Blood

1. McGuire, *Brandywine Battlefield Park*. McGuire tells me that three battles vie for the title of "largest": Brandywine, Long Island, and Monmouth.

2. Irving, *Washington*, 3:249. Trevelyan, *American Revolution*, 4:227.

3. McGuire, *Philadelphia Campaign*, 203.

4. Heathcote, *Washington*, 6–7.

5. McGuire, *Philadelphia Campaign*, 173. The location of Procter's battery was still visible at the time of the Bache Map survey of 1863.

6. McGuire, *Philadelphia Campaign*, 170. Conway, *Life of Thomas Paine*, 104.

7. McGuire, *Philadelphia Campaign*, 190, 194–96, 239.

8. McGuire, *Philadelphia Campaign*, 194–96, 213. Trevelyan, *American Revolution*, 4:229.

9. McGuire, *Philadelphia Campaign*, 215–16.

10. Lengel, *Washington*, 242. "Papers Relating," 58.

11. McGuire, *Philadelphia Campaign*, 235, 239.

12. McGuire, *Philadelphia Campaign*, 234. *Lafayette at Brandywine*, 68–74, 88.

13. Trevelyan, *American Revolution*, 4:230–31.

14. Smith, *Battle of Brandywine*, 23, 197.

15. McGuire, *Philadelphia Campaign*, 244–48, 181, 170.

16. "Papers Relating," 60.

17. Morgan, *True La Fayette*, 113–14.

18. McGuire, *Brandywine Battlefield Park*. Townsend: West Chester *Village Record*, February 12, 1861. McGuire, *Philadelphia Campaign*, 268–69.

19. McGuire, *Philadelphia Campaign*, 270.

20. Irving, *Washington*, 3:253. Futhey and Cope, *Chester County*, 72.

21. Futhey and Cope, *Chester County*, 77, 81.

22. Pyle, "Old-Time Life," 190. *Delaware Archives*, 3:1414–16. Scharf, *Delaware Archives*, 1:211.

23. Chastellux, *Travels*, 118.

24. *Lafayette at Brandywine*, 76–77. Harper, *West Chester*, ch. 38.

25. *Lafayette at Brandywine*, 75–88. Darlington, *Directory*. Wyeth, *Andrew Wyeth*, 122.

26. "Letter from Chester County," 365. "Birmingham Township Churches."

27. "Birmingham Township Churches."

28. "Letter from Chester County," 364–66.

29. Peterson, "Battle-Grounds."

30. *Delaware County American*, July 6, 1870.

31. *Lafayette at Brandywine.*

32. *West Chester, Past and Present*, appendix.

33. West Chester *Village Record*, May 26, 1819. *Delaware County American*, May 14, 1856.

34. *Lafayette at Brandywine*, 17.

35. *Brandywine Story.*

4. "Rushing Water and Buzzing Wheels"

1. Gilpin, *Wye*, 20, 39.

2. *The Wye Valley Walk*, 36. Peterken, *Wye Valley*, x.

3. Bathe and Bathe, *Oliver Evans*, 1935. Welsh, "Brandywine Mills," 27.

4. *Pennsylvania Gazette*, March 16, 1791.

5. *Pennsylvania Gazette*, November 10, 1773.

6. Hunter, "Wheat, War," 511.

7. Weslager, *Forgotten River*, 118. Montgomery, *Reminiscences*, 16. Welsh, "Brandywine Mills."

8. Hoffecker, *Brandywine Village.*

9. *Pennsylvania Gazette*, January 23, 1793.

10. Wilkinson, "Brandywine Borrowings." Fairbanks, "House of Thomas Shipley."

11. Moore and Jones, *Traveller's Directory*, 4. Wilkinson, "Brandywine Borrowings."

12. *Pennsylvania Gazette*, February 28, 1771.

13. *Pennsylvania Gazette*, March 16, 1785.

14. Currie, *Historical Account*, 210–11.

15. Montgomery, *Reminiscences*, 10–11.

16. *William Canby of Brandywine.*

17. Montgomery, *Reminiscences*, 18–19.

18. Maynard, "Log House." Cobbett, *Hints*, 12–13.

19. Montgomery, *Reminiscences*, 21–22. Canby, *Family History*, 58.

20. La Rochefoucauld-Liancourt, *Travels.*

21. *Pennsylvania Gazette*, December 12, 1765. Lea, "One Hundred Years Ago."

22. La Rochefoucauld-Liancourt, *Travels.* Canby, *Brandywine*, 17.

23. Jordan, *Colonial and Revolutionary Families*, 1:429–30.

24. Rink, *Printing*, 44. Hancock and Wilkinson, "Gilpins."

25. Hunter, *Papermaking*, 351–55. Hancock and Wilkinson, "Gilpins."

26. Gravell, *American Watermarks.*

27. Bryant, *Picturesque America*, 1:227–29.

28. Crowninshield and du Pont, *Tancopanican*, 2:9. Gurney, *Journey*, 364. Wallace, *Rockdale*, 29. Mulrooney, *Black Powder*, 122.

29. Welsh, "Brandywine Mills," 25.

30. La Rochefoucauld-Liancourt, *Travels.*

31. This and the following account are from Montgomery, *Reminiscences*, 8–29.

32. Howe, "Banks of Brandywine!"

33. Windle, *Life in Washington*, 128–29.

34. Wilkinson, *Brandywine*, 121. Rockland is shown in Joseph Taylor's detailed 1849 map and John Rubens Smith's 1835 paintings.

35. N. C. Wyeth, *The Wyeths*, 193.

36. Bassler, "William Young."

37. *Delaware County Republican*, November 10, 1865.

38. Silvia, Oral Interviews.

39. Hergesheimer, *Old House*, 34.

5. Thunderous Age of Black Powder

1. Downing, *Landscape Gardening*, viii, 18, 59, 64–65.

2. Bryant, *Picturesque America*, 1:224.

3. Carr, *Du Ponts*, 55.

4. Wilkinson, "Brandywine Borrowings," 3.

5. Carr, *du Ponts*, 66. Quimby, *Eleutherian Mills*. Wilkinson, *E. I. du Pont, Botaniste*, 52.

6. Carr, *du Ponts*, 39, 41.

7. Scharf, *Delaware*, 1:291. Low, "Youth of 1812."

8. Wilkinson, "Brandywine Borrowings."

9. Sisson, "From Farm to Factory."

10. Canby, *Brandywine*, 140.

11. Wilkinson, "Mills on the Brandywine." For painters: *Four Decades*.

12. Crowninshield and du Pont, *Tancopanican*, 6:59–60.

13. *Pennsylvania Gazette*, February 16, 1791.

14. Baldwin, *Brandywine Creek*, 150.

15. Jenkins, "Banks," 214. Carr, *du Ponts*, 116.

16. Bacyk and Rowe, *Gun Powder*.

17. Dutton, *Du Pont*, 38. Wilkinson, *E. I. du Pont, Botaniste*.

18. Fleming, "History of the Winterthur," 21. Wilkinson, *E. I. du Pont, Botaniste*, 61–62, 73.

19. Crowninshield and du Pont, *Tancopanican*, 1:14, 6:16.

20. Crowninshield and du Pont, *Tancopanican*, 2:6–7, 3:46–47; spelling regularized.

21. Mulrooney, *Black Powder*, 68.

22. Myers, *Narratives*, 226–27. Trollope, *Domestic Manners*, 42.

23. Kalm, *Travels*, 1:74.

24. West Chester *American Republican*, February 27, 1822.

25. "Rivers, Brandywine," March 13, 1822.

26. West Chester *American Republican*, February 27, 1822. Canby, Samuel, Diaries.

27. Bounds, *Bancroft's Mills*, 14.

28. West Chester *American Republican*, February 5, 1839. Bryant, *Picturesque America*, 1:226.

29. MacElree, *Down the Eastern*, 144–49.

30. West Chester *American Republican*, August 26, 1856.

31. Rink, *Printing*, 18–19.

32. Durrett, *Filson*, 10–11.

33. Rink, *Printing*, 35–38. Harper, *West Chester*, 577. Reed, *In Memoriam*.

6. Industry and War

1. Wilmington *Evening Bulletin*, June 1, 1854.

2. Canby, *Brandywine*, 146. *New York Daily Times*, October 24, 1859.

3. Montgomery, *Reminiscences*, 9–10, 15.

4. Williams, *Man and Nature*, 107. Dare, *Railroad Guide*, 82–91. *New York Times*, July 13, 1853.

5. *New York Times,* July 9, 1853.

6. Philadelphia *Christian Recorder,* September 19, 1863.

7. Livesay, "Lobdell." White, *American Locomotive,* 181–82.

8. *Delaware County Republican,* September 23, 1859.

9. Jordan, *Colonial and Revolutionary Families,* 1:426. Calarco, *Places,* 144, 374. *Pennsylvania Gazette,* April 3, 1782.

10. *Delaware County American,* September 12, 1860.

11. Taylor, *Selected Letters.* Harper, *West Chester,* 529.

12. Taylor, *Two Continents,* 94, 158–59.

13. *West Chester, Past and Present,* 58.

14. Harper, *West Chester,* 703. *Delaware County Republican,* September 6, 1861.

15. West Chester *Village Record,* February 1, 1862.

16. *Delaware County Republican,* July 19, 1861.

17. Taylor, *Philadelphia,* 45. Hancock, "Civil War," 37–40. Hancock, *Delaware During.* Scharf, *Delaware,* 1:340.

18. *Delaware's Industries,* 60. Montgomery, *Reminiscences,* 14.

19. Du Pont, *How the Church Was Builded.* Silliman, *Story of Christ Church,* 43. Henry, *Life of Alexis.*

20. Dutton, *Du Pont,* 98–100.

21. Wilkinson, *Brandywine Home,* 102 n. 44, 111. *Delaware County Republican,* February 27, 1863.

22. *Delaware County American,* July 7, 1869.

23. *Philadelphia Record,* October 8, 1890. James, *Alfred I. du Pont,* 92.

24. James, *Alfred I. du Pont,* 127.

25. Oral Histories Interviews.

26. James, *Alfred I. du Pont,* 20, 28, 31, 38.

7. River of Nature

1. *West Chester, Past and Present* 14, 22. "Letter from Chester County," 364–66. Harper, *West Chester,* 529.

2. Canby, *Brandywine,* 155. Higgins, "Garden." Ashland Hollow actually lies just west of the Brandywine Valley along Red Clay Creek.

3. Klein, *Gardens,* 18. Myers, *Narratives,* 229.

4. Harshberger, *Botanists,* 77–85.

5. Belden, "Marshall's." *West Chester . . . Most Important Suburb,* 14. *West Chester, Past and Present,* 70–71. Harper, *West Chester,* 554–56. 1853 map: Rodebaugh, *Chester County,* 37–38.

6. Randall, *Longwood,* 9, 35, 41.

7. Baldwin, *Reliquiae.* The plants mentioned are *Physalis pennsylvanica, Potamogeton lucens,* and *Turritis laevigata.*

8. Darlington, *Florula Cestrica,* 31, 37. The book was revised as *Flora Cestrica.*

9. Fringe tree in Nuttall, *North American Sylva,* 2:156.

10. Darlington, *Florula Cestrica,* 35, 107. Chester County Historical Society marked the site of Darlington's birthplace in 1913.

11. Harshberger, *Botanists,* 225–26. Tatnall, *Catalogue.* Skullcap is *Scutellaria saxatilis.*

12. Burns, *Ornithology,* 12.

13. Hunter, *Alexander Wilson,* 149–50.

14. Rhodes, *Audubon,* 66–69. Wilson, *Life and Letters,* 93.

15. Pennock, "Birds," 88. Shields and Benson, *Catalyst,* 43.

16. McGuire, *Philadelphia Campaign*, 2–3.

17. Osborn, *Cope*.

18. Booth, *Memoir*.

19. Plank and Schenck, *Piedmont Geology*. Pope, "Windsor Forest."

20. Canby, *Brandywine*, 139. Volkman, "Delaware Rocks."

21. Robinson, *Catalogue*. Myers, *Narratives*, 320.

22. Carpenter and Spackman, "Miscellaneous Localities."

23. Lesley, *Geology*, 64.

24. *West Chester, Past and Present*, 99. Fowler, "Fishes."

25. West Chester *Daily Local News*, February 11, 1893.

26. Wilson, *Victorian Thames*, xii. DeMare, *Time on the Thames*, 15, 18.

27. DeMare, *Time on the Thames*, 17. Murray, *Picturesque Tour*, 3–4.

28. *Up the River*, 1–6. Bolland, *Victorians*, 9. DeMare, *Time on the Thames*, 17.

29. Canby, *Brandywine*, 163, 220.

30. West Chester *Daily Local News*, July 31, 1886.

31. West Chester *Daily Local News*, September 1, 1908; April 4, 1910.

32. Wilmington *Journal Every Evening*, December 30, 1929. "Wilmington: House-boats."

33. *Delaware County Republican*, November 10, 1865. West Chester *Daily Local News*, May 17, 1917.

34. West Chester *Daily Local News*, April 23, 1895. MacElree, *Down the Eastern*, 159.

35. West Chester *Daily Local News*, August 13, 1904.

36. N. C. Wyeth, *The Wyeths*, 409.

37. West Chester *Daily Local News*, September 21, 1908.

38. West Chester *Daily Local News*, July 20, 1908.

39. C. Edwin Smith in West Chester *Daily Local News*, n.d., clippings file, Chester County Historical Society.

40. Bryant, *Picturesque America*, 1:231. Thompson, "Wilmington Park System."

41. Wilmington *Morning News*, December 15, 1905.

42. Milford, "Nonprofit." Obama, *Presidential Proclamation*.

43. James, *Alfred I. du Pont*, 37.

44. Wilmington *Morning News*, November 11, 1961.

45. Wilmington *Journal Every Evening*, May 24, 1957. Wilmington *Morning News*, November 11, 1961.

46. Whyte, *Last Landscape*, 16–18.

8. Literary Pastoral

1. Corn, *Wyeth*, 16.

2. Canby, *Family History*, 25.

3. Taylor, *Poetical Works*, 142. "The Prophet of the Brandywine" in Lippard, *Washington*, 301–2.

4. Hergesheimer, *Old House*, 26–27, 34.

5. Rink, *Printing*, 43.

6. [Parke,] "Elegy," 210–11.

7. Richards, "Elegiac Ode," 1:203.

8. "The Brandywine" (1788).

9. Chandler, *Poetical Works*, 31–32, 49.

10. Lippard, *Blanche*, 181, 260.

11. "The Prophet of the Brandywine," in Lippard, *Washington*, 305, 318.

12. Lippard, *Blanche*, 181, 132, 143.

13. Reynolds, *Lippard*, 16.

14. Reynolds, *Lippard*, 15, 72.

15. Smithers, *Lofland*.

16. Lofland, *Poetical and Prose Writings*, 167.

17. Lofland, *Poetical and Prose Writings*, 115, 435. Lofland, *Harp*, 171.

18. Lofland, *Poetical and Prose Writings*, 435, 152.

19. Foust, *Bird*, 34. Everhart, *Poems*, 136–37.

20. *Banks of Brandywine*. Lanier, *Centennial*, 9:467.

21. Hakutani, *Dreiser's*, 188–89.

22. Hayes, Diary, October 1903, December 1906.

23. Hayes, Diary, January 16, 1903. Hayes, *Brandywine Days*, 120–21.

24. Horgan, *Certain Climate*, 153. Baldwin, *Historic Brandywine*, 26.

25. Hergesheimer, *Old House*, 36–40, 96, 183.

26. Canby, *Age of Confidence*, 198. Aslet, *American Country House*, 118.

27. Sinclair, *Money Writes!*, 92–95.

28. Fleming, "History of Winterthur."

29. Ellerslie: see, Cline, *Zelda Fitzgerald*, 203–4; Turnbull, *Fitzgerald*, 171–79; Buller, *Fairy Tale*, 116–17; Wilson, *Shores*, 373–83; Toll, *Judge Uncommon*, 93–98.

30. Fitzgerald, *My Lost City*, 122.

31. Fitzgerald, *Afternoon*, 137–41.

9. "Painters of True American Art"

1. Dorst, *Written Suburb*, 61. *New York Times*, June 3, 1975.

2. Abstractions: *Woman's Day*, August 1963, clippings file, Chester County Historical Society.

3. Neagle: *West Chester, Past and Present*, appendix. Herzog: West Chester *Daily Local News*, May 23, 1894.

4. Bryant, *Picturesque America*, 220–22.

5. Homer, *Eakins*.

6. Wallace, *Mifflin*, 2–6. Mifflin, *Fleeing Nymph*, 52.

7. Ferber, *Pastoral*, 21–22.

8. West Chester *Daily Local News*, December 31, 1881; February 6, 1882; March 13, 1883; March 28, 1882.

9. West Chester *Daily Local News*, May 27, 1882; May 29, 1882.

10. West Chester *Daily Local News*, December 7, 1901. Hayes, Diary, 1902.

11. "Papers Relating."

12. George O. Bartlett and William French attribution from Library Company of Philadelphia.

13. West Chester *Daily Local News*, May 20, 1889; October 14, 1904.

14. West Chester *Daily Local News*, June 7, 1898.

15. Lewis, *Herzog*.

16. Gorman, *Cope*.

17. Wilmington *Sunday Supplement*, October 15, 1933. Hayes, Diary, February 17, 1910. Beckman, "Etchings," 89–90.

18. Gorman, *Chalfant*. Bryant, *Picturesque America*, 10:222, 231.

19. De Mare, *Time on the Thames*, 15. Irving, *Irving Gift*, 149.

20. Schneer, *Thames*, 121–24.

21. Abbott, *Pyle*.

22. Maynard, *Buildings of Delaware*, 74.

23. *Howard Pyle: The Artist*.

24. May and May, *Pyle*, 109. Pitz, *Brandywine Tradition*, 117.

25. May and May, *Pyle*, 107. Pitz, *Brandywine Tradition*, 111.

26. Pitz, *Brandywine Tradition*, 106, 109.

27. N. C. Wyeth, *The Wyeths*, 811.

28. May and May, *Pyle*, 108.

29. N. C. Wyeth, *The Wyeths*, 46–47.

30. N. C. Wyeth, *The Wyeths*, 86, 135. Pitz, *Brandywine Tradition*, 113.

31. Lykes, "Pyle."

32. N. C. Wyeth, *The Wyeths*, 246. Michaelis, *N. C. Wyeth*, 171.

33. N. C. Wyeth, *The Wyeths*, 384, 376. Podmaniczky, *Wyeth*, 1:40. Podmaniczky, *The Wyeths*, 10.

34. Podmaniczky, *The Wyeths*, 7–8.

35. N. C. Wyeth, *The Wyeths*, 436.

36. Thoreau: Maynard, *Walden*, 236–37. Maynard, "Thoreau Manuscript Leaf." N. C. Wyeth, *The Wyeths*, 595, 283.

37. Fitzgerald, *Conversations*, 86. Meryman, *Wyeth: A Secret*, 81. Michaelis, *N. C. Wyeth*, 273.

38. N. C. Wyeth, *The Wyeths*, 737–38.

39. Michaelis, *N. C. Wyeth*, 330.

40. Mortenson, *Illustrations*. Fitzgerald, *Rivers*, 53–54. N. C. Wyeth, *The Wyeths*, 807.

41. Logsdon, *Wyeth People*, 16. Pitz, *Brandywine Tradition*, 216. Logsdon and Kuerner, *All in a Day's Work*.

42. Andrew Wyeth, *Andrew Wyeth*, 24.

43. N. C. Wyeth, *The Wyeths*, 252, 813.

44. Andrew Wyeth, *Andrew Wyeth*, 20.

45. "Service of Dedication," 50. N. C. Wyeth, *The Wyeths*, 644, 503.

46. Thompson, *Chris*, 294, 316. Bob Duggan blog, September 2012, BigThink.com.

47. Andrew Wyeth, *Andrew Wyeth*, 122, 153.

48. N. C. Wyeth, *The Wyeths*, 844.

49. Corn, *Andrew Wyeth*, 58.

50. Meryman, *Wyeth: A Secret*, 82. Hergesheimer, *Old House*, 35–39.

51. *Woman's Day*, August 1963, clippings file, Chester County Historical Society.

52. Frascina, *Pollock*, 167. *Woman's Day*, August 1963, clippings file, Chester County Historical Society.

53. Andrew Wyeth, *Andrew Wyeth* (1995), 153.

54. Meryman, *Wyeth* (1968), 71. *Woman's Day*, August 1963, clippings file, Chester County Historical Society.

55. Wilmington *Evening Journal*, January 11, 1969. Dorst, *Written Suburb*, 54.

56. Nixon, "Toasts."

57. Jamie Wyeth, *Farm Work*, 23. Zeidner and Edgeworth, *Brandywine*, 58, 201.

58. Quillman, *100 Artists*, 60, 6.

59. Hergesheimer, *Old House*, 39.

Bibliography

❧

Abbott, Charles D. *Howard Pyle: A Chronicle*. New York: Harper & Brothers, 1925.

Ackroyd, Peter. *Thames: Sacred River*. London: Chatto and Windus, 2007.

Aslet, Clive. *The American Country House*. New Haven, Conn.: Yale University Press, 1990.

Bacyk, Ted and David, and Tom Rowe. *Gun Powder Cans and Kegs*. Maynardville, Tenn.: Rowe Publications, n.d.

Baldwin, William. *Reliquiae Baldwinianae*. Philadelphia: Kimber and Sharpless, 1843.

Baldwin, William C. *Brandywine Creek: A Pictorial History*. West Chester, Pa.: self published, 1977.

———. *Historic Brandywine Guide Book*. 3rd ed. West Chester, Pa.: Bradford Village Press, 1960.

Banks of Brandywine. Broadside. Boston: Hunts & Shaw, 1836.

Bassler, Margaret A. "The Story of William Young and Rockland." Historical Society of Delaware, n.d.

Bathe, Greville, and Dorothy Bathe. *Oliver Evans: A Chronology of Early American Engineering*. Philadelphia: Historical Society of Pennsylvania, 1935.

Beckman, Thomas. "The Etchings of Robert Shaw." *Delaware History* 24, no. 2 (Fall/Winter 1990): 75–108.

Belden, Louise Conway. "Humphry Marshall's Trade in Plants of the New World for Gardens and Forests of the Old World." *Winterthur Portfolio* 2 (1965): 107–26.

"Birmingham Township Churches—Society of Friends." Clippings files, Chester County Historical Society.

Bolland, R. R. *Victorians on the Thames*. Tunbridge Wells, UK: Midas Books, 1974.

Booth, James C. *Memoir of the Geological Survey of The State of Delaware.* Dover: S. Kimmey, 1841.

[Bounds, Harvey.] *The History of Bancroft's Mills, 1831–1961.* c. 1961.

"The Brandywine." *American Museum* (February 1788): 186.

The Brandywine Story, 1777–1952. Brandywine Battlefield Park Commission, 1952.

Brooks, Seal T. "The Beaver Valley Rock Shelter." *Bulletin of the Archaeological Society of Delaware* 4, no. 5 (January 1949): 22–24.

Bryant, William Cullen. *Picturesque America.* 2 vols. New York: D. Appleton, 1872–1874.

Buller, Richard P. *A Beautiful Fairy Tale: The Life of Lois Moran.* Pompton Plains, N. J.: Limelight Editions, 2005.

Burns, Franklin L. *The Ornithology of Chester County, Pennsylvania.* Boston: Richard G. Badger, 1919.

Calarco, Tom. *Places of the Underground Railroad.* Santa Barbara, Calif.: Greenwood, 2011.

Canby, Henry Seidel. *The Age of Confidence: Life in the Nineties.* New York: Farrar & Rinehart, 1934.

———. *The Brandywine.* New York: Farrar and Rinehart, 1941.

———. *Family History.* Cambridge, Mass.: Riverside Press, 1945.

Canby, Samuel. Diaries. No. 314, Hagley Museum and Library.

Cannon, Patt, and Carol Kipp. *Centreville: The History of a Delaware Village, 1680–2000.* Centreville, Del.: Centreville Civic Association, 2001.

Carpenter, G. W., and George Spackman. "Miscellaneous Localities of Minerals." *American Journal of Arts and Science* 10 (February 1826): 218–24.

Carr, William H. A. *The du Ponts of Delaware.* New York: Dodd, Mead, 1964.

Catalogue of the Collection, 1969–1989. Chadds Ford: Brandywine River Museum of Art, 1991.

Chandler, Elizabeth M. *Poetical Works.* Philadelphia: Lemuel Howell, 1836.

Chase, Susan M. *Within the Reach of All: An Illustrated History of Brandywine Park.* Montchanin: Friends of Wilmington Parks, 2005.

Chastellux, Marquis de. *Travels in North America.* New York: Gallaher & White, 1828.

Cline, Sally. *Zelda Fitzgerald: Her Voice in Paradise.* London: John Murray, 2002.

Clio. "Written at the Retreat; An Admired Spot on the Banks of the Brandywine." Philadelphia *Evening Fire-Side* 1, no. 36 (August 17, 1805): 282.

Cobbett, William. *Hints to Emigrants.* Liverpool: W. Bethell, 1817.

Connelley, William E. *Doniphan's Expedition and the Conquest of New Mexico and California.* Topeka, Kans.: author, 1907.

Conway, Moncure D. *The Life of Thomas Paine.* Reprint, New York: B. Blom, 1969.

Corn, Wanda M. *The Art of Andrew Wyeth*. Greenwich, Conn. New York Graphic Society, 1973.

Craig, Peter Stebbins. *The 1693 Census of the Swedes on the Delaware*. Winter Park, Florida: SAG Publications, 1993.

Crowninshield, Louise du Pont, and Pierre S. du Pont, eds. *Tancopanican Chronicle 1830–1834*. Multivolume. Wilmington, Del.: authors, 1949.

Currie, William. *A Historical Account of the Climate and Diseases of the United States of America*. Philadelphia: T. Dobson, 1792.

Danson, Edwin. *Drawing the Line: How Mason and Dixon Surveyed the Most Famous Border in America*. New York: Wiley, 2001.

Dare, Charles P. *Philadelphia, Wilmington and Baltimore Railroad Guide*. Philadelphia: Fitzgibbon and Van Ness, 1856.

Darlington, William. *Address Before the Chester County Horticultural Society*. West Chester, Pa., 1846.

———. *Address to the Chester County Cabinet of Natural Science*. West Chester, Pa.: Simeon Siegfried, 1826.

———. *Directory of the Borough of West Chester for 1857*. West Chester, Pa.: Wood & James, 1857.

———. *Florula Cestrica*. West Chester, Pa.: Simeon Siegfried, 1826.

Delaware Archives: Revolutionary War. 3 vols. Wilmington: Charles L. Story, 1919.

Delaware's Industries. Philadelphia: Keighton, 1891.

De Mare, Eric. *Time on the Thames*. London: Architectural Press, 1952.

Dorst, John D. *The Written Suburb*. Philadelphia: University of Pennsylvania Press, 1989.

Downing, A. J. *A Treatise on the Theory and Practice of Landscape Gardening*. New York: Wiley and Putnam, 1841.

Dunlap, A. R. *Dutch and Swedish Place-Names in Delaware*. Newark: University of Delaware Press, 1956.

Du Pont, Joanna Maria. *How the Church Was Builded* [Christ Church Christiana Hundred]. New York: Daniel Dana, 1859.

Durrett, Reuben T. *John Filson: The First Historian of Kentucky*. Louisville: Filson Club, 1884.

Dutton, William S. *Du Pont: One Hundred and Forty Years*. New York: C. Scribner's Sons, 1942.

Everhart, James B. *Poems*. Philadelphia: J. B. Lippincott, 1868.

Fairbanks, Jonathan L. "The House of Thomas Shipley. . . ." *Winterthur Portfolio* 2 (1965): 142–59.

Ferber, Linda S. *Pastoral Interlude: William T. Richards in Chester County*. Chadds Ford, Pa.: Brandywine River Museum of Art, 2001.

Fitzgerald, Carol. *The Rivers of America: A Descriptive Bibliography*. New Castle, Del.: Oak Knoll, 2001.

Fitzgerald, F. Scott. *Afternoon of an Author.* New York: Scribner, 1968.

———. *Conversations.* Ed. Matthew J. Bruccoli and Judith S. Baughman. Oxford: University of Mississippi Press, 2004.

———. *My Lost City: Personal Essays, 1920–1940.* New York: Cambridge University Press, 2005.

Fleming, E. McClung. "History of the Winterthur Estate." *Winterthur Portfolio* 1 (1964): 9–51.

Four Decades: The Hotel du Pont Collection. Wilmington: Delaware Art Museum, 1982.

Foust, Clement E. *The Life and Dramatic Works of Robert Montgomery Bird.* New York: Knickerbocker Press, 1919.

Fowler, Henry W. "Records of Pennsylvania Fishes." *American Naturalist* 41, no. 481 (January 1907): 5–21.

Fox, George. *Journal.* Multivolume. London: Friends' Tract Association, 1891.

Frascina, Francis, ed. *Pollock and After: The Critical Debate.* 2nd ed. London: Routledge, 2000.

Futhey, J. Smith, and Gilbert Cope. *History of Chester County.* Philadelphia: Louis H. Everts, 1881.

Gilpin, William. *Observations on the River Wye.* 2nd ed. London: R. Blamire, 1789.

Goldsmith, Oliver. *The Deserted Village, A Poem.* London: W. Griffin, 1770.

Goodheart, Adam. "History's Backyard: America's First State Celebrates Its 'Founding River' and More." *National Geographic* (April 2013).

Gorman, Joan H. *George Cope, 1855–1929.* Chadds Ford, Pa.: Brandywine River Museum of Art, 1978.

———. *Jefferson David Chalfant, 1856–1931.* Chadds Ford, Pa.: Brandywine River Museum of Art, 1979.

Gravell, Thomas L., and George Miller. *American Watermarks 1690–1835.* New Castle, Del.: Oak Knoll, 2002.

Gurney, Joseph John. *A Journey in North America.* Norwich, UK: Josiah Fletcher, 1841.

Hakutani, Yoshinobu. *Theodore Dreiser's Uncollected Magazine Articles, 1897–1902.* Newark: University of Delaware Press, 2003.

Hancock, Harold B. "Civil War Comes to Delaware." *Civil War History* 2, no. 4 (December 1956): 29–46.

———. *Delaware During the Civil War: A Political History.* Wilmington: Historical Society of Delaware, 1961.

Hancock, Harold B., and Norman B. Wilkinson. "The Gilpins and Their Endless Papermaking Machine." *Pennsylvania Magazine of History and Biography* 81, no. 4 (October 1957): 391–405.

Harper, Douglas R. *West Chester to 1865: That Elegant & Notorious Place.* West Chester, Pa.: Chester County Historical Society, 1999.

Harshberger, John W. *The Botanists of Philadelphia and Their Work*. Philadelphia: T. C. Davis & Sons, 1899.

Hayes, John Russell. *Brandywine Days: Or, The Shepherd's Hour-Glass*. Philadelphia: Biddle Press, 1910.

———. Diary. RG 5/180, John Russell Hayes Papers, Friends Historical Library of Swarthmore College.

Heathcote, Charles W. *Washington in Chester County*. West Chester, Pa.: Chester County Historical Society, 1932.

Henry, Allan J. *The Life of Alexis Irénée du Pont*. 2 vols. Philadelphia: William F. Fell, 1945.

Hergesheimer, Joseph. *From an Old House*. New York: Knopf, 1926.

Higgins, Adrian. "A Garden That Takes the Long View." *Washington Post*, November 2, 2006, H01.

Hoch, Bradley R. *The Lincoln Trail in Pennsylvania*. University Park: Pennsylvania State University Press, 2001.

Hoffecker, Carol E. *Brandywine Village*. Wilmington, Del.: Old Brandywine Village, 1974.

———. *Wilmington: A Pictorial History*. Virginia Beach, Va.: Donning, 1982.

———. *Wilmington, Delaware: Portrait of an Industrial City, 1830–1910*. Charlottesville: University Press of Virginia, 1974.

Holmes, Oliver Wendell, Sr. *Pages From an Old Volume of Life*. Boston: Houghton, Mifflin, 1891.

Homer, William I. *Eakins at Avondale*. Chadds Ford, Pa.: Brandywine River Museum of Art, 1980.

Horgan, Paul. *A Certain Climate: Essays in History, Arts, and Letters*. Middletown, Conn.: Wesleyan University Press, 1988. 5 vols. Philadelphia: University of Pennsylvania Press, 1987.

Horle, Craig W., Alison Duncan Hirsch, Marianne S. Wokeck, and Joy Wiltenburg, eds. *The Papers of William Penn, Vol. 4: 1701–1718*. Philadelphia: University of Pennsylvania Press, 1987.

Howard Pyle: The Artist, the Legacy. Wilmington: Delaware Art Museum, 1987.

Howe, Mrs. S. J. "The Banks of Brandywine!" *Peterson's Magazine* 14, no. 3 (September 1848): 107.

Humphrey, Elizabeth, and Michael Kahn. *Brandywine*. Wilmington, Del.: Jared, 1990.

Hunter, Brooke. "Wheat, War, and the American Economy During the Age of Revolution." *William and Mary Quarterly* 62, no. 3 (July 2005): 505–26.

Hunter, Clark, ed. *The Life and Letters of Alexander Wilson*. Philadelphia: American Philosophical Society, 1983.

Hunter, Dard. *Papermaking: The History and Technique of an Ancient Craft*. 1943. Reprint, New York: Dover, 1978.

Irving, Washington. *The Irving Gift*. Buffalo: Phinney & Co., 1857.

———. *Life of Washington*. 5 vols. Philadelphia: J. B. Lippincott, 1871.

James, B. B., and J. F. Jameson, eds. *Journal of Jasper Danckaerts 1679–1680*. New York: Scribner's, 1913.

James, Marquis. *Alfred I. du Pont: The Family Rebel*. Indianapolis: Bobbs-Merrill, 1941.

Jenkins, Howard M. "The Banks of the Brandywine." *Harper's New Monthly Magazine* 19 (June–November 1889): 208–14.

Johnson, Amandus. *The Swedes on the Delaware, 1638–1664*. Philadelphia: International Printing Company, 1927.

Jordan, John W., ed. *Colonial and Revolutionary Families of Pennsylvania*. 3 vols. 1911. Reprint, Baltimore: Clearfield, 2004.

Kalm, Peter. *Travels*. 2 vols. New York: Dover, 1964.

Klein, William M. *Gardens of Philadelphia and the Delaware Valley*. Philadelphia: Temple University Press, 1995.

Lafayette at Brandywine. West Chester, Pa.: West Chester Historical Society, 1896.

La Rochefoucauld-Liancourt, François-Alexandre-Frédéric, duc de. *Travels through the United States of North America*. 2 vols. London: R. Phillips, 1799.

Lanier, Sidney. *Centennial Edition of the Works*. Multivolume. Baltimore: Johns Hopkins University Press, 1945.

Lea, William. "One Hundred Years Ago." Spruance Material, Acc. 1168, Folder 3, Hagley Museum and Library.

Lemon, James T. *The Best Poor Man's Country*. Baltimore: Johns Hopkins University Press, 1972.

Lengel, Edward G. *General George Washington: A Military Life*. New York: Random House, 2005.

Lesley, J. P., ed. *The Geology of Chester County*. Harrisburg, Pa.: Second Geological Survey, 1883.

"Letter from Chester County." *Hazard's Register of Pennsylvania* 1, no. 6 (June 1828): 364–66.

Lewis, Donald S. *American Paintings of Herman Herzog*. Chadds Ford, Pa.: Brandywine River Museum of Art, 1992.

Lidz, Maggie. *The Du Ponts: Houses and Gardens in the Brandywine, 1900–1951*. New York: Acanthus Press, 2009.

Lippard, George. *Blanche of Brandywine: Or, September the Eleventh, 1777*. Philadelphia: G. B. Zieber, 1846.

———. *Washington and His Generals: Or, Legends of the Revolution*. Philadelphia: G. B. Zieber, 1847.

Livesay, Harold C. "The Lobdell Car Wheel Co., 1830–1867." *Business History Review* 42, no. 2 (Summer 1968): 171–94.

Lofland, John. *The Harp of Delaware*. Philadelphia: Atkinson & Alexander, 1828.

———. *The Poetical and Prose Writings*. Baltimore: J. Murphy, 1853.

Logsdon, Gene. *Wyeth People*. 1969. Reprint, Dallas: Taylor, 1988.

Logsdon, Gene, and Karl J. Kuerner. *All in a Day's Work . . . From Heritage to Artist*. Wilmington, Del.: Cedar Tree Books, 2007.

Low, Betty-Bright P. "The Youth of 1812." *Winterthur Portfolio* 11 (1976): 173–212.

Lykes, Richard Wayne. "Howard Pyle, Teacher of Illustration." *Pennsylvania Magazine of History and Biography* 80, no. 3 (July 1956): 339–70.

MacElree, Wilmer W. *Along the Western Brandywine*. West Chester, Pa.: F. S. Hickman, 1912.

———. *Around the Boundaries of Chester County*. West Chester, Pa., 1934.

———. *Down the Eastern and Up the Black Brandywine*. West Chester, Pa.: F. S. Hickman, 1912.

May, Jill P., and Robert E. May. *Howard Pyle: Imagining an American School of Art*. Urbana: University of Illinois Press, 2011.

Maynard, W. Barksdale. *Architecture in the United States, 1800–1850*. New Haven, Conn.: Yale University Press, 2002.

———. *Buildings of Delaware*. Charlottesville: University of Virginia Press, 2008.

———. "A Log House for an Architect: Benjamin Henry Latrobe at Iron Hill." *Delaware History* 31, no. 2 (Fall/Winter 2005/6): 97–124.

———. "Thoreau Manuscript Leaf Found at N. C. Wyeth Studio." *Thoreau Society Bulletin* 243 (Spring 2003): 3.

———. *Walden Pond: A History*. New York: Oxford University Press, 2004.

McGuire, Thomas J. *Brandywine Battlefield Park*. Mechanicsburg, Pa.: Stackpole, 2001.

———. *The Philadelphia Campaign*. Vol. 1, *Brandywine and the Fall of Philadelphia*. Mechanicsburg, Pa.: Stackpole, 2006.

McWilliams, James E. *A Revolution in Eating: How the Quest for Food Shaped America*. New York: Columbia University Press, 2005.

Meginnis, Susan. Henry Clay Village map, based on 1902 survey. Hagley Museum, 1973.

Meryman, Richard. *Andrew Wyeth*. Boston: Houghton Mifflin, 1968.

———. *Andrew Wyeth: A Secret Life*. New York: HarperCollins, 1996.

Michaelis, David. *N. C. Wyeth: A Biography*. New York: Knopf, 1998.

Mifflin, Lloyd. *The Fleeing Nymph: And Other Verse*. Boston: Small, Maynard, 1905.

Milford, Maureen. "Nonprofit Trust Shapes Growth." *New York Times*, November 5, 1989, R21.

Montgomery, Elizabeth. *Reminiscences of Wilmington*. Philadelphia: T. K. Collins, 1851.

Moore, S. S., and T. W. Jones. *The Traveller's Directory*. Philadelphia: Mathew Carey, 1804.

Morgan, George. *The True La Fayette*. Philadelphia: J. B. Lippincott, 1919.

Mortenson, C. Walter. *The Illustrations of Andrew Wyeth: A Check List*. West Chester, Pa.: Aralia Press, 1977.

Mowday, Bruce E. *Along the Brandywine River*. Charleston, S.C.: Arcadia, 2001.

Mulrooney, Margaret M. *Black Powder, White Lace: The du Pont Irish and Cultural Identity in Nineteenth-Century America*. Hanover, N.H.: University Press of New England, 2002.

Murray, John Fisher. *A Picturesque Tour of the River Thames*. London: Henry G. Bohn, 1853.

Myers, Albert Cook, ed. *Narratives of Early Pennsylvania, West New Jersey and Delaware: 1630–1707*. New York: Scribner's, 1912.

Nixon, Richard. "Toasts of the President and Andrew Wyeth." February 19, 1970. American Presidency Project online.

Nuttall, Thomas. *The North American Sylva*. 2 vols. Philadelphia: Rice and Hart, 1859.

Obama, Barack. *Presidential Proclamation: First State National Monument*. Washington, D.C.: White House, March 25, 2013.

Oral Histories Interviews. Acc. 2026, Box 1, Hagley Museum and Library.

Osborn, Henry F. *Cope: Master Naturalist*. Princeton, N.J.: Princeton University Press, 1931.

"Papers Relating to the Battle of the Brandywine." *Proceedings of the Historical Society of Pennsylvania* 1, no. 8 (December 1846): 40–63.

[Parke, John.] "Elegy to General Sir W[illiam] H[ow]e." In Parke, John. *The Lyric Works of Horace*. Philadelphia: Eleazer Oswald, 1786, 210–11.

Pennock, Charles J. "The Birds of Chester County." *29th and 30th Quarterly Reports of the Pennsylvania Board of Agriculture* (October–December 1885): 78–91.

Peterken, George. *Wye Valley*. London: HarperCollins, 2008.

Peterson, Charles J. "The Battle-Grounds of America. No. 1—Brandywine." *Graham's Magazine* 24 (January–June 1844): 226–28.

Pitz, Henry C. *The Brandywine Tradition*. Boston: Houghton Mifflin, 1969.

Plank, Margaret O., and William S. Schenck. *Delaware Piedmont Geology*. Newark: Delaware Geological Survey, 1998.

Podmaniczky, Christine B. *N. C. Wyeth: Catalogue Raisonné of Paintings*. 2 vols. Chadds Ford, Pa.: Brandywine River Museum of Art, 2008.

———. *The Wyeths in Chadds Ford: The Early Years*. Chadds Ford: Brandywine River Museum of Art, 1997.

Pope, Alexander. "Windsor Forest." In Pope, Alexander, *Poems*, multivolume. Chiswick: C. Whittingham, 1822. 1:193–206.

Pyle, Howard. "Old-Time Life in a Quaker Town." *Harper's New Monthly Magazine* 62 (December 1880–March 1881): 178–90.

Quillman, Catherine. *100 Artists of the Brandywine Valley*. Atglen, Pa.: Schiffer, 2010.

Quimby, Maureen O'Brien. "Brandywine Valley Estates: Two Centuries of Garden Tradition." Hagley Museum, 1991.

———. *Eleutherian Mills*. Greenville, Del.: Hagley Museum, 1973.

Randall, Colvin. *Longwood Gardens: 100 Years of Garden Splendor*. Kennett Square, Pa.: Longwood Gardens, 2005.

Read, Thomas Buchanan. *Paul Redding: A Tale of the Brandywine*. Boston: A. Tompkins and B. B. Mussey, 1845.

Reed, Laura. *In Memoriam Sarah Walter Chandler Coates*. Kansas City: Hudson-Kimberly, 1898.

Reynolds, David S. *George Lippard*. Boston: Twayne, 1982.

Rhodes, Richard. *Audubon: The Making of an American*. New York: Knopf, 2004.

Richards, George. "Elegiac Ode, Sacred to the Memory of General Greene." In *American Poems, Selected and Original*, vol. 1. Litchfield, Conn.: Collier and Buel, 1793.

Richie, Margaret Bye, Gregory D. Huber, John D. Milner, and Geoffrey Gross. *Stone Houses: Traditional Homes of Pennsylvania's Bucks County and Brandywine Valley*. New York: Rizzoli, 2005.

Rink, Evald. *Printing in Delaware 1761–1800*. Wilmington, Del.: Eleutherian Mills Historical Library, 1969.

"Rivers." Clippings files, Wilmington Public Library.

"Rivers, Brandywine." Clippings files, Chester County Historical Society.

Robinson, Samuel. *A Catalogue of American Minerals*. Boston: Cummings, Hilliard, 1825.

Rodebaugh, Paul A. *Chester County Notebook*. West Chester, Pa., Taggart Printing, 1987.

Rush, William. *Medical Inquiries and Observations*. Multivolume. Philadelphia: Thomas Dobson, 1794.

Scharf, J. Thomas. *History of Delaware*. 2 vols. Philadelphia: L. J. Richards, 1888.

Schneer, Jonathan. *The Thames*. New Haven, Conn.: Yale University Press, 2005.

"Service of Dedication of the Markers Placed at Brandywine Battlefield." *Second Report of the Pennsylvania Historical Commission* (1918).

Sesqui-Centennial Gathering of the Clan Darlington. Lancaster, Pa.: E. C. Darlington, 1853.

Shields, David, and Bill Benson. *Catalyst for Conservation: The Brandywine Conservancy's Success in Saving King Ranch Lands in Pennsylvania*. Chadds Ford, Pa.: Brandywine Conservancy, 2011.

Silliman, Charles A. *The Story of Christ Church Christiana Hundred and Its People*. Wilmington, Del.: author, 1960.

Silverman, Sharon Hernes. *The Brandywine Valley*. Mechanicsburg, Pa.: Stackpole, 2004.

Silvia, Mary Laird. Oral interviews of Rockland, Delaware, ca. 2003. Hagley Museum and Library.

Sinclair, Upton. *Money Writes! A Study of American Literature*. Long Beach, Calif.: author, 1927.

Sisson, William A. "From Farm to Factory" [Henry Clay Mill]. *Delaware History* 21 (1984/85): 31–52.

Smith, George. *History of Delaware County*. Philadelphia: Henry B. Ashmead, 1862.

Smith, Samuel S. *The Battle of Brandywine*. Monmouth Beach, N.J.: Philip Freneau Press, 1976.

Smithers, William W. *The Life of John Lofland*. Philadelphia: W. M. Leonard, 1894.

Stetson, George E. "The 1704 House Built in Chester County, Pennsylvania, by William Brinton the Younger." Master's thesis, University of Delaware, 1961.

Tatnall, Edward. *Catalogue of the Phaenogamous and Filicoid Plants of New Castle County, Delaware*. Wilmington, Del.: J. T. Heald, 1860.

Taylor, Bayard. *Poetical Works*. Boston: Houghton, Mifflin, 1894.

———. *Selected Letters*. Ed. Paul C. Wermuth. Lewisburg, Pa.: Bucknell University Press, 1997.

———. *The Story of Kennett*. New York: G. P. Putnam, 1866.

Taylor, Frank H. *Philadelphia in the Civil War*. Philadelphia: The City, 1913.

Taylor, Marie Hansen. *On Two Continents*. New York: Doubleday, Page, 1905.

Thompson, Priscilla M. "Creation of the Wilmington Park System Before 1896." *Delaware History* 18, no. 2 (Fall/Winter 1978): 75–92.

Thompson, Thomas R. *Chris: A Biography of Christian C. Sanderson*. Philadelphia: Dorrance, 1973.

Toll, Seymour I. *A Judge Uncommon: A Life of John Biggs, Jr.* Philadelphia: Legal Communications, 1993.

Trevelyan, Sir George Otto. *The American Revolution*. Multivolume. Reprint, New York: D. McKay, 1964.

Trollope, Frances. *Domestic Manners of the Americans*. New York: Knopf, 1949.

Turnbull, Andrew. *Scott Fitzgerald*. New York: Ballantine, 1971.

Up the River from Westminster to Windsor. London: Hardwicke & Bogue, 1876.

Vincent, Francis. *A History of the State of Delaware*. 2 vols. Philadelphia: John Campbell, 1870.

Volkman, Arthur G. "Delaware Rocks." *Delaware Today* (December 1973): 55–62.

Wallace, Anthony F. C. *Rockdale: The Growth of an American Village in the Early Industrial Revolution*. New York: Knopf, 1980.

Wallace, Paul A. W. *Lloyd Mifflin: Painter and Poet of the Susquehanna.* Harrisburg: Pennsylvania Historical and Museum Commission, 1965.

Wamsley, James S. *The Brandywine Valley: An Introduction to Its Cultural Treasures.* New York: Abrams, 1992.

Welsh, Peter C. "The Brandywine Mills: A Chronicle of an Industry, 1762–1816." *Delaware History* 7, no. 1 (March 1956): 17–36.

Weslager, C. A. *The Delaware Indians.* New Brunswick, N.J.: Rutgers University Press, 1972.

———. *Delaware's Forgotten River: The Story of the Christina.* Wilmington, Del.: Hambleton, 1947.

———. *Dutch Explorers, Traders and Settlers in the Delaware Valley, 1609–1664.* Philadelphia: University of Pennsylvania Press, 1961.

———. *Red Men on the Brandywine.* Wilmington: Hambleton, 1953.

West Chester, Past and Present: Centennial Souvenir. West Chester, Pa.: *Daily Local News,* 1899.

West Chester, Pennsylvania: The Most Important Suburb of Philadelphia. West Chester, Pa.: Board of Trade, 1888.

White, John H., Jr. *A History of the American Locomotive.* New York: Dover, 1979.

Whyte, William H. *The Last Landscape.* Garden City, N.Y.: Doubleday, 1968.

Wiley, Samuel T. *Biographical and Historical Cyclopedia of Delaware County, Pennsylvania.* New York: Gresham, 1894.

Wilkinson, Norman B. "Brandywine Borrowings from European Technology." *Technology and Culture* 4, no. 1 (Winter 1963): 1–13.

———. *The Brandywine Home Front During the Civil War.* Wilmington, Del.: Kaumagraph, 1966.

———. *E. I. du Pont, Botaniste.* Charlottesville: University Press of Virginia, 1972.

———. "The Mills on the Brandywine." In Baldwin, *Historic Brandywine Guide Book.*

William Canby of Brandywine, Delaware. Philadelphia: Friends' Book Association, 1883.

Williams, William H. *Man and Nature in Delaware: An Environmental History of the First State, 1631–2000.* Dover: Delaware Heritage Press, 2008.

"Wilmington: Houseboats." Clippings files, Wilmington Public Library.

Wilson, Alexander. *Life and Letters.* Ed. Clark Hunter. Philadelphia: American Philosophical Society, 1983.

Wilson, David G. *The Victorian Thames.* Dover, N.H.: Sutton, 1993.

Wilson, Edmund. *The Shores of Light.* New York: Vintage, 1952.

Wilson, Woodrow. *A History of the American People.* 5 volumes. New York: Harper & Brothers, 1902.

Windle, Mary J. *Life in Washington*. Philadelphia: Lippincott, 1859.

Wyeth, Andrew. *Andrew Wyeth: Autobiography*. Boston: Little Brown, 1995.

Wyeth, Jamie. *Farm Work*. Chadds Ford, Pa.: Brandywine River Museum of Art, 2011.

Wyeth, N. C. *The Wyeths: The Letters of N. C. Wyeth, 1901–1945*. Ed. Betsy James Wyeth. Boston: Gambit, 1971.

The Wye Valley Walk. Wye Valley Walk Partnership, 2011.

Zebley, Frank R. *Along the Brandywine*. Wilmington: William N. Cann, 1940.

———. Photograph collection [Brandywine views]. 1930–1947. Delaware Public Archives, Dover.

Zeidner, Lisa, and Anthony Edgeworth. *Brandywine: A Legacy of Tradition in du Pont-Wyeth Country*. Charlottesville: Thomasson-Grant, 1995.

Index

❧ ❧

100 Artists of the Brandywine, 207

Abolitionism, 114, 161
Ackroyd, Peter, 10, 11
Adams, John (printer), 106, 107
Agriculture, 33, 38, 79
Alapocas Run State Park, 138
Americana, 171, 172, 173
American Ornithology (Wilson), 134, 135
American Revolution: battlefield tourism, 63;
    Quakers during, 6, 72, 80; Valley Forge, 49;
    Wyeth's passion for, 198, 199. *See also*
    Brandywine, Battle of; Brandywine
    Battlefield
Amtrak Bridge, 217
Annals of the Former World (McPhee), 141
Antiquarianism, 178–79, 195, 199
Antiques, 171–72, 173
Apsley Mill, 81
Arcadia, 159
Architecture: from Quaker settlement, 31;
    Victorianism, 140. *See also* Churches;
    Houses
Art: Brandywine River Museum of Art, 197,
    206; Delaware Art Museum, 8
Artists, 1–2; *100 Artists of the Brandywine*, 207;
    at Brandywine, 179–82; Brandywine
    Tradition, 179, 207; in Chadds Ford, 183;
    Doughty, 82; influence of Brandywine on,
    185–86; local, 183–84; Otis, 79; Peale, 74,
    96; Pyle, 1, 9, 39, 40–41, 42, 58, 166, 179,
    186–89, 206, 208; at Turner's Mill, 187,
    190. *See also* Wyeth, Andrew; Wyeth, N. C.
Artists, topographical, 79
Audubon, John James, 134–35

Augustine Cut-Off Bridge, 215
Automobiles, 12, 89, 151, 169–70, 172,
    178–79, 192

Bache, Alexander Dallas, 122
Baldwin, William, 131, 140
Bancroft, George, 63
Bancroft, Joseph, 104
Bancroft, William P., 152, 153
Bancroft Mills, 104
Bancroft Mills Bridges, 215
Barns-Brinton House, 32
Bartlett, George O., 182
Barton, William, 132
Bartram, John, 128–29
Beauties of the Brandywine, 182
Beaver Valley Rock Shelter, 17
Biddle, Chapman, 118–19
Biggs, John, 174, 175
Bird, Robert Montgomery, 165
Birds, 133–36. *See also* Wildlife
Birds of America (Audubon), 135
Birmingham, Pa., 31
Birmingham Meeting, 53, 56, 60–61, 62, 161
Birmingham Park, 146
Björk, Eric, 39
Blanche of Brandywine (Lippard), 162–64
Blue-bottle flowers, 33
Blue rock, 137–38
Boats, 148
Boone, Daniel, 106–7
Bordley, John Beale, 38
Botanists/botany, 99–101, 128–30, 131–33.
    See also Horticulture
Bowen, John S., 63

Brandywine: importance of, 1–2; length of, 10; mystique of, 157; name of, 4–5, 25; path of, 1; variety of, 5–6. *See also* Paradox

Brandywine, Battle of, 34, 47–67; anniversary of, 193–94; effects of, 57–58; historical plaques, 198; in literature, 162–64; officers at, 49; and poetry, 160, 161, 165, 166; Pyle's stories of, 189–90; relics from, 64–65, 113, 198; strategy at, 48; Townsend's reminiscences of, 51, 52; wounded, 56. *See also* Brandywine Battlefield; Howe, William; Lafayette, Marquis de; Washington, George

The Brandywine (Canby), 3–4, 158–59, 195, 199

Brandywine Battlefield, 131–32; map of, 58; paintings of, 65, 181, 194, 203–4; photograph of, 13; preservation of, 14, 47–48, 66–67; tourism at, 58–65, 116, 117–18. *See also* Brandywine, Battle of

Brandywine Battlefield (Smith), 65

Brandywine Conservancy, 14, 43, 66, 136, 156

Brandywine Corn Meal, 4–5

Brandywine Creek State Park, 153–54

Brandywine Granite Quarry, 138

Brandywine River Museum of Art, 197, 206

Brandywine Paper Mills, 80–81

Brandywine Tradition, 179, 207

Brandywine Valley Association, 155

Brandywine Village, Del., 73

Brandywine Walk, 109

Breck's Mill, 95–96

Bridges, 211–17; Cope's Bridge, 147, 211; importance of, 105; Market Street Bridge, 78–79, 104, 216–17; in paintings, 181–82, 184; Penn Central Bridge, 143, 213; Smith's Bridge, 184–85, 214; Washington Memorial Bridge, 2–3, 216

Bridges, covered, 184–85, 214

Bridges, railroad, 110–11, 112–13, 143, 213, 214, 215–16, 217

Brinton (family), 33–34

Brinton, Amos, 203

Brinton, Francis, 37

Brinton, John Hill, 180

Brinton, William, 33

Brinton 1704 House, 33, 34, 180

Brinton Association of America, 33

Caleb Brinton House, 203

Edward Brinton House, 203

Brinton's Bridge, 213

Brinton's Ford, 203

British, 20, 25, 77, 79

Britishness, 6–10

Broom, Jacob, 93

Bunce, Oliver B., 180

Burroughs, John, 167–69

Cabinet of Natural Sciences, 133

Camping, 116, 147

Camp meetings, 147

Canby, Henry Seidel, 3–4, 7, 79, 95, 110, 128, 138, 146, 158–59, 172, 195, 199

Canby, James, 133

Canby, Oliver, 43, 158

Canby, William M., 152

Canoeing, 150–151, 154

Cedarcroft, 115, 116

Cemeteries, 98, 133

Chadds Ford, Pa.: art academy at, 179, 187; artists in, 181, 183; effects of railroad on, 112–13. *See also* Brandywine, Battle of

Chads, Betty, 32

John Chads House, 32

Chandler, Elizabeth Margaret, 161

Chateau Country, 3, 13

Checochinican, 28

Chester County, 6, 8, 9, 12–13, 27, 31, 198

Chester County Historical Society, 64, 65, 198

Chestnut trees, 150

Christ Church Christiana Hundred, 120–21

Christina River, 18

Churches: Christ Church Christiana Hundred, 120–21; Mother Archie's Church, 196; Old Swedes Church, 39–41, 187

Civil War, 55, 66, 117–22

Cobbett, William, 77

Conservation, 14, 43, 66, 136, 155–56

Coolidge, Calvin, 131

Cope, Edward Drinker, 137

Cope, Emmor B., 122

Cope, George, 183–84

"Cope Map," 122

Cope's Bridge, 147, 211

Cornwallis, Charles, 48, 52

Cox, Hannah, 114

Cox, John, 114

Creek, *vs.* river, 5

Cropper, John, 55–56

CSX Bridge, 215–16

Dams, effects of, 43

Danckaerts, Jasper, 25

Darlington, Abraham, 6

Darlington, Deborah, 6

Darlington, William, 6, 13, 29, 129, 131–33, 140

Dawes, Rumford, 97

Deborah's Rock, 106, 147

Deborah's Rock (Tatnall), 182
Declaration of Independence, 53, 56
Deforestation, 102–3, 150
De Foss, Mattias, 39
Delaware, 28, 113–14
Delaware Art Museum, 8
Delaware Paper Mills, 88
Delaware Valley, 21–26, 27
De Mare, Eric, 145–46
"The Deserted Village" (Goldsmith), 14
Development, 12–15, 66–67
De Vries, David, 18–20, 22
Dickinson, John, 81
Dixon, Jeremiah, 44–45, 113
Doughty, Thomas, 82
Dower House, 35–37, 169, 170–71
Downing, Andrew Jackson, 91–92
Down the Eastern and Up the Black Brandywine
    (MacElree), 168
Dreiser, Theodore, 166–67
Droughts, 142
Duff, James, 197–98
DuPont (company), 183
du Pont (family), 3, 89; cemetery, 98; Fitzgerald
    on, 175; and horticulture, 8; houses of, 101,
    125–26, 173; land ownership, 154; love of
    trees, 30–31; and paradox, 91; passion for
    family history, 91; wealth of, 13, 125; Wyeth
    on, 192
du Pont, Alexis, 120, 121
du Pont, Alfred I., 13, 124
du Pont, "Boss Henry," 120, 125
du Pont, Charles I., 96
du Pont, Eleuthera, 99–101
du Pont, Eleuthère Irénée, 30, 92–95, 96–97,
    98, 99
du Pont, Elise, 128
du Pont, Henry Francis, 173, 174
du Pont, Irénée, 125–26
du Pont, Josephine, 94–95
du Pont, Pete, 128
du Pont, Pierre, 130–31
du Pont, Pierre Samuel, 93, 98
Du Pont, Captain Samuel Francis, 120, 121
du Pont, Sophie, 99–101
Dutch, 18, 20, 21–22, 24–25
Dutch West India Company, 20
Dynamite, 183

Eakins, Thomas, 180
"Eccentric Earl of Ellerslie," 174–76
Ecology, 43, 102–3, 141–44, 149. *See also*
    Wildlife
Eisenhower, Dwight D., 202

Eleutherian Mills, 97–98
Ellerslie, 174
Empson, Cornelius, 26
England, rivers in, 10, 11, 15, 69–70, 145–46,
    185–86
Englishness, 6–10
Erosion, 141–42
Evans, Oliver, 71, 110
Everhart, Benjamin, 141
Everhart, James B., 166

Faden, William, 58
Filson, John, 15, 106–7
Finns, 22
First State National Monument, 2, 14–15, 16,
    28, 38, 41, 153
Fish, 43, 149. *See also* Wildlife
Fish Creek, 24
Fisher, Miers, 80
Fitzgerald, F. Scott, 170, 174–76, 193
Fitzgerald, Zelda, 174, 175, 193
Flag, American, 54
Flanking maneuvers, 48, 50, 55, 212
Flooding, 102–5, 143–44, 150
Flora Cestrica (Darlington), 132
Fort Casimir, 22, 24
Fort Christina, 21–25, 41
Fox, George, 26, 61
Fox hunting, 7
French, 76, 79
French, William, 182
From an Old House (Hergesheimer), 171, 202
Furniture, 172
Futhey, J. Smith, 63

Gardening, 8
Gardens, 127–28; in Chateau Country, 13;
    Longwood Gardens, 34–35, 128, 129,
    130–31; Marshall Park, 129–30; at
    Nemours, 125; Peirce's Park, 129–31;
    Winterthur, 30–31, 128
Garrett, Thomas, 114
Geology, 137–41
Gettysburg, Battle of, 47, 122
Gideon Gilpin House, 49
Gillylen, John, 38
Gilpin (family), 34–35, 80
Gilpin, Gideon, 59
Gilpin, Hanna, 34
Gilpin, Joseph, 34
Gilpin, Joshua, 80, 81, 83
Gilpin, Rachel, 130
Gilpin, Thomas, 80
Gilpin, Vincent, 74

Gilpin, William, 15, 69
Gilpin's Mill, 80, 82, 83, 135
Gilpin's Mill on the Brandywine (Doughty), 82
Gish, Lillian, 170, 193
Goldsmith, Oliver, 14
Graham's Magazine, 61
Granogue, 125–26
Gravell, Thomas, 81–82
Greatrake, Laurence, 81
Greene, Nathanael, 160
Greenhouses, 130–31
Gunpowder, 92, 93–94, 96–99; during Civil
    War, 120; explosions, 109–10, 121, 122–24;
    in Spanish-American War, 124; workers,
    124–25. *See also* Powder yards
Gurney, Joseph, 83

Hagley Museum, 89, 99, 126
Hagley Yard, 97–98, 102, 110, 121
Harper's, 187
Hartman, William D., 141
Harvey, Chalkley, 114
Hayes, John Russell, 11, 149, 167–69, 178, 184
Helga pictures, 196
Hergesheimer, Joseph, 11, 12, 35–37, 89, 159,
    169–73, 193, 202, 208
Historical associations: Chester County
    Historical Society, 64, 65, 198; Historical
    Society of Pennsylvania, 63, 181; Pennsyl-
    vania Historical Commission, 198
Historical Society of Pennsylvania, 63, 181
History. *See* Past
Hoff, Clayton M., 154–55
Holly Island, 97
Holme, Thomas, 27
Holmes, Oliver Wendell, Sr., 6
The Homestead, 179, 191–92
Horticultural Hall, 127
Horticulture, 8, 91–92. *See also* Botanists/
    botany
Houseboats, 148
Houses, 31–34; Barns-Brinton House, 32;
    Brinton 1704 House, 33, 34, 180; Caleb
    Brinton House, 203; Edward Brinton
    House, 203; Cedarcroft, 115, 116; John
    Chads House, 32; Dower House, 35–37,
    169, 170–71; of du Ponts, 101, 125–26, 173;
    Ellerslie, 174; Gideon Gilpin House, 49; The
    Homestead, 179, 191–92; log cabins, 22, 31;
    Marshallton, 129; restoration of, 32, 35–37;
    Tatnall Houses, 73; Abiah Taylor House,
    32, 35; unrestored, 37; Windtryst, 190
Howe, William, 47, 48, 51, 57
Hugh Wynne, Free Quaker (Mitchell), 166

Hundreds, 6
Hurricanes, 143–44

I-95 Bridge, 216
Indian Hannah, 28
Indians. *See* Native Americans
Indian Town, 28
Industrial Revolution, 71
Industry: beginnings of, 23; during Civil War,
    119; growth of, 70, 110; juncture with
    agriculture, 79; and picturesqueness, 180;
    pollution by, 87; and railroad, 111–12. *See
    also* Gunpowder; Milling; Mills; Paradox
Insects, 142
Irish, 77, 79, 83
Iron Bridge, Hagley, 215
Iron-casting foundry, 111
Irving, Washington, 13, 48, 57

Jefferis, Emmor, 51
Jefferis's Bridge, 211–12
Jefferis's Ford, 48, 50, 51, 117
Johnson, Adam, 196

Kaat, Linda, 67
Kalm, Peter, 29, 103, 138
Kennedy, John F., 202
Kentucky, 15, 106
Kirk, Samuel, 42–43
Knyphausen, Wilhelm von, 49, 50, 53
Kuerner's Farm, 196

Lafayette, Marquis de, 49, 53, 58, 59–60, 64,
    65, 73
Lancaster, Pa., 105
Land: hundreds, 6; preservation of, 155; price
    of, 66
Landa, Mary, 204
Land preservation, 155
Landscape Gardening (Downing), 91–92
Lanier, Sidney, 116, 166–67
The Last Leaf (Pyle), 40–41
The Last of the Chestnuts (Wyeth, N. C.), 150
Latimer (family), 92
Latitude, measurement of, 45
Lea, Thomas, 73
Lee, Harry, 55
Lee, Robert E., 55
Lenape Bridge, 212
Lenape Indians, 17–18, 19, 22, 43
Lenape Park, 146
Leopold, Luna, 141
Lewis, Sinclair, 170, 172
Lidz, Maggie, 30, 128, 173

Lincoln, Abraham, 15
Lindeström, Peter, 24
Lippard, George, 10, 159, 162–64
Literature: Battle of Brandywine in, 162–64;
   Brandywine in, 159–60, 166–67; British
   influence on, 168; Dreiser, 166–67;
   Fitzgerald, 174–76; Hergesheimer, 11, 12,
   35–37, 89, 159, 169–73, 202, 208; Lippard,
   10, 159, 162–64; Neal, 160; past in, 168;
   Taylor, 31, 103, 115–17, 159. *See also* Poetry
Lobdell Car Wheel Company, 111–12
Lofland, John, 164–65
Log cabins, 22, 31
London, 145
Longwood Gardens, 34–35, 128, 129, 130–31
Longwood Meeting, 114
Lossing, Benson, 63

MacElree, Wilmer, 5, 150, 168
Map of Historical Chester County, 198
*Map of Reconnaissance of the Valley of
   Brandywine Creek*, 122
Maps: "Cope Map," 122; at Hagley Museum,
   126; *Map of Historical Chester County*, 198;
   *Map of Reconnaissance of the Valley of
   Brandywine Creek*, 122; of Pennsylvania,
   27–28
Market Street Bridge, 78–79, 104, 216–17
Marquand, John, 172
Marshall, Humphry, 129
Marshall, James, 73
Marshall, John, 54
Marshall Park, 129–30
Marshallton house, 129
Maryland, boundary of, 44–45
Mason, Charles, 44–45, 113
Mason-Dixon Line, 44–45, 113
Tyler McConnell Bridge, 215
McGuire, Tom, 67
McKinly, John, 58
McPhee, John, 140–41
Mencken, H. L., 170, 173, 193
Methodists, 147
Mifflin, Lloyd, 180
Milles, Carl, 41
Milling: demise of, 149–50; early, 42–43;
   effects of western expansion on, 110; and
   Evans, 71, 73; growth of, 73–75; import of to
   U.S., 95; paper mills, 80–81, 83, 87–90,
   135; plans for, 24; potential for, 72; during
   Revolution, 72
Mills, 23; Bancroft Mills, 104; Breck's Mill,
   95–96; Gilpin's Mill, 80, 82, 83, 135;
   Old Barley Mill, 43; in paintings, 184; plans

for, 23; Turner's Mill, 187, 190; Walker's
   Mill, 96
Milner, John, 32, 35
Minquas Indians, 19, 22
Minquas Kill, 18, 20
Minuit, Peter, 21
Mitchell, S. Weir, 166
Modernism, 178
Modernity: excluded from Wyeth's art, 179,
   199; intrusion of, 12. *See also* Automobiles;
   Development
Monigle, Joe, 126
Montgomery, Elizabeth, 84–85
Mother Archie's Church, 196

National Register of Historic Places, 31
Native Americans, 17–18, 19, 21, 22, 28, 43
Native Tree Society, 30
Nature: Quakers' appreciation of, 128; retreat
   to, 11–12; Westtown School, 136. *See also*
   Paradox
Neal, John, 160
Nemours mansion, 125
Nemours Foundation, 125
New Yorker, 140
Niles, Hezekiah, 107
Nixon, Richard, 33–34, 205
Northeast Boulevard Bridge, 217
North Market Street Bridge, 216–17
North Point, Battle of, 56
Nostalgia, 10–11. *See also* Past
Notman, John, 109

Observations on the River Wye (Gilpin),
   69–70
O'Doherty, Brian, 157
Okie, Brognard, 35–37
Old Barley Mill, 43
Old Swedes Church, 39–41, 187
"Old-Time Life in a Quaker Town" (Pyle), 9,
   39–40, 187
Olmsted, Frederick Law, 152
The Orchards, 148–49
Ornithologists, 133–36
Otis, Bass, 79
"Outside the Cabinet-Maker's" (Fitzgerald),
   175–76

Paine, Thomas, 50, 77
Painter's Bridge, 213
Painter's Bridge (Tatnall), 181–82
Paleontology, 137
Palmer, Joseph, 140–41
Paper/paper mills, 80–82, 83, 87–90, 135

Paradox, 2–3, 14, 82, 86, 91, 92, 146, 148, 174, 177–78
Parke, John, 160
Parker, James, 50
Parks, 138, 146, 152, 153–54
Past: and art, 206; in Hayes's writing, 168; Hergesheimer's love of, 171–73; in romanticism, 165; Wyeth's love of, 197–98, 199
Paul Redding (Read), 162
Peale, Charles Willson, 74, 96
Peale, Franklin, 96
Peale, Titian, 96
Peirce, Joshua, 130
Peirce's Park, 129–31
Penn, William, 26, 27, 128
Penn Central Bridge, 143, 213
Pennock, Charles J., 136
Pennsylvania: boundary of, 44–45; Delaware divided from, 28; founding of, 27; maps of, 27–28; Quaker settlement of, 28; race in, 9
Pennsylvania Historical Commission, 198
People's Party, 114–15
Perkins, Granville, 180
Peterson, Charles Jacob, 61–63
Philadelphia, 57, 61, 122
Photographers, 182–83
Picnicking, 85, 116, 147
Picturesque America, 82, 92, 180
Pinckney, Charles C., 49
Pine Street Bridge, 217
Plants, study of, 127. *See also* Botanists/botany; Horticulture
Pocopson Creek, 146
Poetry: about Brandywine, 160; "An Admired Spot on the Banks of the Brandywine," 8–9; and Battle of Brandywine, 160, 161, 165, 166; Chandler, 161; English rivers in, 10, 69–70; Everhart, 166; Hayes, 11, 167–69, 178, 184; Lofland, 164–65; Mifflin, 180; Pope, 138; Read, 161–62; "Tintern Abbey," 69, 70
Poetry, topographic, 160–61
Pollution, 87, 144, 148, 151–52, 155, 178
Pope, Alexander, 138, 160
Powder yards: explosions at, 97–98, 121, 122–24; Hagley Yard, 97–98; trees in, 101–2. *See also* Gunpowder
Preservation, 3, 13, 16. *See also* Conservation; First State National Monument
Printers, 106–7, 160
Printz, Johan, 22–23
Promenades, 85, 109
Property, 74–75. *See also* Land
Publishing, growth of, 159

Pulaski, Casimir, 49
Pyle, Howard, 1, 9, 39, 40–41, 42, 58, 166, 179, 186–89, 206, 208
Pyle's Bridge, 213–14

Quakers: abolitionism by, 114; during American Revolution, 6, 72, 80; appreciation of natural beauty, 128; connection to Britain, 6; effects of Battle of Brandywine on, 57; Fox, 26, 61; Penn, 26, 27, 128; settlement of Pennsylvania, 28; settlement patterns, 38; Westtown School, 136, 137
Quarries, 138

Race, in Pennsylvania, 9
Railroad, 110, 111–13, 119, 146
Read, Thomas Buchanan, 161–62
Recreation, 84–86, 146–49, 151
Relics, from Battle of Brandywine, 64–65, 113, 198
Revolutionary War. *See* American Revolution; Brandywine, Battle of; Brandywine Battlefield
Richards, George, 160
Richards, William Trost, 180–81
Ring, Benjamin, 49
Rising, Johan, 23–24, 25
Rising Sun Bridge, 215
Rivers: *vs.* creeks, 5; English, 8–9, 10, 11, 15, 69–70, 145–46, 185–86
Rivers of America series, 158
Robbins, Roland Wells, 89
Rochefoucauld, Francois de La, 78, 79, 83–84
Rock, 137–41
Rockland, Del., 87–90, 104, 184, 214
Rockland Bridge, 214
The Rocks, 18, 20, 22, 41
Romanticism, 82, 83, 165, 208
Rothrock, Joseph, 12, 129
Rowan, Archibald Hamilton, 77
Rozier, Ferdinand, 135
Rush, Benjamin, 45, 56

Saltpeter, 93
Sanderson, Christian, 65, 198–99
Schneer, Jonathan, 185, 186
Schoepf, Johann, 83
Science/scientists, 127, 136–38. *See also* Botanists; Ornithologists
Selig, Robert, 67
Serpentine, 139–40
Settlement: influence of Brandywine on, 15; of Pennsylvania, 28; Quaker patterns of, 38; Swedish, 18, 21–26

Seventy-Six (Neal), 160
Sharpless, Isaac, 136–37
Shaw, Robert, 184
Shaw's Bridge, 212
Shields, David, 14, 66
Shipley, Thomas, 42
Shipley, William, 42
Sims, Joseph E., 96
Skating, 85
Slavery, 44, 113–14
Slaves, treatment of, 84
Smillie, James, 82
Smith, Russell, 65
Smith, Samuel, 55
Smith's Bridge, 184–85, 214
Spanish-American War, 124
Stargazers Stone, 44
Steadman, Edmund C., 116
Steelworks, 151
Stidham, Tymen, 25–26
Stidham Mill, 43, 216
The Story of Kennett (Taylor), 31–32, 103, 115
Strickland, William, 110
Strong, Ann Louise, 155
Stroud Preserve Bridge, 211
Stuyvesant, Peter, 22, 24, 25
Suburbs, 172
Swanendael, 18, 19
Sweden/Swedes: anniversaries of landing of, 41; Old Swedes Church, 39–41, 187; settlement in New World, 18; settlement of Delaware Valley, 21–26
Sword, James Brade, 181
Sycamore trees, 197

"Tancopanican Chronicle," 99–101
Tatnall, Edward, 76, 79, 133
Tatnall, Henry Lea, 181–82
Tatnall, Joseph, 72, 158
Tatnall Houses, 73
Taylor, Bayard, 31, 103, 115–17, 159
Abiah Taylor House, 32, 35
Tenant Farmer (Wyeth, A.), 32, 158, 202
Tender Is the Night (Fitzgerald), 175
Testorf, Helga, 196, 207
Textile mills, 104
Thames, River, 10, 11, 145–46, 185–86
Thames Valley, 15
Thirteenth Amendment, 113–14
Thompson's Bridge, 214
"Tintern Abbey" (Wordsworth), 69, 70
Tobacco, 22
Tourism: and automobile, 151; of Brandywine Battlefield, 58–65, 116, 117–18; and

railroad, 112–13, 146; in Wye Valley, 69–70. *See also* Recreation
Tourists, 1, 100, 206–7
Townsend, Joseph, 50, 51, 52, 56
Townsend, Joseph (nephew), 63
Townsend's bunting, 135
Traditionalism, 10. *See also* Past
Trees: chestnut, 150; deforestation, 102–3, 150; at Hagley Museum, 97, 99; at Longwood Gardens and Tyler Arboretum, 34–35; Native Tree Society, 30; at Peirce's Park, 130; in powder yards, 101–2; preservation of, 12; surviving, 29–31; sycamore, 197; tulip, 29, 30
Trevelyan, George Otto, 48, 52, 53
Tulip trees, 29, 30
Turner, Eliza, 190
Turner, Jessica, 154
Turner, J. M. W., 185, 186
Turner, Joseph C., 190
Turner's Mill, 187, 190
Twaddle, William, 89
Tyler Arboretum, 35

Underground Railroad, 114
U.S. 1 Bridge at Chadds Ford, 213

Valley Forge, 49
Valley of the Brandywine (Richards), 180–81
Van Buren Street Bridge, 216
Victorianism, 140

Walker's Mill, 96
Walter, Thomas U., 127
War of 1812, 56, 93–95
Washington, George, 47, 49, 50, 53, 56–57, 72, 73
Washington Memorial Bridge, 2–3, 216
Watermarks, 80, 81–82
Water supply, shrinking of, 149–50
Water tower, 153
Watson, Elkanah, 44
Wealth: of Brandywine Valley, 12–13; and culture, 76; of du Ponts, 13, 125; and houses, 31; and preservation, 3; in Rockland, 87–88; in Wilmington, 109, 110
Weather, 45
Weber, Carl, 181
Wernwag, Lewis, 79, 104, 214, 216
West Chester, Pa., 127, 133, 160
Western expansion, 106–7, 110
Westtown School, 136, 137
Weymouth, George "Frolic," 14, 206
White, Kirk, 143–44

Whyte, William, 12, 155

Wildlife, 20–21, 29, 133–36, 149

Willing, Thomas, 42

Wilmington, Del.: effects of Battle of Brandywine on, 57–58; Englishness of, 9; Fitzgerald on, 175; flooding in, 104; founding of, 42–43; growth of, 75–77, 152, 153; printers in, 160; recreation in, 84–86; wealth in, 109, 110

Wilmington & Northern Rockland Branch Railroad Bridge, 214

Wilson, Alexander, 134

Windsor Forest, 138

Windtryst, 190

Winterthur, 30–31, 128, 173

Wire Bridge, 216

Wise, Henry A., 55–56

Wolman, Gordon "Reds," 141

Wood, Enoch, 82

Woodlawn section of First State National Monument, 38

Woodlawn Trustees, 153

Wordsworth, William, 69, 70

World War I, 130

Writers. *See* Literature

Wyeth, Andrew, 2, 4, 157–58; antiquarianism of, 178–79, 195, 199; Battle of Brandywine in art of, 203–4; on Brandywine, 11; at Brinton's Mill, 203–4; charged with sentimentalism, 178; childhood, 192, 196; and commodification of Americana, 173; and critics, 178; early work, 194–95, 199; encounter with, 207–8; fame of, 202–3, 205, 206–7; focus on Brandywine landscape, 201–3, 205; Helga pictures, 196; influence of, 205–6; influence of Battle of Brandywine on, 205; influence of father on, 201; and Kuerner's Farm, 196; on Lafayette, 60; love of history, 197–98, 199; modernity excluded from art of, 199; and Mother Archie's Church, 196; palette of, 199–201; and paradox, 177–78; and sycamore trees, 197; *Tenant Farmer*, 32, 158, 202

Wyeth, Betsy, 203, 204

Wyeth, Jamie, 192, 198, 200, 201, 206, 207

Wyeth, Nat, 178

Wyeth, N. C., 2, 87; on Andrew's work, 195, 197, 200; antimodern mindset, 192; Battle of Brandywine in art of, 194; death of, 201; friendship with Sanderson, 198; *The Homestead*, 179, 191–92; at Lafayette Hall, 189–90; landscape paintings, 192–93; *The Last of the Chestnuts*, 150; palette of, 199

Wye Valley, 69–70

Yong, Thomas, 20–21

Young, William, 88

Young Millwright and Miller's Guide (Evans), 71

Acknowledgments

❧ ☙

I began this project in 2002, at the time I was writing *Buildings of Delaware* in the Buildings of the United States series. A newcomer to the region, I was surprised to find that there was no comprehensive, modern history of the Brandywine, clearly Delaware's preeminent cultural resource.

Having previously written a history of Walden Pond, I assumed a "river book" would represent about the same level of challenge. I should have recalled that the Brandywine's watershed is 77 times bigger than Walden Woods—in fact, the size of New York City—and features a myriad of human dramas going back centuries. Eventually the book took eleven years to write, on and off, as its bibliography grew to include entries about everything from Daniel Boone to Precambrian geology to the fluorescent study of watermarks, all of which, it turns out, have some Brandywine connection.

The 2013 announcement of First State National Monument lit a fire in me to complete this project. I hoped that I could make an intellectual contribution, however modest, to that rare endeavor: the creation of a brand-new unit of the National Park Service in a state that never had one before.

For their invaluable assistance I wish to thank Karen Baumgartner and Mary Landa, Andrew Wyeth Office; Margaretta Brokaw; Heather Campbell Coyle, Delaware Art Museum; James Duff, Thomas Padon, Christine B. Podmaniczky, and Audrey Lewis of the Brandywine River

Museum of Art, and Bethany Engel for very kindly assisting with the photographic costs; Michael Kahn; Maggie Lidz, Winterthur Museum; Craig Lukezic, Delaware Division of Historical and Cultural Affairs; Terry Maguire; Tom McGuire; Bruce E. Mowday; John McPhee, Lars Hedin, Dean Clayton Marsh, Edward Tenner, and David Wilcove, Princeton University; Pamela C. Powell, Chester County Historical Society; Niquole Primiani, New Jersey Historical Commission; Heather Isbell Schumacher, Delaware Historical Society; David D. Shields, Brandywine Conservancy; Sharon Silverman; Halsey Spruance, Delaware Museum of Natural History; Joyce Hill Stoner; Paul Weagraff, Delaware Division of the Arts; Sarah J. Weatherwax, The Library Company of Philadelphia; Kirk White, U.S. Geological Survey; Jamie Wyeth; and Victoria Wyeth. Thanks also to my mother, Isabel Barksdale Maynard, and to my sister, Mims Maynard Zabriskie. Robert Lockhart and the staff of University of Pennsylvania Press have very capably seen the book through to publication, along with Edward Wade and Westchester Publishing Services.

I wish to acknowledge the generous support of Fair Play Foundation, which provided a publication grant. Special thanks to Blaine T. Phillips, Jr., of The Conservation Fund for his interest in this project.

As with my previous books, my greatest debt is to my wife, Susan Matsen Maynard.

Illustration Credits

ↁ

Frontispiece, pages 7, 86, 94, 101, 112, 123, 212. Courtesy Hagley Museum and Library.

Page 23, PL. 5, Page 78. Courtesy of the Delaware Historical Society.

PL. 7, Page 118, PL. 8. Chester County Historical Society, West Chester, Pa.

Page 36. Reprinted from Joseph Hergesheimer, *From an Old House*. New York: Knopf, 1926.

Page 40. Reprinted from Woodrow Wilson, *A History of the American People*. New York: Harper & Brothers, 1902.

Page 62. Reprinted from Wilmer W. MacElree, *Along the Western Brandywine*. West Chester, Pa.: F. S. Hickman, 1912.

PL. 10. Photograph by the author.

PL. 11. *Summer Freshet*, 1942 tempera © Andrew Wyeth. Private Collection.

Page 171. Courtesy Haverford College Quaker & Special Collections (Haverford, Pa.).

Page 188. Courtesy Delaware Art Museum.

Page 195. Courtesy Andrew Wyeth Office.

Page 200. Courtesy Michael Kahn.

The following were provided by the Brandywine River Museum of Art:

[PL. 1] N. C. Wyeth
Popular Magazine, cover illustration, 1915
Oil on canvas
Private collection

[PL. 2] Thomas Doughty
View on the Brandywine River: Gilpin's Paper Mill, ca. 1825–1830
Oil on wood panel
Collection Brandywine River Museum of Art
Museum Purchase, 2005

[Page 19] Andrew Wyeth
First Traders on the Brandywine, 1940
Pen and ink on paper
Collection Brandywine River Museum of Art
Gift of Lammot du Pont Copeland, 1981
© Andrew Wyeth

[PL. 3] N. C. Wyeth
William Penn, Man of Vision-Courage-Action, 1933
Oil on canvas
Collection Brandywine River Museum of Art
Gift of the Penn Mutual Life Insurance Company, 1997

[PL. 4] N. C. Wyeth
In a Dream I Meet General Washington, 1930
Oil on canvas
Collection Brandywine River Museum of Art
Purchased with funds given in memory of George T. Weymouth, 1991

[Page 55] Andrew Wyeth
The Fight at the Rocky Hill Ford, 1940
Pen and ink on paper
Collection Brandywine River Museum of Art
Gift of Lammot du Pont Copeland, 1981
© Andrew Wyeth

[PL. 6] Thomas Doughty
Gilpin's Mill on the Brandywine, 1830
Oil on canvas
Collection Brandywine River Museum of Art
Museum purchase, 1986

[PL. 9] George Cope
Trout in the Brandywine, 1904
Oil on canvas
Collection Brandywine River Museum of Art
Gift of Mrs. S. Hallock du Pont, 1979

[PL. 12] N. C. Wyeth
The Last of the Chestnuts, ca. 1916
Oil on canvas
Collection Brandywine River Museum of Art
Gift of Amanda K. Berls, 1980

[PL. 13] Horace Pippin
Birmingham Meeting House III, 1941
Oil on fabric board
Collection Brandywine River Museum of Art
Museum Volunteers' Purchase Fund and other funds, 2011

[PL. 14] N. C. Wyeth
Country Gentleman, cover illustration, 1944
Oil on hardboard (Renaissance Panel)
Collection Brandywine River Museum of Art
Bequest of Margaret S. Butterfield, 2005

[PL. 15] Andrew Wyeth
Pennsylvania Landscape (At Lafayette's Headquarters), 1942
Tempera on panel
Collection Brandywine River Museum of Art
Bequest of Miss Remsen Yerkes, 1982
© Andrew Wyeth